FOUR DAYS IN HITLER'S GERMANY

Mackenzie King's Mission to Avert a Second World War

Four Days in Hitler's Germany

Mackenzie King's Mission to Avert a Second World War

ROBERT TEIGROB

UNIVERSITY OF TORONTO PRESS
Toronto Buffalo London

ISBN 978-1-4875-0550-9

Printed on acid-free, 100% post-consumer
recycled paper with vegetable-based inks.

Library and Archives Canada Cataloguing in Publication

Title: Four days in Hitler's Germany : Mackenzie King's mission
to avert a Second World War /
Robert Teigrob.
Names: Teigrob, Robert, 1966– author.
Description: Includes bibliographical references and index.
Identifiers: Canadiana 20190087501 | ISBN 9781487505509 (hardcover)
Subjects: LCSH: King, William Lyon Mackenzie, 1874–1950. | LCSH: Hitler,
Adolf, 1889–1945. | LCSH: World War, 1939–1945 – Diplomatic history. |
LCSH: Canada – Foreign relations – Germany – History – 20th century. |
LCSH: Germany – Foreign relations – Canada – History – 20th century.
Classification: LCC D754.C2 T45 2019 | DDC 940.53/220971–dc23

This book has been published with the help of a grant from the Federation
for the Humanities and Social Sciences, through the Awards to Scholarly
Publications Program, using funds provided by the Social Sciences and
Humanities Research Council of Canada.

University of Toronto Press acknowledges the financial assistance to its
publishing program of the Canada Council for the Arts and the Ontario Arts
Council, an agency of the Government of Ontario.

Canada Council   Conseil des Arts
for the Arts   du Canada

ONTARIO ARTS COUNCIL
CONSEIL DES ARTS DE L'ONTARIO
an Ontario government agency
un organisme du gouvernement de l'Ontario

Funded by the   Financé par le
Government   gouvernement
of Canada   du Canada

MIX
Paper from
responsible sources
FSC   FSC® C016245
www.fsc.org

It is what we prevent, rather than what we do that
counts most in Government.

Mackenzie King, 1936

Contents

Contents

Illustrations

Acknowledgments

Thanks to all of my colleagues in the History Department at Ryerson University for their support and counsel. Several whose expertise intersects with this subject deserve special recognition: Ross Fair, Catherine Ellis, Tomaz Jardim, Carl Benn, and David Mackenzie shared their insights and pointed me to helpful source materials; Ingrid Hehmeyer tutored me in the nuances of the German language, lent me the camera that captured some of the images in this book, and, together with Norbert Schappacher, enriched my knowledge of the history and culture of Berlin; Arne Kislenko helped plant the seed for this project by connecting me with Freie Universität Berlin back in 2010 and giving me an expert tour of the city.

Ryerson's history department, Office of the Dean of Arts, and faculty association provided funding that helped to cover some of the research, travel, and production costs associated with this book. Stefan Fergus performed his usual magic with the index, and his keen eye caught a few typos and inconsistencies in word usage.

The truly *fabelhaft* staff at the Freie Universität Berlin International Summer Program (FUBiS) – in particular, program director Sophia Krause – have been a perennial source of assistance and hospitality. Staff at the Koblenz and Berlin chapters of the German Bundesarchiv and at Library and Archives Canada provided invaluable assistance; the latter's Alexandra McEwen was especially helpful in following up on some loose ends. Susan Ross of the Canadian War Museum was of great assistance in securing some of the photographs. Ryerson history student Matthew Czipf tracked down newspaper articles and other sources, and students in my classes in international and German history at both Ryerson and FUBiS sparked new questions and insights that enriched aspects of this study. Alexander Freund at the University of Winnipeg helped me think through some important issues when I wrote the book chapter that initiated this larger project, "One Fuhrer, Two Kings: A Canadian Prime Minister in Nazi Germany and the Dilemma of Responsibility," which he was kind enough to include in his forthcoming edited collection *History, Memory, and Generation: German-Canadian Experiences in the Twentieth Century* (University of Manitoba Press). The anonymous readers at the University of Toronto Press furnished superb commentary that strengthened the final product considerably.

Once again, the staff at the University of Toronto Press have been a pleasure to work with. Acquisitions editor (and, full disclosure, great friend) Lennart Husband championed the project diligently, while managing editor Frances Mundy handled production duties with characteristic professionalism. To anyone seeking a crack copyeditor I would recommend without reservation Terry Teskey, who boasts a surfeit of both *savoir faire* and good humour.

My siblings, nieces, nephews, and parents are a constant source of support and encouragement; the latter now drill me regularly in German, a language they initially reserved for confidential discussions about *die Kinder*. My wife Suzanne is my greatest champion and source of inspiration, and I dedicate this book to her.

Glossary of Commonly Used German Words and Abbreviations

Allgemeine Elektricitäts-Gesellschaft (AEG): General Electricity Company

Bundesarchiv: German Federal Archives

Deutsche Demokratische Republik (DDR): German Democratic Republic, aka East Germany

Deutsch-Englische Gesellschaft (DEG): German-English Fellowship Society

Deutsche Arbeitsfront (DAF): German Labour Front

Einsatzgruppen: literally, "special task force"; mobile Nazi death squads

Freikorps: literally, "free corps"; in Weimar Germany, right-wing paramilitary groups

Gedenkstätte Deutscher Widerstand: German Resistance Memorial, Berlin

Gemütlichkeit: warmth, hospitality

Gleichschaltung: Nazi program of coordination/synchronization

Hitlerjugend: Hitler Youth

Kraft durch Freude (KdF): Strength through Joy, a program of the DAF

Kristallnacht: literally, "night of crystal," or "night of broken glass"; the anti-Jewish pogroms that swept across German-held territory on 9 and 10 November 1938.

Lebensraum: living space

Nationalsozialistische Deutsche Arbeiterpartei (NSDAP): National Socialist German Worker's Party (Nazi Party)

Reichsarbeitsdienst (RAD): Reich Labour Service

Reichsluftfahrtministerium (RLM): Reich Ministry of Aviation

Reichspräsidentenpalais: Reich President's Palace

Schönheit der Arbeit (SdA): Beauty of Work, a program of the DAF

Schutzstaffel (SS): literally, "protection squad"; Nazi paramilitary organization

Sozialistische Einheitspartei Deutschlands (SED): Socialist Unity Party of Germany, the ruling communist party of East Germany

Staatsoper: State Opera

Stadtschloss: literally, "city castle"; here, the Berlin residence of the House of Hohenzollern

Sturmabteilung (SA): literally, "storm detachment"; Nazi paramilitary organization

Sturmbannführer: literally, "assault unit leader"; a high-ranking SS officer

Trümmerfrau: "rubble women," those assigned to clear debris from German cities following the Second World War

Welthauptstadt Germania: World Capital Germania, name for Albert Speer's proposed remaking of Berlin

Wehrmacht: literally, "defence force"; the unified armed forces of Nazi Germany

Crerar's map of Berlin (overleaf page spread): Nazi-era tourist map of Berlin used by Colonel H.D.G. Crerar during his visit to the city in June, 1937, just prior to Mackenzie King's own. From Library and Archives Canada, Crerar fonds, MG30 E157, vol. 10, file "Notes on Visit to Germany" (2F-L, 2K: Visit to Germany).

Sites plotted on the map visited by King include:

7: Pergamon Museum
40: Staatsoper (State Opera House)
48: Britische Botschaft (British Embassy)
49: Reichspräsidenten-Palais (Reich President's Palace)
50: Auswärtiges Amt (Foreign Office)
51: Reichskanzlerpalais ([Old] Reich Chancellery)
63: Reichsluftfarhrtministerium (Reich Ministry of Aviation)
72: Reichskriegsministerium (Reich War Ministry, aka Bendlerblock)
87: Planetarium und Zoo
96: Reichssportfeld (Reich Sports Field, aka Olympicstadion)

Unnumbered sites visited by King include:

Friedrichstrasse train station, across the street from 19.
The Anton Weber home in the Diplomatic Quarter, just south of 75.
Hotel Adlon, adjacent to 47 on the south side of Pariser Platz, a square flanked on the west by the Brandenburg Gate.
Templehof Airport, here labelled Zentral Flughafen (Central Airport), bottom right.
Hitlerjugend (Hitler Youth) headquarters, just north of 16 (top right)
Deutsche Arbeitsfront (German Labour Front) Headquarters, just east of 61.
Reichsarbeitsdienst (Reich Labour Service) headquarters, just west of 94.

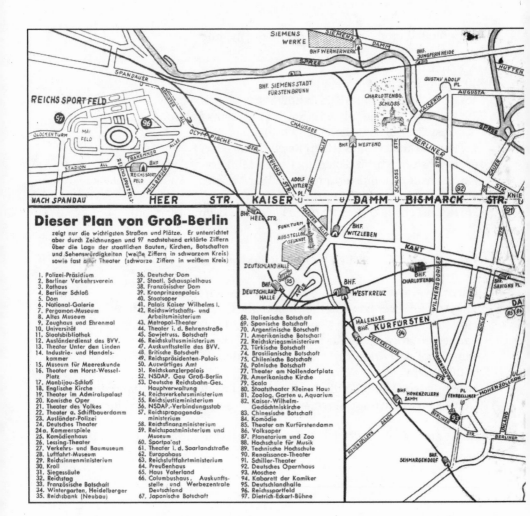

Dieser Plan von Groß-Berlin

zeigt nur die wichtigsten Straßen und Plätze. Er unterrichtet aber durch Zeichnungen und 97 nachstehend erklärte Ziffern über die Lage der staatlichen Bauten, Kirchen, Botschaften und Sehenswürdigkeiten (weiße Ziffern in schwarzem Kreis) sowie fast aller Theater (schwarze Ziffern in weißem Kreis)

1. Polizei-Präsidium
2. Berliner Verkehrsverein
3. Rathaus
4. Berliner Schloß
5. Dom
6. National-Galerie
7. Pergamon-Museum
8. Altes Museum
9. Zeughaus und Ehrenmal
10. Universität
11. Staatsbibliothek
12. Ausländerdienst des BVV.
13. Theater Unter den Linden
14. Industrie- und Handelskammer
15. Museum für Meereskunde
16. Theater am Horst-Wessel-Platz
17. Monbijou-Schloß
18. Englische Kirche
19. Theater im Admiralspalast
20. Komische Oper
21. Theater des Volkes
22. Theater a. Schiffbauerdamm
23. Ausländer-Polizei
24. Deutsches Theater
24a. Kammerspiele
25. Komödienhaus
26. Lessing-Theater
27. Verkehrs- und Baumuseum
28. Luftfahrt-Museum
29. Reichsinnenministerium
30. Kroll
31. Siegessäule
32. Reichstag
33. Französische Botschaft
34. Wintergarten, Heidelberger
35. Reichsbank (Neubau)

36. Deutscher Dom
37. Staatl. Schauspielhaus
38. Französischer Dom
39. Kronprinzenpalais
40. Staatsoper
41. Palais Kaiser Wilhelms I.
42. Reichswirtschafts- und Arbeitsministerium
43. Matropol-Theater
44. Theater i. d. Behrenstraße
45. Sowjetruss. Botschaft
46. Reichskultusministerium
47. Auskunftsstelle des BVV.
48. Britische Botschaft
49. Reichspräsidenten-Palais
50. Auswärtiges Amt
51. Reichskanzlerpalais
52. NSDAP. Gau Groß-Berlin
53. Deutsche Reichsbahn-Ges. Hauptverwaltung
54. Reichsverkehrsministerium
55. Reichsjustizministerium
56. NSDAP.-Verbindungsstab
57. Reichspropaganda- ministerium
58. Reichsfinanzministerium
59. Reichspostministerium und Museum
60. Sportpalast
61. Theater i. d. Saarlandstraße
62. Europahaus
63. Reichsluftfahrtministerium
64. Preußenhaus
65. Haus Vaterland
66. Columbushaus, Auskunftsstelle und Werbezentrale Deutschland
67. Japanische Botschaft

68. Italienische Botschaft
69. Spanische Botschaft
70. Argentinische Botschaft
71. Amerikanische Botschaft
72. Reichskriegsministerium
73. Türkische Botschaft
74. Brasilianische Botschaft
75. Chilenische Botschaft
76. Polnische Botschaft
77. Theater am Nollendorfplatz
78. Amerikanische Kirche
79. Scala
80. Staatstheater Kleines Haus
81. Zoolog. Garten u. Aquarium
82. Kaiser-Wilhelm-Gedächtniskirche
83. Chinesische Botschaft
84. Komödie
85. Theater am Kurfürstendamm
86. Volksoper
87. Planetarium und Zoo
88. Hochschule für Musik
89. Technische Hochschule
90. Renaissance-Theater
91. Schiller-Theater
92. Deutsches Opernhaus
93. Moschee
94. Kabarett der Komiker
95. Deutschlandhalle
96. Reichssportfeld
97. Dietrich-Eckart-Bühne

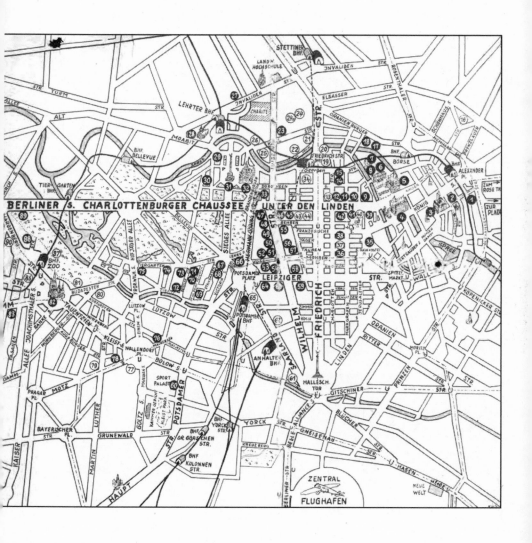

FOUR DAYS IN HITLER'S GERMANY

Mackenzie King's Mission to Avert a Second World War

Prologue: Values, Interests, and Foreign Relations

Following Donald Trump's stunning victory in the 2016 US presidential election, heads of state the world over, many of whom had very publicly expressed alarm over the prospect of the immensely unqualified and bigoted reality television personality moving into the White House, issued *pro forma* official statements of congratulation. Canadian prime minister Justin Trudeau's feel-good bromide was typical: "The relationship between our two countries serves as a model for the world," Trudeau proclaimed blithely. "Our shared values, deep cultural ties and strong integrated economies will continue to provide the basis for advancing our strong and prosperous partnership."[1]

One world leader took special care not to follow script. Germany's Angela Merkel offered salutations that, given her country's close and often dependent relationship with the United States since the end of the Second World War, were remarkable for their implicit censure and explicit conditionality. "Germany and America are connected by values of democracy, freedom and respect for the law and the dignity of man, independent of origin, skin colour, religion, gender, sexual orientation or political views," she said in her congratulation-cum-lecture, adding: "I offer the next President of the United States close cooperation *on the basis of these values*."[2]

The German chancellor had good reason to proffer this lesson in civics and diplomacy. Her nation, more than any other in the modern era, has become cognizant of the perils of governance unmoored from the principles of human dignity, and of the international community's responsibility to stand firm against states that flout those principles. In the catastrophe wrought by Nazism the world learnt hard lessons about the outcome of doing business as usual with governments whose conduct towards their neighbours and their own citizens was an affront to the ideals of tolerance, equality, and the rule of law. Today, what happens within states is no longer considered irrelevant to the wider world or off-limits to foreign criticism or intercession. Morality now has a role in the calculus of diplomacy, even if values are frequently overshadowed by strategic and economic interests. The global war instigated by fascism ushered in a revolution in international relations and governance – one that begat the United Nations, the Universal Declaration of Human Rights, and later, such notions as universal legal jurisdiction and the responsibility to protect – that we are to this day still struggling to come to terms with.

Although the Second World War thus marks a watershed, it is possible to overemphasize how diplomacy prior to 1939 differed from that which followed. As early as 1933, some states, organizations, and individuals took a strong stand against the problem of Adolf Hitler based on apprehensions over his regime's stunning repression of internal "enemies" and deliberate inflammation, even before the shooting started, of the international order. Boycotts, sanctions, condemnations, and anti-fascist alliances were debated, invoked, revoked, and reissued. Leftists, anti-racist and human rights' groups, religious bodies, labour unions, artists, and intellectuals constructed popular fronts against fascism at home and abroad, and some of their number travelled to Spain to fight the fascists head on. Certain governments tried to isolate themselves from right-wing dictatorships, or to quarantine those dictatorships from the rest of the world. Others sought to rally the international community to a collective defence against fascist aggression. Still others strove to placate the belligerent dictators who seemed to be pulling the world towards war, believing these leaders' grievances to be valid or hoping their aims were limited. Many states tried several approaches in turn, and even simultaneously. International relations operated in a state of profound confusion and profound flux.

In casting about for a suitable strategy for dealing with fascist governments, Canada was no different. As the Depression decade ground on, however, the nation emerged as arguably the most consistent apologist among the Western democracies for the policy of appeasement and for the Third Reich itself, insisting to the British Commonwealth and League of Nations that fear of German aggression was overblown. At a time when the United States and Britain were reducing their commercial interactions with Hitler's regime, the Canadian government was completing an agreement to increase trade with Germany and permitting significant expansion of that nation's consular service in Canada.

This did not render Canada primarily or even particularly answerable for the failure of appeasement; the nation was too remote, too small, too young to be of much influence. However, coupled with the fact that the country was the least willing among the Western democracies to accept Jewish refugees fleeing fascist persecution, interwar Canada exhibits highly unflattering patterns of intolerance at home and a tolerance for intolerance abroad.[3]

The individual most responsible for these domestic and international decisions was William Lyon Mackenzie King, who served as prime minister from 1921 to 1930 and again from 1935 to 1948, and assigned himself the file of secretary of state for external affairs for all but his last two years as prime minister. This is not to imply that King was an inherently malevolent man. The prime minister sought peace above all, and pursued a diplomatic strategy he was confident would achieve that goal. And much of the time, he was simply speaking for Canada and reflecting the dominant view of its people; the successes and failures of his interwar diplomacy thus belong to the citizens of his country as a whole. That said, the shortest route to understanding how the Canadian state came to adopt its attitudes and strategies towards the crisis bred by fascism is through Prime Minister King, shaper and servant of Canadian opinion and policy. And the episode that most clearly reveals these attitudes and their origins, manifestations, and consequences is the four days King spent in Berlin in the summer of 1937 as a guest of the Nazis. That visit left the Canadian prime minister enthusing over the regime's transformation of Germany and confident that, in no small part because of his own intercession, Europe was destined for a just and lasting peace.

In recounting King's diplomatic initiative, this study raises questions about the proper response to governments that flout international law, the rights of those within and beyond their borders, and the peace and stability of the globe. Under which circumstances should democracies engage with, shun, reprimand, or seek to transform unlawful, authoritarian regimes? Are foreign nations whose interests are intertwined with the economic well-being of a country like Canada exempt from our criticism, regardless of their indifference or threat to human rights and international justice and peace? Should morality factor into decisions regarding diplomatic relations and international trade, even if this threatens prosperity? How can multi-ethnic states best align their commitments to the global community with efforts to maintain domestic harmony? What are our responsibilities to those seeking refuge from the violence, persecution, and anarchy wrought by state and non-state aggression? Should answers to these questions be fashioned in isolation or in dialogue with like-minded states?

Such questions, rarely posed prior to the rise of twentieth-century totalitarian regimes, have become part of the modern diplomatic calculus, but how seriously do we take them? Why was Merkel's carefully qualified congratulation so unusual among international leaders? In an age when democracy and the liberal international order are facing some of their gravest challenges since the 1930s, when autocratic populists are again stoking ethnic and national rivalries in order to build support for regressive domestic and international schemes, these are not hypothetical dilemmas. Many well-meaning people from the interwar era took approaches that inadvertently strengthened the forces of violence and hatred, and we ignore their example at our peril.

It is easy, of course, to look back and denounce the errors in judgement of previous generations, to assert that we would not have fallen prey to the same biases, hubris, and faulty judgement when confronted by something as ominous as Nazism. To study history with equanimity, however, is to recognize that some of the choices we make today will be looked upon with mortification by later generations required to live with the outcomes of those choices. While it is surely impossible to get everything right as we navigate the labyrinth of foreign relations, the story of Canada's response to Hitler's Germany suggests that certain habits of mind are essential to crafting a constructive response to the wider world: humility regarding our own suppositions; careful scrutiny of the preponderance of evidence, one focused on the deeds, not merely the words, of foreign actors; a willingness to look beyond parochial interests and tackle pressing issues in collaboration with others; a keen sensitivity towards the most vulnerable, informed by an unwavering defence of human rights and equality. The liberal order that was constructed with such care and urgency following history's most ruinous war surely warrants the taking of such pains.

In retracing the footsteps of Prime Minister King's visit to Germany, this book also gives space to two parallel storylines. The first involves a survey of the changes to the built environment wrought by the conflict King and others worked so strenuously to avoid. The Berlin toured by King in 1937 was almost wholly annihilated during the war, turning the task of reconstructing his visit into a grim excavation of an urban landscape brutalized by repressive ideologies, aerial assaults, political dismemberment, and walled and militarized borders.

Such an excavation serves as testament to the consequences of a war of aggression inaugurated by a state so reprehensible that its enemies would accept nothing less than its unconditional surrender – and would then occupy and divide, imposing separate and ideologically opposed governments and a hated border that Germans would wait forty-five years to erase. Importantly, to chronicle the annihilation and reconstruction of Berlin is to illustrate and interrogate the Allied decision to deploy area (that is, indiscriminate) bombing against cities inhabited mostly by non-combatants – the majority of them children, women, and the elderly – a tactic whose contribution to the defeat of Nazism remains hotly debated. Allied raids pounded Berlin alone with roughly seventy thousand tons of bombs that killed thirty-five thousand of its inhabitants and led 40 per cent of remaining residents to flee.[4] The work to restore the city's infrastructure, housing, economy, and health standards to pre-war levels would go on for decades, during which time hunger, disease, and exposure claimed further victims. Would we countenance the deployment of area bombing in wars conducted in our name today? Should the international community do more to prevent warring factions from targeting civilians – sadly, a tactic that has not gone out of fashion in the conflicts of the twenty-first century? To answer these questions, we must be wide-eyed and frank about the consequences of past assaults on urban civilians and spaces.

The second parallel story traces the highly commendable efforts of Berliners, and Germans as a whole, to acknowledge and confront the past through commemorative sites preserved and created throughout the post-war era, a project of remembrance that continues to the present. As we follow King's path through Berlin and its surrounding environs, we will encounter remnants of and memorials to the region's complicated and conflict-ridden past, evidence of a degree of willingness to own up to history that is unparalleled among modern nation-states. None of the questions raised about what and how to commemorate have come with easy answers, and the forthright debates undertaken by post-war Germans provide something of a guide for other peoples – like Canadians – who have come to realize that they, too, have a responsibility to reconcile past wrongs they had previously attempted to deny or rationalize away. Only through a collective commitment to this process will we demonstrate, to reprise Chancellor Merkel, a true allegiance to the rule of law and the dignity of all humankind.

1

Of Lions and Lyons

June 26, 1937, a Saturday: A Paris-to-Berlin overnight train approaches the German border; the weather is fair and clouds dot the twilight summer sky. In a railcar hastily added to the train that morning specifically to accommodate him, Canadian prime minister William Lyon Mackenzie King tugs on the sleeve of one of his long-suffering secretaries, Edward Pickering, to point out one particular billowy mass. The secretary is "amazed," as King wrote the next day in his diary, by a "cloud formation which was exactly that of a seated lion ... facing towards Germany." It is an undeniable portent, a symbol of "security" and "strength" that confirmed that the prime minister's current mission – a four-day visit to preach peace to a government seemingly bent on expansion at any cost – was the cornerstone of a divine plan to vanquish the metaphorical and considerably more menacing clouds then gathering over Europe: those of war.[1]

This was neither the first nor last appearance of the king of the jungle on King's trip to Europe. Visiting Scotland a week earlier to take in his ancestral homeland, the prime minister was led by an elderly local to the gravestone of a purported forbear, William Lyon, which was crowned by a carving of his animal-kingdom homonym. A few days later the prime minister purchased a number of Scottish mementos and antiques, including a pair of bronze lion doorstops that he trusted would "please Pat and Derry," the canine companions of King, and his neighbour Joan Patteson. On 27 June, his first morning in Berlin, King's gaze was drawn to a pair of stone lions flanking the steps of a museum; later that day he entered the Berlin zoo through the Loewentor (Lion Gate) with its twin sculpted lions "glorious in power and majesty." He then encountered the authentic specimens roaring in their cages and a "little lion carried by a keeper which I patted twice on the head – it all seemed significant," he wrote that night in his diary, reflecting on the recurring cat motif. Opening his Bible that same evening, King chanced upon Acts 27 (given the date, no mere coincidence for the numerologist prime minister), wherein the Apostle Paul, on board a ship buffeted by a violent Mediterranean storm, is visited by an angel. The heavenly messenger assures Paul that although he must "be brought before Caesar," God would ensure his safety and that of his shipmates. Just two days from being brought before German chancellor Adolf Hitler, King was buoyed by the scriptural lesson, writing: "Could any words be plainer than those! or their meaning or significance clearer. God grant I may be used to serve His holy will."[2]

Adherents of bibliomancy – the practice of gaining supernatural guidance by randomly selecting a passage from a sacred text – face a stiff challenge here, as we know in broad brushstrokes where this is headed: all would *not* be well in the wake of King's peace initiative, as the Fuhrer would in due course, and in accordance with a long-predetermined plan, lead his country and the world to catastrophe. Far better for the prime minister and humanity (not to mention bibliomantics) would have been a chance encounter with the warning found in 1 Peter 5:8, wherein the lion symbolizes not security or majesty but the Devil himself, "seeking someone to devour." And while Hitler had little use for scripture, doubtless he would have embraced an analogous interpretation of the ways of the lion expressed by Friedrich Nietzsche, who has the beast, through sheer triumph of will, smashing old notions of morality in order to remake the world.[3]

Sadly, King's benign reading of feline symbology would come to epitomize the spectacularly ill-informed image of Hitler and Nazism that he would bring back to Canada and broadcast to the world. As a result of interviews with top officials, information gleaned from guided tours of various Nazi departments and initiatives, and, not insignificantly, his own and nimble intermediation, the prime minister concluded that war was highly unlikely. The men he communed with – including Joachim von Ribbentrop, Rudolph Hess, Hermann Göring, and the Fuhrer himself – had assured him of Nazi Germany's irenic intentions, and King found their pledges sincere. Indeed, and notwithstanding the rough treatment the Nazi government had received at the hands of the foreign press and certain uninformed and imprudent British politicians, King judged his hosts honourable men and reliable international partners with whom he anticipated productive diplomatic relations, even enduring personal friendships. The true threat to peace, the prime minister concluded, came from those who would condemn and isolate the Nazi regime and seek to thwart what were in truth only limited and justifiable German territorial and diplomatic readjustments. King sailed for home believing that he had found the path to Hitler's heart, that he had helped the Fuhrer to embrace the life-affirming aspects of the Nazi agenda and shun any actions that would threaten the magnificent transformation of Germany the prime minister had witnessed during his visit.

Mackenzie King was certainly not alone in misreading the omens in the 1930s, but it would be difficult to find a democratic leader who missed the mark by a wider margin or held onto salutary views of the Fuhrer and his movement, in the face of outrage after outrage, more stubbornly or ingenuously. Andrew Nagorski's history of Americans who visited or lived in Germany during Hitler's ascent and rule found that "many were superficial in their observations, some were deliberately blind, and a few became Nazi apologists. But most of the Americans came to understand what was happening around them, even if they often found it hard to grasp the full implications" as they sought to make sense of "a society undergoing a horrific transformation in the name of a demented ideology ... The best of them, listening closely to the drumbeat of German militarism, recognized the looming danger."[4] Unlike Mackenzie King, many of Nagorski's subjects had more than four days in Germany to reach their verdicts. By 1937, however, these and other foreign visitors to the Third Reich had broadcasted far and wide their increasingly dystopian alarms in a flurry of newspaper and magazine articles and bestselling books. Humanity was on edge for good reason – the Nazis, eyewitnesses had repeatedly warned the world, seemed primed to plunge civilization into the abyss.

Mackenzie King was no stranger to these dark appraisals, but his own survey of Hitler's Germany led him to dismiss these dire warnings and to confidently submit a rather different set of prognostications for international affairs. This raises an important though ultimately enigmatic question: Did the prime minister's misapprehensions matter to the wider course of events? What we can say for certain is that his tone-deaf estimations of, and communications with, Nazi apparatchiks did absolutely nothing to alter Hitler's suspicion that Western leadership was naive and pliable; indeed, King's conversations may well have enhanced the Fuhrer's impression that the British in particular would continue to fold in the face of the increasingly outrageous international gambles dictated by his mania for more German *Lebensraum* (living space). At the same time, King's glad tidings to newly appointed prime minister Neville Chamberlain following the visit – that the alleged threat from Hitler's Germany was a chimera conjured by a toxic mix of jingoism, fear, and misinformation – were precisely what his British opposite did not need to hear. Would a more responsible set of observations from King, communicated clearly to all involved, have made an iota of difference? We will never know. But it is nigh impossible to find the good in King's initiative, one that was, it must be acknowledged, undertaken with the most commendable objective of averting a second world war.

This is a story of why King's mission to Berlin proved so personally unenlightening, and of some of the consequences that his delusions reaped for the prime minister, his country, and the international order.

2

Arrival

A little before 9 a.m. on 27 June, Mackenzie King and his assistant private secretary Edward Pickering arrived in Berlin. King was sixty-two years old, and at the midway point of more than two decades as Canada's prime minister. He sensed, not without foundation, a certain kinship to the people of Germany. He had been born in a small town in southwestern Ontario made up primarily of ethnic Germans who named their community Berlin in tribute to their land of origin. Young Willie, as he was then called, absorbed enough of the German language from his neighbours, and later from a stint at Humboldt University in old-world Berlin, to give the occasional prepared speech in German once he entered politics.[1]

The First World War was not kind to German Canadians nor to the town of Berlin, whose nickname, "Canada's German Capital," created obvious complications after Britain, in the name of its entire empire, declared war on the Central Powers. In the conflict's first days the more Anglophilic Berlin townsfolk manifested their disdain for their new enemy by removing a bust of Kaiser Wilhelm I from a local park and depositing it into a nearby lake. Verbal and physical harassment of ethnic Germans in Berlin, as across the country, was common throughout the war. The town's name was particularly galling to self-styled patriots, and was rechristened "Kitchener" by public plebiscite in June 1916 to honour the controversial British imperialist and general, who had been sailing for negotiations in Russia earlier that month when he was sent to his grave by a German mine in the North Atlantic.[2]

The King family was not around to witness the jingoistic crusade to expunge Berlin's German-ness (a transformation that Mackenzie himself opposed). They had moved one hundred kilometres east to Toronto in 1893 after the family patriarch, John, determined that the larger city would offer more clients for his law practice. Although not especially well off, the King family lived as if they were, hiring servants they could barely afford – as well as a governess to tutor their four children in German and other subjects. However, it was Mackenzie, second oldest and the firstborn son, whom his parents judged the most promising of their offspring. They doted on him accordingly, to the exasperation of his siblings.[3]

Part of the family's fixation on status arose from his mother Isabel's lineage. She was the daughter of prominent politician and journalist William Lyon Mackenzie, a radical democrat who in 1837 attempted to overthrow the elitist government of Upper Canada and replace it with an American-style republic. Although her father was later pardoned for that insurrection, its failure and his decade of exile in New York state that followed brought a certain ignominy to the family name that Isabel, and later her eldest son, strove to redress. However financially draining to John and Isabel, the tutoring of Mackenzie, as he came to be known, was a component of this project, and it served its purpose. He excelled in high school and progressed rapidly through various post-secondary degrees, including one in law, before heading to the University of Chicago and then Harvard for graduate work in political economy. An MA at Harvard in 1898 was followed by the same school's conferring of a PhD in 1909 for "Oriental Immigration to Canada," a report King completed for the Canadian federal government.[4]

The young King was a devout Presbyterian and a committed advocate of the Progressive Era's Social Gospel movement. This general outlook and his growing expertise in economics and politics provided the logical foundations for a career in the public sector. In 1900, following an offer extended by a friend of his father, King took a job as the editor of the Liberal government's *Labour Gazette,* and in short order was made deputy minister of the newly created Department of Labour. In 1908, he ran successfully for the federal seat of Waterloo North, a riding that included his hometown of Berlin, and shortly after was named the nation's first minister of labour.[5]

Defeated in the 1911 election, Mackenzie King was out of politics through much of the 1910s. However, his reputation as a labour fixer caught the eye of John D. Rockefeller, Jr, whose corporation was facing a public-relations crisis after it responded violently to recent worker militancy. King consulted for the Rockefellers from 1914–1918, though not, as some critics charged, to dodge the war – his stateside job began well before the outbreak of the conflict and King, nearly forty when the war began and largely unacquainted with demanding physical activity, would likely have been rejected for service. While in Rockefeller's employ King maintained his connections to the Canadian Liberals, and ran unsuccessfully for the party in 1917.[6]

Prior to that election, most Liberal candidates outside Quebec abandoned their long-time leader Wilfrid Laurier over his opposition to conscription, and joined the wartime Union government of Conservative leader Robert Borden. Despite his 1917 electoral defeat, King's loyalty to his party and its leader paid off. Before Laurier died in February 1919, he made it clear that King was his preferred successor; at the leadership convention in August of that year, the ambitious protégé was duly elected to replace the august patriarch. King's success as a mediator while with the Department of Labour and his stand against conscription helped to separate him from other candidates and secure favour among the party's powerful Quebec wing.[7] The Liberals won their first federal election with King as leader in 1921, and except for a Conservative party interlude between 1930 and 1935, King held the office of prime minister until his resignation in 1948.

If the Liberal bigwigs of today's image-obsessed era were vetting King as a potential candidate – even for a safe Liberal riding, much less for party leader – they might well judge him unelectable. He was bland and workmanlike, an uninspiring speaker possessing a "high-pitched, whiny voice" and little charisma. By his own reckoning he was unphotogenic and physically unimposing – balding, short, paunchy.[8] He lacked the attractive partner – or any partner – and the wholesome, accomplished offspring commonly trotted out to verify the candidate's own character and capacity to inspire.

Few Canadians of King's generation, however, could deny his political capacities. He was admittedly never beloved as a national leader like contemporaries Franklin Roosevelt and Winston Churchill – although King helped to steer his country through the same traumatic miasma of the Depression and Second World War years. Yet King, exercising an enviable capacity to find and build middle ground, sound out the public mood, defer controversial decisions until the winds were in his favour, and employ some very dexterous and occasionally crooked political stickhandling, earned an unprecedented five electoral victories and more than twenty-one years in power. He was passionate about Canadian unity, and governed with an eye to the interests of Quebecers. He oversaw Canada's transformation into both a welfare state and a fully autonomous nation, presiding over such milestones as the 1931 Statute of Westminster, which allowed Canada its own foreign policy, and the 1946 Naturalization Act, which finally defined citizens of the country as Canadians, not Britons; King was the first to receive a certificate of citizenship. During the Second World War, he managed to hold his party and the country together when the issue of conscription threatened once again to tear both apart. For these feats of nation-building and -sustaining, historian Margaret MacMillan called King Canada's Bismarck.[9]

Time has not diminished respect for his political IQ. In a 2016 *Maclean's* magazine survey of Canadian academics, King regained the title of greatest prime minister that he claimed in a similar 1997 poll and then lost – by a slim margin – in 2011. Survey participants from all three polls praised his longevity, ability to weather enormous domestic and international crises, masterful political judgement, and devotion to national unity. Particularly impressive was King's consonance with the public mood, operating as he was in an era before opinion polls and focus groups. The prime minister, respondents noted, "intuitively understood and responded to popular attitudes" and demonstrated a "canny ability to detect opinion trends." As a federal politician, King's reputation is without equal.[10]

Mackenzie King the man, however, has not aged nearly as well. A series of revelations and re-evaluations since his death in 1950 have bruised his image to the point where this extraordinarily successful national leader offers little in the way of a usable legacy – indeed, King's "bland and workmanlike" persona came to be seen as a cover for a man who was secretly salacious and approximately bonkers. Post-mortem testimonials from his colleagues and staff (he had few friends) depicted a humourless, thin-skinned, Oedipal, and cravenly opportunistic glory-seeker who was cringingly sycophantic to both the famous and those who might be of use to him. His reputational crown slipped further as rumours proliferated (and were later confirmed in King's own bizarre diary, published in stages between 1971 and 1981) that the prime minister was gripped and guided by the spirits of dead family members, world leaders, and pets, by certain angles of the hands of clocks, by signs manifested in clouds and dollops of shaving cream, and by numerical coincidences. While historians continue to praise his considerable administrative and tactical skills – even as they often hunt in vain for the principles undergirding his many feats of political endurance – aspiring Canadian politicians gain little leverage by casting themselves as the guardians of the Mackenzie King legacy. Woodrow Wilson, FDR, Churchill, John F. Kennedy, Margaret Thatcher, Ronald Reagan, Wilfrid Laurier, Lester Pearson, Trudeau the Elder – all boast candid disciples, exploitable coattails, and a commonly held understanding of their core political values. King's name, rarely invoked even by the party he built into twentieth-century Canada's "natural" governor, has become something of a national embarrassment, one that cannot be uttered without at least some leavening (and usually puckish) allusions to his undeniable oddities.[11] This paragraph is but one case in point.

The diary itself has become a centrepiece of Canadian lore. King began it in 1893 when he was eighteen and logged entries nearly every day until his death in 1950, raw material for the memoirs that he would never write. In his will King ordered that all but the diary passages he indicated as significant be destroyed, but his literary executors soon found themselves poring over a trove of revelations about the public and private King that they could not bear to incinerate. With the consent of the Liberal government led by King's successor, Louis St. Laurent, the executors transcribed the diaries, more than seven and a half million words in all. When they were released to the public, Canadian political history's reputation for dowdiness suffered a staggering, if not terminal, blow.[12]

King's private ruminations proved irresistible to a range of authors, and C.P. Stacey was surely the most unexpected. A professor of history and retired Canadian military officer whose previous works offered rather staid analyses of his country's military and political past, Stacey was nearly seventy and working on a general survey of Canada at war when King's literary executors permitted him to utilize the diary for his research. Stunned at what he discovered, Stacey put the survey on hold and instead delivered to his publishers a work well outside his typical field (and some would argue his expertise), *A Very Double Life: The Private World of Mackenzie King* (1976). The book became a sensation and the first of many lurid pseudo-psychoanalytical meditations on what made "Weird Willie" tick. Stacey, whose ability to divine a sexually loaded Freudian craving behind nearly every opaque diary reflection on guilt, regret, or wasted time may have revealed as much about himself as his subject, christened King's diary "the most important Canadian political document of the twentieth century."[13]

The diary is certainly the most indispensable record of his 1937 mission to Berlin, not only for its characteristic candour and detail but because, outside the newspapers, almost no data on the trip from the

German perspective survived the war. Employing King's recollections to help piece together the story raises understandable concerns over bias and faulty recollection. However, these concerns are leavened by the fact that the typewritten portions of the diary (the preponderance of the entries) were dictated to secretary Edward Pickering, who was also a witness to the events described and took his own notes during the trip's most important meetings. It is also a fact that although King's goal was the opposite, his diary often paints a distinctly unflattering picture of its protagonist. This is especially true of the handwritten entries, penned when the prime minister was alone and free to divulge his most candid and frequently solipsistic impressions of his feats of political logic and dexterity.

Elihu Root, US president William McKinley's secretary of war, once commented that his boss "had a way of handling men so that they thought his ideas were their own. He cared nothing about the credit, but McKinley *always had his way.*" Others described McKinley as "a sweet-tempered man who forswore carrying grudges." Mackenzie King was, on these matters, the anti-McKinley: a leader who relied heavily on the counsel of his many capable advisors but who cared very much about the credit; a well-mannered and outwardly kindly man who was nevertheless a hanging judge when it came to those he felt had wronged him. Like McKinley, however, King had his way more often than not, and both were students of the "slow-and-steady school of leadership."[14] The prime minister played the long game and placed emphasis on public consensus and what he considered the greater good rather than the divide-and-rule calculations employed by politicians cravenly partial to their "base."

King's decision to visit Berlin was, for a man who generally operated with such caution, uncharacteristically spontaneous, a last-minute add-on to a voyage to the British Isles. He had set sail from Montreal aboard the RMS *Empress of Australia* on 24 April, bound for the 12 May coronation of King George VI and Elizabeth Bowes-Lyon, the Windsors shunted onto the throne by the abdication of George's brother Edward VIII.[15] Meetings in London were to follow the royal celebrations, and then King would travel north to Scotland, his ancestral homeland, for a week of sightseeing.

It was a time of great uncertainty for Britain and the Empire, as the change at Buckingham Palace was accompanied by a change at 10 Downing Street; Conservative prime minister Stanley Baldwin had announced that he would resign shortly after the coronation and turn

2.1 Members of the Canadian legation to the 1937 Imperial Conference sail for Britain aboard the RMS *Empress of Australia*, 1 May 1937. *Left to right*: Minister of Defence Ian Mackenzie, Minister of Finance Charles Dunning, Senator Raoul Dandurand, Prime Minister Mackenzie King, Minister of Justice Ernest Lapointe, and Minister of Mines and Resources Thomas Crerar (no relation to H.D.G. Crerar). (Library and Archives Canada, C-087864)

power over to his chancellor of the exchequer, Neville Chamberlain. Since representatives from the British dominions and colonies would be assembled in London, and since the new prime minister was eager to confer with those same representatives about the challenges ahead, the home government proposed an Imperial Conference following the coronation. While attendees could not have known it, it would be the last of the fifteen such conferences held intermittently since 1887.[16] This one was dominated by the matter that ultimately rendered the concept of imperial conferences an anachronism – the crisis in Europe that would incite a conflict whose immensity and savagery bankrupted both the great colonial powers and the remaining pretences of the "white man's burden."

While at the conference King was introduced to the German ambassador to London, Ulrich Friedrich Wilhelm Joachim von Ribbentrop, representative of the government most responsible for that European crisis. A member of the German nobility via his formal adoption at age thirty-eight by a titled but distantly related "aunt," Ambassador Ribbentrop, now forty-four, was a notoriously dim dilettante and social climber. His machinations in support of Hitler's appointment to chancellor earned him a central role in the new government, despite the near-universal conviction that this ersatz aristocrat and former champagne salesman lacked the training, character, and intellect for high office. A year after his meeting with King, he would be appointed Germany's foreign minister and emerge as the regime's second-most-fervent warmonger, and later, a leading and eager facilitator of the Final Solution. Following the war, Ribbentrop was the first of the Nuremberg defendants to be hanged; his execution followed a trial that laid bare his mindless fanaticism (he expressed a grovelling devotion to the Fuhrer all the way to the noose) as well as his more general mindlessness (asked by the incredulous prosecution how such an obvious mediocrity had gained a station so far beyond his abilities, German diplomat and naval officer Ernst von Weizsäcker explained that "Hitler never noticed Ribbentrop's babbling, because Hitler always did all the talking"). Even his fellow accused in the dock at Nuremberg hated him to a man.[17]

King's first impressions of the ambassador were of an entirely different sort; the prime minister was instantly taken by a man he judged "exceedingly friendly, and pleasant, both in appearance and manner."[18] Doubtless King already knew that the wine merchant had plied his trade in Canada before the Great War, and Ribbentrop played his Canadian card effectively, charming the prime minister with recollections of his days in the Dominion, including a stint living in Ottawa. King responded by proclaiming his formidable grasp of the German character by way of his affiliations with the Canadian and German Berlins, and both men agreed on the urgent need to improve British-German relations. Reflecting on a private lunch with Ribbentrop two weeks later, King called the man that fellow Nazi elites detested for his flagrant careerism, vanity, hypersensitivity, and obsequiousness towards elites "a man I could get along with quite easily."[19]

The amity towards an individual of such qualities says something about King's own traits and affinities, and this sense of mutual bonhomie may explain why the prime minister failed to fully consider the implications of one of his rare genuinely oracular spiritual sessions. At his lunch with King, Ribbentrop wore a white scarf around his neck that, to the prime minister, gave the appearance of a head disconnected from its body. This brought to mind a previous meeting with "a lady in New York" (doubtless a medium) who, while conversing with King, saw his head metamorphosize into that of Hitler, floating on "a sort of a plate as though he had been cut around the throat." Rather than perceiving in these signs the fates awaiting Ribbentrop, Hitler, and/or Germany itself, King concluded that the woman and her ghoulish vision had simply presaged upcoming conversations with Reich officials that would see King "opening a door in the establishment of friendship."[20]

A year before the Imperial Conference, Ribbentrop and King had exchanged cordial letters proposing a bilateral trade agreement, a pact that had been approved by Canada's Parliament just prior to King's departure for the coronation. When they met in person, the ambassador's sense that King might be counted among Germany's better friends was confirmed. Indeed, Ribbentrop was in the midst of drawing up a list of "eminent Britons" whose comparative warmth towards the Nazi regime warranted special invitations to Germany. After meeting King, Ribbentrop added one non-Briton: "the Canadian prime minister, Mackenzie King who is very friendly towards Germany and whose visit I consider particularly important in view of the significance of the Dominions for British Foreign policy."[21]

With King now before him over lunch, Ribbentrop extended the invitation, which included a promise that the prime minister would have an audience with German chancellor Adolf Hitler. King was flattered. It was, the prime minister believed, a testament to his keen grasp of the German people and the difficult situation they had faced since the Great War. Not all were similarly educated about the "German question." At the reception where King and Ribbentrop had first met, Conservative member of parliament Winston Churchill interrupted their genial conversation. At the time, the future British prime minister was wandering in the political wilderness, shunned by many in his own party over his hostility towards the Nazis. Ribbentrop, King noted, cooled immediately, "indicating, I thought, a sort of feeling that Churchill did not fully understand Germany."[22]

Ribbentrop's evident warmth towards the Canadian prime minister was thus an auspicious signal. King was tantalized by the prospect of adding Germany to his itinerary, confident that expressions of kindness and understanding were a far surer route to stabilizing

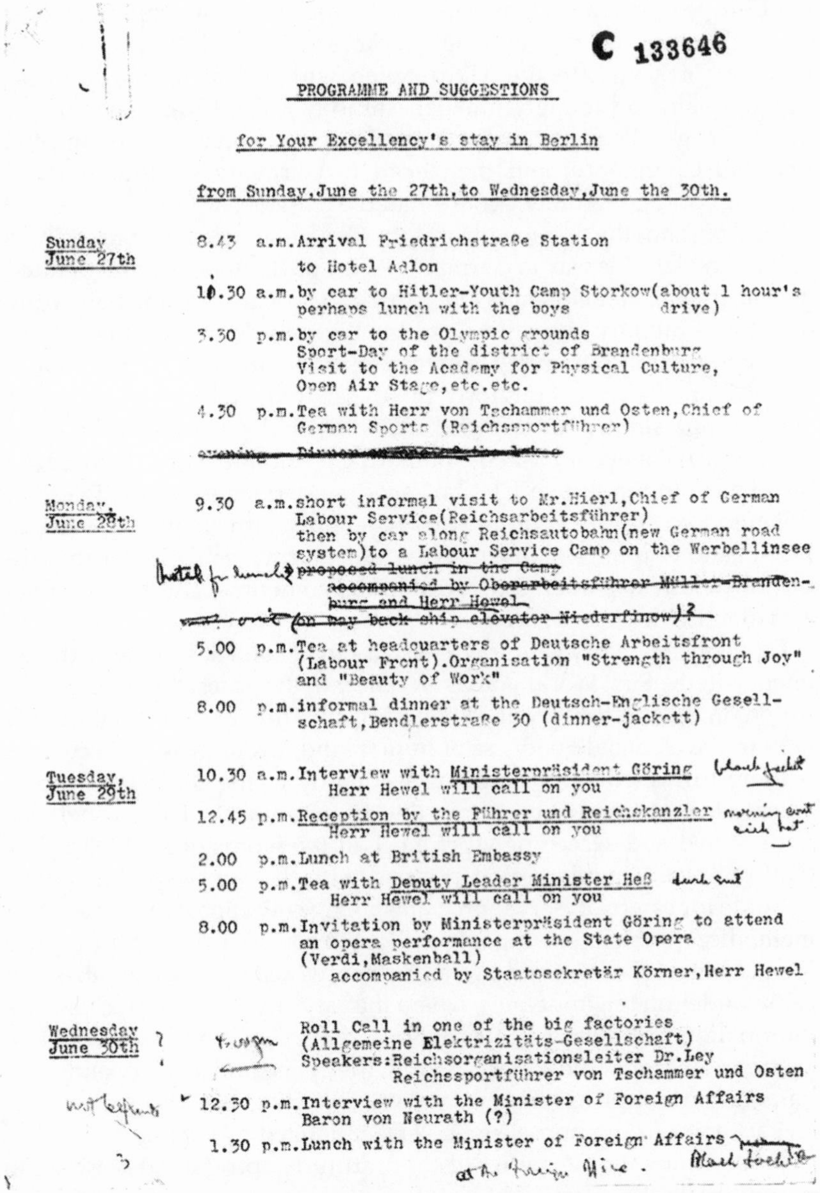

C 133646

PROGRAMME AND SUGGESTIONS

for Your Excellency's stay in Berlin

from Sunday, June the 27th, to Wednesday, June the 30th.

Sunday
June 27th

8.43 a.m. Arrival Friedrichstraße Station
to Hotel Adlon

10.30 a.m. by car to Hitler-Youth Camp Storkow (about 1 hour's
perhaps lunch with the boys   drive)

3.30 p.m. by car to the Olympic grounds
Sport-Day of the district of Brandenburg
Visit to the Academy for Physical Culture,
Open Air Stage, etc. etc.

4.30 p.m. Tea with Herr von Tschammer und Osten, Chief of
German Sports (Reichssportführer)

~~evening   Dinner~~ *(struck through)*

Monday,
June 28th

9.30 a.m. short informal visit to Mr.Hierl, Chief of German
Labour Service (Reichsarbeitsführer)
then by car along Reichsautobahn (new German road
system) to a Labour Service Camp on the Werbellinsee
hotel for lunch ~~proposed lunch in the Camp~~
~~accompanied by Oberarbeitsführer Müller-Branden-~~
~~burg and Herr Hewel~~
~~(on way back ship elevator Niederfinow)?~~

5.00 p.m. Tea at headquarters of Deutsche Arbeitsfront
(Labour Front). Organisation "Strength through Joy"
and "Beauty of Work"

8.00 p.m. informal dinner at the Deutsch-Englische Gesellschaft, Bendlerstraße 30 (dinner-jackett)

Tuesday,
June 29th

10.30 a.m. Interview with Ministerpräsident Göring *(black jacket)*
Herr Hewel will call on you

12.45 p.m. Reception by the Führer und Reichskanzler *(morning coat + silk hat)*
Herr Hewel will call on you

2.00 p.m. Lunch at British Embassy

5.00 p.m. Tea with Deputy Leader Minister Heß *(dark suit)*
Herr Hewel will call on you

8.00 p.m. Invitation by Ministerpräsident Göring to attend
an opera performance at the State Opera
(Verdi, Maskenball)
accompanied by Staatssekretär Körner, Herr Hewel

Wednesday ?
June 30th

(handwritten notes)
Roll Call in one of the big factories
(Allgemeine Elektrizitäts-Gesellschaft)
Speakers: Reichsorganisationsleiter Dr.Ley
Reichssportführer von Tschammer und Osten

12.30 p.m. Interview with the Minister of Foreign Affairs
Baron von Neurath (?)

1.30 p.m. Lunch with the Minister of Foreign Affairs
at the foreign office.   Black frock?

2.2 The itinerary prepared for King by Ribbentrop's office; handwritten
notations are those of a member of the prime minister's staff. (Library and
Archives Canada, C-133646)

the European situation than the kind of toughness synonymous with the aptly marginalized (in King's reckoning) Churchill. After vetting the idea of a visit to the Third Reich with British prime minister Chamberlain and foreign minister Anthony Eden, King resolved that he would go ahead with his planned trip to Scotland following the Imperial Conference, and then head to Germany for four days of meetings and government-coordinated excursions.[23]

King was not the first member of the Canadian delegation to the conference to make his way to Germany. When the London meetings ended in mid-June, Colonel Henry Duncan Graham Crerar, Canadian Army director of military operations and intelligence, flew to visit Hamburg and then Berlin to conduct his own, personally funded reconnaissance of the Third Reich. Crerar, forty-nine years old, was of a background and outlook similar to King and many other English Canadian elites of the era: a college-educated, southern Ontario Protestant who traced his lineage to the British Isles; a Canadian nationalist who advocated full autonomy for his country and yet retained strong emotional ties to Britain and Empire; a man who was polite, formal, and outwardly a little dull, and who garbed considerable and sometimes ruthless personal ambition in the cloak of *noblesse oblige*.[24]

Unlike King, Harry Crerar was also a career soldier, serving with distinction in the First World War as an officer in the gruesome battles of attrition on the Western Front. While King's worldview was built upon a faith in the essential goodness of humankind, Crerar's experience with warfare furnished some haunting testimony to the contrary. Temperament also set Crerar apart from the prime minister. The colonel was understated and exceedingly practical, in the words of his biographer Paul Dickson "singularly unconcerned with the public spotlight." His aptitude for careful observation, painstaking collection of evidence, and methodical problem-solving was evident to his instructors at Kingston's Royal Military College, and Crerar further refined these sensibilities as a commander on the front lines, where the capacity to gather and process information was often a matter of life and death.[25] While King could be a sharp observer of the material world, the prime minister's openness to paranormal as well as sensory data was entirely at odds with the exclusively "normal," no-nonsense universe inhabited by Crerar.

These contrasting experiences and attitudes provide at least some grounding to the question of how two prominent individuals from the same country could embark upon nearly identical and coterminous trips, and then return to Canada with vastly divergent travelogues. In

2.3 H.D.G "Harry" Crerar was Canadian Army director of military operations and intelligence when he travelled to Germany in 1937, two weeks before King's visit. This photograph was taken during the Second World War, during which Crerar was promoted to Commander of the Canadian First Army. (City of Vancouver Archives, AM54-S4-: Port P1588, Matthewhews, James Skitt, Major)

their respective reckonings of their time in Germany, King would come to play the part of Voltaire's Professor Pangloss, the sunny optimist seeking to instill that same bearing in his pupil Candide, while Crerar assumed the role of the jaded Martin, a philosopher striving to open Candide's eyes to the darkness in men's souls. While the prime minister's basic agenda in journeying to Berlin – to lower the temperature on

Anglo-German relations and to demonstrate that kindness, not toughness, would maintain the peace – clearly shaped his report from Germany, Crerar's agenda, too, coloured his own findings. Since the end
of the Great War the colonel had campaigned tirelessly for increased
military preparedness, a call he issued with greater urgency as fascism
gained ground in Europe.[26] Though both men returned with testimonials whose general thrust plainly supported their personal crusades, this
is not to say each was equally guilty of distortion or myopia. Rendering
judgement on that front requires measuring their respective findings
against those of other eyewitnesses and other information available at
the time, not to mention the truths made manifest by hindsight. An eye
to those comparators reveals rather unambiguously which visit proved
more instructive.

One simple measure of this King-Crerar discrepancy involves the
tactics they employed to document their respective trips. Where King,
as was his wont, outlined his activities and ideas in daily dictations to
Pickering along with his own handwritten addendums, Crerar operated
like a scout in enemy territory, one who feared he could well be sur-
veilled by his hosts. "I deliberately took no notes," he wrote in his confidential "Report on Visit to Germany" prepared afterward for Canadian
officials, "as a suitcase in a hotel bedroom does not provide safe custody
in Germany of today." Crerar also went out of his way to seek the views
of non-Nazis, treating his official docents like hostile witnesses to the
reality of life under Hitler. (Crerar's friend, the Canadian-born Bank of
England director Sir Edward Peacock, had put the colonel in touch with
some German contacts who promised a more objective view of the Nazi
project.)[27] King demonstrated a roughly inverse attitude to the trustwor-
thiness of the Third Reich representatives whose acquaintance he made
just two weeks after Crerar's visit. Over time, the course of world events
would bring a partial meeting of the minds, with King leading the call
for Canadian participation in the war against fascism and Crerar emerging as Canada's top field commander in that same conflict, although
they continued to clash over the precise nature and extent of Canada's
participation. In June 1937, however, the amount of daylight between
the two men on the German question was enough to blind.

It is unclear why the prime minister's assistant private secretary
Edward Pickering, rather than his personal secretary Edouard Handy,
accompanied King to Berlin, as both staffers travelled with the Canadian legation to London for the Imperial Conference. Perhaps King
valued the twenty-nine-year-old Pickering's experience over that of

Handy, twenty-six, as the former had worked for King since the summer of 1929, while Handy had joined the King entourage only in 1936. Any suppositions that the senior employee had jockeyed for the opportunity to visit Germany must be tempered by the widespread acknowledgement that working for Mackenzie King exacted a considerable toll on his subordinates' spirits. Pickering would later gain wide renown as a successful senior executive at the CBC and the Simpson's department store chain and a noted patron of Toronto's arts community, but he is often presented as a bumbling incompetent in the prime minster's diaries. Indeed, while King had a habit of dressing down his staff over "a poorly written memo, a simple mistake of human error or any one of a thousand other reasons," Pickering's alleged miscues in particular seemed to exasperate the PM. Immediately following the trip to Germany, King dictated to Handy that "it is sad to see a man [Pickering] bury his talent in a napkin, stand in the way of his own promotion and advancement." Both King and Pickering were doubtless relieved when the latter left the prime minister's employ for the CBC a year later.[28]

Pickering was hardly alone in tasting the bitterness of a King underling. Gordon Robertson, a later King staffer who went on to become Canada's top-ranking civil servant, recalled that his boss would often "use his power, whether as prime minister or simply as employer, to dominate and to humiliate people who could not defend themselves".[29] King ably demonstrated this talent the day before arriving in Berlin, dictating *to Pickering himself* the frustrations of trying to usher in a new millennium of world peace while surrounded by rank incompetents. Reflecting on the ways in which his 1918 book on the humane resolution of labour disputes, *Industry and Humanity*, and indeed his entire life's journey had laid the groundwork for steering "this hour and moment" of global crises towards reconciliation, King continued:

> With my mind filled with thoughts of the kind, I felt a little upset at having a lot of trivial things brought before me for possible reading today, and in discovering that no one of my Secretarial staff or in connection with the Legation had discovered or would let me know that the banks would not be opened on Saturday revealing again the old truth that if anything had to be done, one has to do it oneself. I had a distressing and confusing half an hour searching for the identification signature to permit my getting a letter of credit cashed, and another half hour's complications in getting money for Germany and for France on Saturday morning with even the staff in [travel agency Thomas] Cook's offices being reduced to half what they were, under some new law which has just come into force.[30]

King the august spokesman for the plight of the common man seems here to have given way to King the courtly grandee who bristled at labour regulations that inconvenienced him and "who never admitted he was adequately served," to quote another of his exasperated secretaries.[31] Both personas were authentically King, and the prime minister's inability to recognize the dissonance between them was part and parcel of a man who, despite a lifetime of penning ruminations on his every quotidian experience, feeling, and idea, manifested an often startling inability to acknowledge his own inconsistencies and deficiencies. To a significant degree, King was a stranger to himself.

In spite of the alleged blunderings and apathy of his staff, King's transport to Berlin went off without a hitch. This circumstance the prime minister owed not to his support team, but to his own intermediations, the generosity of the foreign governments involved, and the guidance of "unseen powers and ministering hands that are invisible."[32] And now King set foot, along with Pickering – the ministering hand that, though visible, often seemed more hindrance than help – on the platform of Friedrichstrasse Station in the Mitte district of Berlin.

Opened in 1882 as part of the original Berlin Statdbahn – the elevated east-west local line through the city – the station was expanded to accommodate U-bahn (subway) service in anticipation of the 1936 Berlin Olympics, a spectacle meant to showcase the Nazi transformation of post-war Germany. Although Polish saboteurs detonated a bomb in the station that killed fourteen and wounded twenty-seven in 1943, the structure largely escaped damage from Allied aerial bombardment during the Second World War, and thus appears today much as it did to the visiting Canadians eight decades ago.[33]

With a few notable exceptions. A year after King's visit, the station would serve as a principal staging area for Britain's *Kindertransport* operation, which delivered nearly ten thousand Jewish children from Germany and other Nazi-held territories to British foster families, boarding schools, and orphanages in the wake of the nationwide assault on Jewish houses of worship, businesses, and neighbourhoods known as *Kristallnacht*; today, a statue memorializing both the rescued children and the 1.6 million murdered in Nazi extermination camps, *Züge in das Leben – Züge in den Tod: 1938–1939* (Trains to Life – Trains to Death: 1938–1939) stands outside the main entrance to the station. Representing the arbitrary and stark disparity between the fates of the handful of children sent west and those transported eastward, the memorial was sculpted in 2008 by Frank Meisler, one of the children fostered in Britain during the war.[34]

2.4 Although surrounded by devastation, Friedrichstrasse station, in the background of this photograph, somehow survived the relentless Allied bombing of central Berlin. This image (looking northwest) from the spring of 1950 gives a good indication of the pace of the rebuilding efforts in the Soviet sector of Berlin. (Bundesarchiv, Bild 183-S95055)

A 1999 plaque on the western exterior wall of the station where the tracks pass over Friedrichstrasse points to another grim episode on the grounds. The English translation reads: "Shortly before the end of Hitler's criminal war two young German soldiers were hanged here by inhuman SS bandits" (*Kurz vor Beendigung des verbrecherischen Hitlerkrieges wurden hier zwei junge deutsche Soldaten von entmenschten SS-Banditen erhängt*). Executions of alleged deserters by the SS (short for Schutzstaffel, "protection squad") were common in the last days of the war, and for whatever reason, this example, in which two young men were hanged from the window bars of the shoe store that stood here in 1945, proved particularly notorious. The memorial's text features stock communist

2.5 Friedrichstrasse station in 2017, looking northeast. (Author photograph)

party terminology for the war and the SS, a testament to the fact that the first version of the plaque appeared in 1952, when the area lay in the Soviet zone of occupation. In a demonstration of the frequently unsettling paradoxes of German history, vandals removed earlier versions of the marker on several occasions following German unification in 1990, owing, it is surmised, to the widespread feeling summed up by German historian Theo Schulte: "that to have served loyally in Hitler's army ... was much more likely to have earned post-war respectability (and a war pension) than to have acted the part of a 'traitor.'"[35]

Mackenzie King's experience at Friedrichstrasse station, by contrast, was entirely convivial. He had enjoyed a good night's rest in his personal sleeping car and woke as the train approached Berlin. Upon entering a city whose chronic interwar demonstrations, strikes, street brawls, and cycle of recriminatory assassinations had been erased through ruthless Sturmabteilung (SA, "storm detachment") and SS patrols and purges of leftists and ethnic minorities, King recorded that he "could not but be impressed with great neatness of the City

2.6 Frank Meisler's 2008 sculpture commemorating the *Kindertransport* operation and those it left behind. Two children facing west smile as they depart for foster care in the United Kingdom, while the expressions of the five bound for killing centres to the east reflect fear and despair. (Author photograph, 2017)

as approached by train." He and Pickering were greeted on the platform by career diplomat Sir Nevile Henderson, the newly appointed British ambassador to Berlin, and thirty-three-year-old German diplomat Walther Hewel, Joachim von Ribbentrop's personal chief of staff; Hewel had been tasked by his boss to chaperone the Canadians during their four-day stay.[36]

An earlier, trip-planning meeting in London between King and Hewel had not gone well; King was unimpressed by the lack of "imagination" on offer from Ribbentrop's subordinate, so much so that the

2.7 Today, the Friedrichstrasse station memorial to two German soldiers executed by the SS is flanked by the windows of a McDonald's restaurant. (Author photograph, 2017)

prime minister resolved – temporarily, as it turned out – to shorten his tour by a day. Yet King seemed destined to get along with Hewel. Both men traded in, and were wowed by, a devotion to ceremony, duty, and the kind of ingratiating flattery that delighted some but could annoy the more aloof. Employing one of those German terms that is at once uncannily precise and difficult to translate, a waiter in post-war Berlin observed that Hewel "specialized in that kind of *Gemütlichkeit* [roughly, warmth and hospitality] that's never quite genuine unless it's a bit artificial." Of King, British High Commissioner to Canada Sir Francis Floud confided that he found the prime minister "excessively friendly."

2.8 Newly appointed British ambassador to Germany Sir Nevile Henderson
greets Prime Minister Mackenzie King on the platform at Friedrichstrasse
station, Berlin, on Sunday morning, 27 June 1937. Walther Hewel, Ribbentrop's
personal chief of staff, stands behind them at left. King is holding his prized
Mackenzie family tartan, a gift received from relatives a week earlier in
Scotland (see chapter 5). (Library and Archives Canada, PA-119012)

"My wife," Floud continued with far too much candour, "says after a conversation with him she feels as if the cat had licked her all over and she ought to go and have a bath."[37]

While not considered especially "imaginative," to reiterate King's charge, Hewel's capacity to charm enabled him to build business and political relationships around the world; that capacity was also based in part on his instinct to conceal the more repugnant aspects of his politics in the company of new contacts like King. In truth, Hewel was one of the earliest and most committed members of the fledgling Nationalsozialistische Deutsche Arbeiterpartei (NSDAP, National Socialist German Worker's Party, "Nazis" for short). He joined the party while still a teen and soon gained a position in the elite Stoßtrupp-Hitler (Shocktroop-Hitler), the leader's personal guard comprised of roughly twenty of his most fanatical loyalists, and the precursor to the SS. In the 1930s, Hewel would join the SS proper, the organization charged with enforcing the Nazis' racial policies and eventually its program of genocide, serving at the esteemed rank of *Sturmbannführer* (assault unit leader, equivalent to a major).[38]

Having done hard time with Hitler in the Landsberg Prison for participating in the failed Beer Hall Putsch of 1923, Hewel developed an unusually close relationship with the rising Nazi leader, a loner otherwise notoriously incapable of forming friendships. It appears that Hitler never forgot Hewel's birthday, presenting greetings and gifts even in the final years of the war, while information from a top-secret file on Hewel created after the conflict goes so far as to state unequivocally that "Hewel was Hitler's best friend." Known as one of the few who could stay awake during Hitler's nightly, repetitive, and mostly hate-filled monologues, Hewel was also one of the few to remain faithfully by his chancellor's side in the Fuhrerbunker to the bitter end. Sturmbannführer Hewel followed his master's suicide with his own, having given the Fuhrer an oath that he would do so, and performed the act exactly as his trusted companion allegedly did – by simultaneously shooting himself in the head while biting into a cyanide capsule. Both pistol and pill had been furnished by Hitler himself.[39]

3

Beholding the Nazi Miracle

Walther Hewel's grisly, unctuous demise seemed very far away in the summer of 1937; instead, as chaperone he laid on lavish doses of the *Gemütlichkeit* – and King drank it up. The prime minister enthused that his chatty German host drove Pickering and himself "in [an] open car through fields of ripening grain, getting [a] lovely view of country for miles beyond [the] suburbs of Berlin," and then treated the Canadians to lunch "beside a lake, and at a delightful spot." Hewel and King engaged in talks the latter described as "interesting," in which Hewel lamented the lack of cooperation from Britain over attempts to check the threat of communism and to address Germany's legitimate grievances, and in which King gathered that the Nazis were "not thinking of war."[1]

Also along for the ride on Germany's newly minted autobahn, according to King's diaries, was "a young officer of the South Movement." The designation is a typo (secretary Pickering blunders again?), as the entourage was on its way to separate girls' and boys' Hitlerjugend (Hitler Youth) camps at Storkow, a bucolic lakeside town about seventy kilometers southeast of the German capital. The youth organizations were by 1936 compulsory for all Germans aged ten to eighteen who were deemed racially pure and free of hereditary diseases; the training they received constituted a foundational component of the government policy of *Gleichschaltung* – roughly, coordination or synchronization – aimed at Nazifying the mentalities and strengthening the bodies of Aryan Germans in preparation for the wars of expansion to come. Here, indoctrination in such matters as Germany's destiny as master of Europe, the necessity of *Lebensraum*, the "science" underpinning Aryan supremacy, and lust for battle combined to produce a generation of soldiers, street thugs, and concentration camp guards whose fanaticism

3.1 and 3.2 (above and opposite) Exuberant Aryan specimens of the
Hitlerjugend being groomed for the impending racial crusade. (From Richter,
Carstensen, and Hitzer, *Germany*, n.p.)

and pitilessness would soon horrify the world. As historian Michael
Kater noted with some understatement, the camp training like that at
Storkow strove to "create conditions under which a German soldier,
as a former Hitler Youth member or leader, would find it difficult to
be guided by a humane conscience." The programs at Storkow would
in fact get worse: in the Second World War, the site became one of the
many subcamps of Sachsenhausen, the main concentration camp complex for the Berlin area, a constellation of facilities where more than
thirty thousand enemies of the state perished.[2]

King's evening dictation to Pickering regarding the stopover read
simply: "Visited a girls' camp, and later a boys' camp, being told of the

Youth faces life with a fresh, open countenance. Slender and supple, nimble as whippets, sturdy as leather, an

extensive methods of these organizations." Given the camps' blatant zeal for regimentation, blind obedience, and militancy, the brief, dispassionate description of the visits is notable. The prime minister had long disdained militarism – he expressed, as historian James Eayrs wrote, "a marked aversion to the military life and the military mind," deeming "the jingo-tory-militarist," as King himself called Canadian martial enthusiasts, a virus to be expunged from the national body politic. Perhaps, then, some unease over the camp regimen accounts for the brevity of the entry in an account of the trip that is otherwise meticulously chronicled. It is also likely that the excursion was overshadowed by the prime minister's thoughts of his upcoming appointment with Hitler, a meeting King's diary references repeatedly in the days leading up to it. And it is a certainty that King, like the many other foreign visitors taken to the camps in an effort to demonstrate Germany's revived spirit, was offered a sanitized tour of these brainwashing yards, *pace* the prime minister's belief that he had been "told of the extensive methods of these organizations." Such sleights of hand were commonplace. Bella Fromm, a Jewish social columnist for Berlin's liberal newspaper *Vossiche Zeitung*, informed an English friend "that he was not crazy" for suspecting that his tour of a concentration camp featured hale and hearty stand-ins for the real state enemies actually incarcerated there. "The trick was an ordinary Nazi routine," she wrote, "with which we were so familiar that it always seemed extraordinary to us that any human being with ordinary intelligence could possibly be taken [in] by it." Canadian journalist Matthew Halton called his own tour of the concentration camp at Dachau "a pre-arranged farce."[3]

Whatever the reason for his laconic initial description of the Hitler-jugend facility, King's reflections a few days later displayed only admiration for the camp's programming. While in Germany, he wrote, he had witnessed nothing less than "a new nation being created – a nation being conscientiously created, particularly through the appropriate training of youth." Naive and distressing, yes, but at the very least King did not take pains to publicly laud the process of mental perversion on display, as did British author Norman Hillson in his delusional 1937 bestseller *I Speak of Germany: A Plea for Anglo-German Friendship.* "So far as the German Youth Camps are concerned," Hillson informed readers, "the impartial observer must come away from them feeling that Dr. Goebbels is justified in his view that in the faces of the modern German you can discern a finer and happier face."[4]

At the same time, and in a pattern on view throughout his visit, the prime minister found no reason to condemn, even in his private reflections, aspects of the fascist project that seemingly ran counter to his sensibilities and begged for greater reflection and commentary. (This from a man otherwise obsessed with reflection and commentary, and one who in diary entries frequently let fly his often startlingly caustic and petty criticisms of his Liberal colleagues, political opponents, private staff, and, in particular, Canadian governor-general Vincent Massey.) By contrast, British political analyst and close Nazi observer Emily Lorimer, reporting on her own official tour of the camps, was disturbed by "the rigid regimentation of the mind" on full display, while Australian journalist Stephen Roberts wrote after his visit that the camps' "outward husk is imposing, but beneath is only mental aridness." H.D.G Crerar, the Canadian army officer who had made his own inspection of Nazi Germany just two weeks before King, expressed a similar dis-ease in his confidential report on the trip. The battle-tested colonel, no stranger to regimentation, found the intensive regulation of German life "from birth till death" alarming, observing that the grinding "rules, regulations and instructions" were reinforced by an unending stream of "vigorous propaganda."[5]

Indeed, Crerar could not help but fret over the confluence of signals that augured a nation girding for war. While he did not have the pleasure of wending along the autobahn in an open car, he did see the new network of roads from the air on his Hamburg-to-Berlin flight. "These roads may have important commercial uses," the colonel allowed. "They most certainly have strategical and tactical values of the greatest significance ... Coupled with this road construction should be noted the increasing number of German Divisions which it is known are being equipped as mobile, mechanized formations." Informed that construction of the entire highway system would be finished in a year or two, he forecasted that its completion would be "as significant as was the opening of the Kiel Canal in 1914." That comparison would have been clear to the many officials in Ottawa who were Great War veterans: the watercourse connecting the North and Baltic seas through the state of Schleswig-Holstein first opened in 1895, but was widened just before the war to accommodate the passage of Germany's new fleet of dreadnought-sized battleships. Crerar also learnt – possibly from Dr. Franz Grüger of the copper manufacturing firm Hirsch Kupfer und Messingwerke, an executive whose business card the colonel brought home – that army barracks were being built at breakneck speed, and vast reserves of iron and steel sequestered for the armaments industry. Although the various citizens he interviewed were not entirely sure where they were heading, they were clearly "on the move, goaded by the Nazi organization, led by Hitler, who superintends the goading process."[6]

These were not the types of observations Mackenzie King was inclined to make. Rather than reading between the lines to parse the claims of his Nazi guides, he simply recorded their statements without qualification, evidently confident in their veracity. Instead of seeking out the opinions of non-party members or opportunities to strike out on his own reconnaissance expeditions, he stuck faithfully to the itinerary set out by Ribbentrop's staff that had the Canadian visitors rubbing shoulders only with party functionaries. After inspecting the Storkow Hitlerjugend camps, the King entourage made its way back to Berlin for another testament to Nazism's infatuation with muscular bodies, regulated minds, and military preparation. The All-German Sports Competition, a series of "races and exercises by young men and women," as King called them, began that afternoon under sunny skies at the site of the previous year's Olympic Games.[7]

Those earlier games had generated sustained worldwide controversy. The International Olympic Committee (IOC) chose Berlin for the event in 1931 as compensation for the cancellation of the 1916 games also awarded to the city, and as a means of celebrating Germany's return from the international ostracism that followed the Great War. Ironically, the selection committee ruled out Barcelona, one of Berlin's primary rivals, because of committee members' grave concerns over the civil strife in Spain; the IOC was also "strongly repelled" by the fascist domination of sport in Italy, sidelining Rome, the other main bidder for the games. After Hitler's seizure of power brought those same conditions to Germany and the Fuhrer began to run roughshod over the games' stated ideals of inclusivity, fair play, and international goodwill, the IOC reconvened to review their decision. They reaffirmed their commitment to Berlin only after receiving (false) assurances that German Jews would be welcomed on the nation's Olympic team. Hitler himself was an early sceptic of the games, believing them to be a distraction from his wider goals, a drain on resources, a platform for race-mixing and hollow sloganeering about international fraternity, and, predictably but inscrutably, "a plot of Freemasons and Jews." However, he came to embrace the opportunity to showcase Germany's economic transformation and the physical supremacy of Aryan peoples. The games would also give the National Socialists a pulpit from which to issue false assurances of their peaceable intent, and provide a pretext for the kind of grand spectacle favoured by the Nazi propaganda machine.[8]

Deliberations over the propriety of participating in the "Nazi Games" vexed political and athletic organizations in the years immediately preceding the event, and active Olympic boycott lobbies in at least seven countries inundated their press and politicians with appeals to stay home. In Canada, the boycott movement was led by leftist and Jewish groups, which urged the Canadian Olympic Committee (COC) to shun Berlin and petition instead for an alternate location. These demands intensified and gathered mainstream support following the 1935 passage of the Nuremberg Laws that stripped Jews of the rights of citizenship and banned marriage and sexual relations between Jews and persons "of German or kindred blood." Reporter Casriel Kurtz of the *Calgary Herald*, hardly a left-wing publication, summed up a common sentiment among boycott advocates: "It is now known conclusively that the Nazis are planning to use the Olympic games as a means of making the people of Germany believe that the world is approving the Nazi dictatorship," he wrote in the fall of 1935. A boycott, on the other hand, would reveal to Germans "that the moral conscience of the world ... brands the Nazi platform as despicable and intolerant."[9]

Advocates of the boycott lost the fight. The international tide turned towards participation when in December 1935 US officials, who traditionally sent one of the largest teams to the Olympics, decided – after acrimonious debate and by the slimmest of majorities – to field a team. The COC, for its part, had voted unanimously to go to Berlin a month earlier, swayed by the views that politics and sports were separate spheres, and that athletes' years of intensive training should not be sacrificed in order to placate "partisan" interests. A combination of indifference towards racist practices and outright antisemitism also nurtured a tolerance for Nazi bigotry, with some Canadian participation advocates arguing that potential maltreatment of Jews would affect only a small percentage of the athletes destined for the Olympics. Germany would have its games, and the world would come to Berlin. Although Jesse Owens emerged as the individual star of the competition, German athletes dominated the events, taking home eighty-nine medals, thirty-three more than the second-place Americans. German nationalism and the belief in Aryan supremacy grew apace. Taking in the ostentatious spectacle that erased traditional boundaries between athletics, nationalism, and militarism, British diplomat Sir Robert Vansittart departed the games with the distinct impression that the host country was "in strict training now, not

3.3 Jewish artist John Henry Amshewitz produced this poster for the British Non-Sectarian Anti-Nazi Council, which called for a boycott of both the Olympics and economic relations with Germany. (University of Warwick Archive, MSS.292/808.91/3)

for the Olympic Games, but for breaking some other and emphatically unsporting world records, and perhaps the world as well."[10]

This high-profile battle over the ethics of the Nazi Olympics raises a vital question for our purposes: Precisely what did outsiders know of Hitler's regime by the summer of 1937? Over the past several decades, scholars have overturned any misconceptions that Canadians of the thirties lacked sufficient information to make sound judgments about Nazism. From 1933 onward, the Canadian press provided extensive and disapproving coverage of the disturbing excesses of the new German regime, including the liquidation of political opponents, the targeting of "unpatriotic" religious leaders, the massive spending on armaments and abrogation of the Treaty of Versailles, and the mounting proscriptions aimed at German Jews and other minorities. King himself heard such views from the pulpit, writing approvingly in his diary of sermons condemning the new Nazi regime's persecution of the Jews and blasphemous worship of the Aryan race.[11]

As Hitler manoeuvered to gain absolute control over the Reich, reports from the British and American press, frequently reprinted or synopsized in the Canadian media, castigated Nazi tyranny and catalogued its crimes with vehemence. Likewise, progressive newspapers like the *Winnipeg Free Press* and the *Toronto Star* – the latter the country's most widely read daily – sounded increasingly vocal alarms. The *Star's* Matthew Halton travelled throughout Germany in late 1933 to produce what became known as his "German series," more than a dozen widely syndicated despatches that began with this unequivocal declaration: "During the last month in Germany, I have seen and studied the most fanatical, thorough-going and savage philosophy of war ever imposed on a nation ... Germany is literally becoming a laboratory and breeding ground for war, unless I am deaf, dumb and blind." Halton wrote of six-year-old children being tutored in "the high ethical values and deeper meaning of war" and of the terrorization of German Jews, in his estimation "a deliberate and implacable intention to wipe the Jews out of the economic and social life of Germany." He reckoned that a visitor's first impressions of "sunshine, energy, resurgence" would be overturned within twenty-four hours, provided their eyes and ears were functional.[12]

In the early years of the Third Reich, however, many conservative publications in Canada and beyond ran counter-stories to those like Halton's, arguing that fascism was preferable to communism, and that much of the shocking reporting from Germany was simply false. Some of these counterclaims came from writers who had not set foot in Germany, or from correspondents in Berlin who feared being expelled for anti-Nazi stories (the fate of at least nineteen between 1933 and 1937), or from those who, on Nazi Party orders, received lavish exchange rates when they converted their foreign currency into Reichsmarks (a.k.a. bribery). Canadian freelance journalist Erland Echlin, for example, published a series in the *Toronto Globe and Mail* and the *Montreal Gazette* contesting Halton's claims; Echlin would be interned by the British in the Second World War when it was discovered he was on the Nazis' payroll.[13]

Over time, the German governments' role in the sanguine reportage faced increased scrutiny, and with the passage of the Nuremberg Laws, even the more conservative Canadian dailies joined in full-throated censure of the Nazi regime. King was a voracious reader of newspapers, and by 1935 his staff were poring over more than forty dailies and "countless magazines" to furnish the prime minister with clippings on domestic and foreign affairs (with special orders to look for "errors, favourable comments, and unjustified criticism" of their boss). And King could hardly have forgotten the resolutions and letters he received from labour and Jewish organizations urging that Canada not send a team to the Berlin Olympics. A recent study of the debates in the Canadian press over the 1936 games concludes that COC officials who endorsed participation in the Berlin games without a dissenting vote did so "not out of ignorance of the events in Nazi Germany, especially during the fall of 1935, but in full knowledge of what was going on."[14] King was certainly privy to that knowledge, which had only deepened by 1937.

Canada's parliament provided another conspicuous platform for launching protests (and admittedly little else) against the disturbing growth of tyranny abroad. Italy's invasion of Ethiopia in the fall of 1935 and Germany's remilitarization of the Rhineland the following spring had provided tangible evidence of the fascists' territorial appetites and indifference to international law, and generated widespread fears of war. Canadian politicians of all stripes denounced the violators – and agreed that this should be the extent of Canada's involvement in the matters, even if the League of Nations endorsed military action to redress the moves. Regarding embattled League member Ethiopia, a Quebec Liberal MP spoke for the majority, using language and logic indicative of the ways in which racial hierarchies shaped Canadian foreign policy. "No interest in Ethiopia, of any nature whatever," he insisted, "is worth the life of a single Canadian citizen." In secret bilateral talks, Britain and France had said essentially the same thing. Regarding the Rhineland crisis, King told the House, "in a word, the attitude of the Government is to do nothing itself and if possible to prevent anything occurring which will precipitate one additional factor into the all important discussions which are now taking place in Europe." This was a more jumbled take on the aphorism King committed to his diary that defined so much of his political praxis: "It is what we prevent, rather than what we do that counts most in Government."[15]

In April 1937, just two months prior to King's Berlin visit, the House of Commons debated Bill 89, a measure to ratify a bilateral trade deal negotiated with Germany the previous year. Toronto Liberal MP Samuel Factor, Ontario's first Jewish MP, issued an extended, passionate denunciation of Nazi crimes for the parliamentary record. The Hitler regime's conduct, he maintained, was "offensive to human civilization ... Medieval barbarities have been perpetrated against hundreds of thousands of people which have shocked the moral conscience of the world ... The German government has passed ghoulish ordinances [against] human beings because of their religious profession." Citing energetic boycott-Germany campaigns underway in the United States and Britain, Factor implored the House to reject the deal brokered by his own party, asking, "what of our conscience?"[16] It was in part a measure of how mildly these protestations resonated that no parliamentarian offered a reply to Factor's plea; instead, the debate shifted abruptly to the economic prospects surrounding Bill 89, which subsequently passed by a wide margin.

By the summer of 1937, then, any Canadian claims of innocence regarding the more disturbing aspects of the Third Reich represented either an astonishing lack of public engagement or an outright lie. This the mass-circulation Canadian magazine *Saturday Night* made clear in an issue released while the prime minister toured Berlin. Responding to German Canadians attending a June 1937 convention in Regina who had complained of the negative Canadian reporting on Nazism, *Saturday Night* charged the attendees with ignoring some incontrovertible and widely acknowledged facts: "The German-Canadians," editors wrote, "were demanding a more sympathetic attitude in the Canadian press towards a Government in Germany which has exercised the most ruthless intolerance that has ever been practiced by a modern civilized state against a racial minority of its population."[17]

And yet here was Mackenzie King, smartly turned out in crisp three-piece suit and tie, fedora in one hand and cane and gloves in the other, standing at attention on the Olympic grounds amidst swastika

3.4 Mackenzie King, left, observing the opening ceremony of the 1937 All-German Sports Competitions. To his left are Robert Ley, head of the German Labour Front, and the diminutive Hans von Tschammer und Osten, Reich Sports Leader. (Library and Archives Canada, PA-119007)

flags and high-ranking, uniformed officials giving the Nazi salute; the photo captures a moment from the opening ceremony of the 1937 All-German Sports Competitions.

In visiting the Olympic complex, situated at the northern end of the three-thousand-hectare Grunewald Forest in western Berlin's tony Charlottenburg District, King was beholding one of the Reich's most extensive construction projects. At its centre stood the one-hundred-thousand-seat Olympiastadion designed by Werner March, son of the architect who had designed an earlier facility on the same site for the cancelled 1916 games. The stadium was praised "by Nazis and non-Nazis alike" for the majestic neoclassical symmetry of its exterior and "the broad sweeping curve of its interior," and the moderate wartime damage it sustained posed a conundrum to post-war officials who sought to erase the more notorious Nazi relics from the built environment.[18]

Supporters of preserving the site pointed to the fact that the Olympics had been awarded to Germany and plans developed for the grounds prior to Hitler's reign, although there is some dispute over how much the Fuhrer influenced the actual construction designs. Detractors noted that the 1936 games constituted one of National Socialism's most conspicuous and successful schemes to gain domestic and international legitimacy and disingenuously advertise its peaceful intentions. And the Olympic site was to witness further outrages: roughly 230 alleged deserters were shot in a ravine at the complex in the closing months of the war, and their replacements – the boys and elderly men of the Volkssturm (people's storm) – were sworn in on the same grounds. Roughly two thousand of these wretched, untrained conscripts would die defending this monument to Aryan supremacy in April 1945. Ultimately the sports complex was preserved, only to become the subject of more public controversy when Berlin made a bid for the 2000 Olympics. Would such a spectacle revive nationalistic urges? Paper over the uncomfortable memories of 1936? Many alarmed Germans organized a committee in support of Berlin's leading rival and eventual winner, Sydney.[19]

Mackenzie King seemed utterly unfazed by the ugly reputation of the 1936 Olympics. After observing the opening ceremonies for the All-German games, he was led to the Fuhrer's own seat in the Olympiastadion to watch track and field events, the special guest of Hans von Tschammer und Osten. Tschammer, an elfin forty-nine-year-old Saxon aristocrat, was *Reichssportführer* (Reich Sports Leader)

3.5 King leans toward Walther Hewel as they take in the opening ceremony of the 1937 All-German Sports Competitions. Sharing their bench are Robert Ley and Hans von Tschammer und Osten; the moustachioed secretary Pickering sits behind Hewel. (Library and Archives Canada, PA-119010)

and the man responsible for enforcing the ban on non-Aryan German Olympians. Like so many Nazi higher-ups – Hewel included – Tschammer seemed the very embodiment of Hannah Arendt's "banality of evil": described as "a good-looking, conceited, pompous man" who exuded "personality in spades, but apparently no character," SA officer Tschammer "knew next to nothing about sport," but ascended the Nazi hierarchy because he was a glad-hander who reflexively carried out even the most ruthless orders from above. His overall mandate as *Reichssportführer* was to employ athletics to promote nationalism, confirm Aryan supremacy, and prepare young

3.6 Reviewing participants in the women's and men's tennis events at the All-German Sports Competitions. *Front row, left to right*: Ley, King, Pickering, and Tschammer. (Library and Archives Canada, PA-119011)

German bodies for victory on the battlefield. His death from natural causes in 1943 allowed him to escape both personal acknowledgement of the ultimate failure of his program and the post-war tribunals that convicted others of his rank.[20]

Tschammer's visit with Mackenzie King on that balmy summer day in 1937 ended with a 4:30 p.m. tea in the stadium's VIP room and a

3.7 King takes the Fuhrer's seat in the VIP box at Olympiastadion next to Tschammer, who found time between opening ceremony and field events to slip into his summer whites. (Library and Archives Canada, PA-119006)

walk to Langemarckhalle, a monument at the western extent of the grounds dedicated to German soldiers who died in the November 1914 Battle of Langemark, Belgium. (King and Tschammer were now standing at the very location where Reich officials would reverently inter the latter's ashes six years later.) Situated as it was in a park for athletics, Langemarckhalle with its inscriptions exhorting Germans to give their lives willingly for the fatherland was one of the more blatant representations of the Nazi conflation of sport and warfare – not to mention the Nazi cult of death. Breaking records at the games was indeed, to reprise Sir Robert Vansittart, fully intended as a prelude to "breaking the world." In his diary King noted simply that the memorial "was now being made a source of inspiration for the youth of Germany."[21] Although Deutsche Arbeitsfront (German Labour Front) chief Robert Ley appears with the prime minister in several photographs from the afternoon's event, for reasons unknown King's meticulous diary entry of his first day in Germany left Ley out of the story.

Around six in the evening, Hewel chauffeured King and Pickering back to the Mitte district. They drove east along the Landwehr Canal, allowing King to catch a glimpse of the house at 70 Konigin Augusta Strasse where he, as a visiting student, had boarded with Humboldt professor Anton Weber and his family in the spring of 1900. By now the street bore a new name, Admiral von Schröder Strasse, a testament to the National Socialist mania for militarizing public space. It was a stately, tree-lined boulevard just one block south of the enormous Tiergarten (animal garden / zoo), a public park and former royal hunting grounds where the younger King had loved to stroll.[22]

A few months after this tour of the neighbourhood, the area was officially designated "the diplomatic quarter" under plans drawn up by Albert Speer for *Welthauptstadt Germania* (World Capital Germania), the rechristened Berlin that was to be the jewel of the civilized world. Four authoritarian allies of the Nazis – Austria, Italy, Spain, and Japan – were subsequently handed prime real estate in the quarter. Their newly constructed, monumental temples to fascism, like the homes and shops throughout the district, were ravaged in the war, but extraterritorial rights prevented post-war German officials from applying the wrecking ball's *coup de grace*, and the embassies lay in ruins for decades. When German reunification returned the capital to Berlin, full renovations of the Italian, Spanish, and Japanese embassies were finally completed, while the Austrians opted to start from scratch. Today, a modernist 1998 building housing a branch of Konrad-Adenauer-Stiftung (Konrad Adenauer Foundation), a political institute named for West Germany's first chancellor and dedicated to the very un-Nazi ideals of peace, democracy, European unity, and international solidarity and development, occupies the former site of the Anton Weber home.[23]

4

Shrugging Off the British Yoke

While SS *Sturmbannführer* Walther Hewel seems to have offered up nothing but rustic Teutonic charm for his Canadian guests, British ambassador Sir Nevile Henderson's own variety of *Gemütlichkeit* left something to be desired. On the job one day short of a month when King arrived, the fifty-five-year-old career diplomat was facing his roughest assignment in Berlin, and not only, or primarily, because of the bullying foreign policies of the Nazis; in fact, Henderson appeared to get along far more cordially with Nazi VIPs than with the growing numbers of Britons who called for toughness towards German provocations. Berlin's noted social columnist Bella Fromm, a Jew chronicling the trajectory of the Hitler regime with mounting anxiety in her diary, wrote that Ribbentrop expected the new British ambassador to "be more sympathetic to rightful German aspirations. That's just what I fear."[1]

When King arrived, Henderson was still smarting from the backlash following his first official speech as ambassador to Germany a few weeks earlier that called on the British to show greater regard for National Socialism – to "lay less stress on Nazi dictatorship and much more emphasis on the great social experiment which is being tried out in this country"; Henderson's salute to the Reich ended with a rousing, and to many Britons galling, toast to the health of Hitler and Germany. By his own admission feeling isolated and chastened – "blamed by every one" – and perhaps somewhat insecure in his new post, Henderson put King on the defensive when the two were alone that evening in the ambassador's study.[2]

With no Canadian embassy yet in Berlin – the 1931 Statute of Westminster had granted the dominions autonomy in foreign affairs,

4.1 Built in 1868 as "Palais Strousberg," the mansion at Wilhelmstraße 70 became the British Embassy in the 1880s. This photograph was taken in August 1937, one month after King and Nevile Henderson bickered – and then made up – here. (Bundesarchiv, Bild 183-C11809)

but in the intervening six years Canada had only begun to establish its own diplomatic infrastructure – Sir Nevile was irked that the Canadian prime minister did not room at the British Embassy, located at Wilhelmstraße 70 amidst an assortment of domestic and foreign bureaucratic offices known as the Government District. Perhaps adding to the snub, Henderson's diplomatic digs literally abutted the Hotel Adlon, where King chose instead to stay. That Henderson had learnt of King's visit through German rather than British officials he considered an additional slight, and he told King so in no uncertain terms.[3]

King could be forgiven for choosing the posh Adlon over the shabby embassy. The British ambassador himself ventilated his contempt for

4.2 The new British Embassy in Berlin, with the new Hotel Adlon adjoining at right. (Author photograph, 2017)

his official accommodation, a once stately but long-neglected mid-nineteenth-century classical mansion that Henderson pronounced "musty, cramped, and dark." Long-overdue, full-scale renovations of the structure were facilitated by Allied bombs – possibly dropped by the Royal Air Force itself – that necessitated the bulldozing of the skeletal remains in 1950 by the East German government. The site remained vacant throughout the Cold War on account of its position adjacent to the East-West border of Berlin, and fifty-five years after war's end, Queen Elizabeth II officially opened the reincarnated, fortress-like British Embassy at Wilhelmstraße 70.[4] The building's modern design is matched by its modern security provisions: because of fears of terrorist attacks, this block of Wilhelmstraße is now a pedestrian-only zone and the embassy's street-level café and library, designed for public use, are now off limits.

King's aversion to the embassy, however, had more to do with the symbolism of a dominion prime minister boarding with the Queen's representative in the German capital. Indeed, the ambassador's protests gave King the perfect opportunity to introduce to Henderson a central concern of his German visit, and indeed, of his entire tenure as prime minister: that Canada was a sovereign entity and would consistently seek new ways to illustrate this fact, despite Britain's intended or inadvertent presumptions of subordinate status.

King's statements and initiatives at the just-completed Imperial Conference in London hammered home this point *ad nauseam*. Here, a draft resolution on foreign affairs "went altogether too far," King informed those assembled, "in linking the Dominions into Imperial obligations;"[5] when a subsequent draft was tabled, King noted that he "took exception to the language of many of [the clauses] without any reservation, pointing out that we could not be a party to any Empire, Imperial, or Commonwealth policy but must maintain freedom to determine our own foreign policy."[6] A separate statement on defence offering the seemingly unremarkable assurances that the dominions would continue to trade with Britain in war as they did in peace "would have to go out," insisted King, as this amounted to a commitment that Canada's Parliament alone could provide;[7] in the discussions on the revised defence report, he wrote, "I had to battle my way through the report from beginning to close, taking exception to words, phrases, clauses, sentences and paragraphs, as we went along."[8] Even a simple reference to the dominions' "common agreement ... in the cause of peace" was too suggestive of a predetermined uniformity of action. King quibbled so mightily over any hint of Empire-wide foreign policy coordination that even newly appointed British prime minister Neville Chamberlain, a man both admired by his Canadian counterpart and today universally synonymous with a forbearance for bad behaviour, "betrayed a little impatience at my attitude," as King confessed in his diary.[9]

These summations of the conference proceedings are King's own, and while the Canadian prime minister had a habit in recounting conversations of embellishing his influence, by all accounts he did exert an outsized effect on the statements released at the meetings and on the patience of many around the table. (To be sure, the prime minister was being encouraged vigorously along these lines by members of the Canadian legation as a whole, and in particular deputy minister of external affairs and resolute Canadian nationalist O.D.

Skelton and minister of justice and resolute guardian of francophone interests Ernest Lapointe.) In fact, in the wake of all three imperial conferences King attended, supporters and critics alike agreed that his views typically won the day, that he "had his way in everything." As historian James Eayrs observed, "In 1937, as in 1923, Mackenzie King, fighting off 'Downing Street domination,' had ended by dominating Downing Street."[10]

King's fortitude in these debates may seem somewhat at odds with his domestic reputation as an epic waffler more comfortable trafficking in compromise than resolute leadership – an individual who, in the words of Canadian historian and novelist Will Ferguson, "had a weather vane where most people had a heart."[11] In instances like those in London, 1937, however, King was drawing red lines abroad so that he would not have to do so at home, where the fallout over foreign policy initiatives and miscalculations could harm both his electoral prospects and the nation's unity (these twin threats were indelibly linked, although in both public pronouncement and diary the prime minister habitually stressed the obligations to unity rather than any crass political calculations). In other words, backbone here, over clauses that threatened to oblige Canada to act at Britain's behest, simultaneously facilitated the kind of open-ended dawdling on Canadian soil that made opponents – and often colleagues – fume. At the same time, this "backbone" was more accurately a defiant stand against taking any kind of stand, against covenanting to a course of action that might prove disadvantageous later on. It was, in true King fashion, a muscular affirmation of the right to fecklessness.

Outside the sheer and abundant desire for political self-preservation, Mackenzie King had understandable reasons for refusing to be boxed in on foreign policy. Interwar Canada was, like most nations that had endured the horrors of the Great War, gripped by unprecedented levels of isolationism and pacifism. Another war involving Britain would doubtless place extraordinary pressure on the dominions to rise once again to the Empire's defence, an obligation responsible for fresh and bitter memories of the previous conflict's carnage, debt, and controversy. The latter outcome was especially abundant in Canada, whose Francophone citizens had begun to talk earnestly of separatism after being conscripted into an overseas war to preserve the empire. And as more recent scholarship has revealed, opposition to conscription was widespread beyond Quebec's borders, with large percentages of farmers, the working class, and ethnic minorities outraged over a federal government that demanded this act of loyalty yet routinely ignored their concerns in peacetime. If nationalism and national survival required, to cite nineteenth-century political theorist Ernst Renan, a collective memory of having "done great things together," wars fought on behalf of the British Empire were decidedly awkward instruments for Canadian nation-building; indeed, another such conflict could incite civil discord that hastened the *unmaking* of a bilingual Canada. "I told the conference," King dictated to Pickering, "I could not begin to imagine how sensitive the people were at home about the European situation, or how closely we were being watched to see whether implicitly we were including Canada to participate in European wars." And as King had informed the Canadian Parliament a year earlier in debates over Germany's remilitarization of the Rhineland, a broken Canada could not but play a diminished role in the peace and stability of Europe: "I believe that Canada's first duty to the league [League of Nations] and to the British empire, with respect to all the great issues that come up, is, if possible, to keep this country united."[12]

As his words suggest, similar motivations underwrote resistance to the injunctions of both Britain and the League of Nations, the interwar organization charged with implementing US president Woodrow Wilson's dream of collective security. While King supported the concept of a supranational international body, he considered the League a forum for reasoned debate and negotiation, not an instrument of coercion via economic sanctions, and most certainly not via military action. When Imperial Conference representatives from the other dominions proposed issuing a statement committing the Commonwealth to any actions taken by the League to maintain peace, King "gave them no quarter," even after Chamberlain passed him a handwritten note pleading for solidarity. "I told him that would not do," King reported; "that any reference to a threat to peace would be equivalent to a declaration of war."[13]

Hindsight has led analysts of the League of Nations to conclude that it was far too weak to face down the challenge from totalitarian aggression. Before 1939, the Canadian prime minister came to precisely the opposite conclusion: that the League covenant's expectation that members would rally to the aid of a besieged nation constituted a gross overstepping of national authority – that the League's authority was dangerously broad. He told the legations in London that his government simply "did not believe in" the implementation of "collective security through the use of force." The world had recently borne witness to the meaning of warfare in the industrial era, and another such conflict featuring still more efficient killing technologies was simply too horrific to imagine (proponents of this view were, of course, proven absolutely correct). To the preponderance of the war's survivors, the old notion of war as "diplomacy by other means" was criminally cavalier. King went so far as to state that Canada would certainly withdraw from the League if the obligation to collective security was enforced – a move that would have made Canada the only industrialized nation *not* under fascist despotism to voluntarily quit the world body. (Ten Latin American countries had departed by 1939, citing onerous financial dues and the League's racial and regional chauvinism.[14])

King was thus aghast when New Zealand prime minister Michael Savage stated that Commonwealth countries, like all League members, ought to ground their foreign policymaking in the organization's basic principles and directives; to do otherwise, he maintained, would render the League toothless. When Chamberlain countered that none of those present sought to thwart the League, Savage directed the British leader's attention to the Canadians. "The truth of the matter," King grouched in his diary entry that evening, "is that Savage does not know what he is talking about most of the time, nor is he able to express himself in a manner to enable others to see any force in any of his arguments."[15] If King's latter criticism regarding Savage's inability to express himself has merit, the flaw is immensely regrettable, for the New Zealand prime minister did in fact appear to know what he was talking about. During the London sessions (and beyond), Savage repeatedly lambasted the policy of appeasement, the approach defended most tirelessly by King and endorsed in the conference's final resolutions.

Musing on his persistent efforts to expunge statements that implied a common front against rogue nations, on the "good deal of watering down" he had effected in the final report, the Canadian PM felt a personal "sense of triumph" over his pivotal role in "getting the [final] report in first class shape." "I think I succeeded in the end," he exulted, "in having given to the report, a turn to our way to an extent greater than even any of us [in the Canadian legation] had thought at the outset would be possible." Conversely, his New Zealand opposite left the conference in a foul mood, declaring that at least some nations were willing to use force in support of peace and the League, and warning that it was possible to pay too high a price to buy off aggressors.[16]

Nor was the *London Spectator* impressed. The newspaper bemoaned both the secrecy surrounding the negotiations and the impotent platitudes discharged for public consumption, and wondered aloud why a certain unnamed participant had even boarded ship for the home country: "At least one of the Dominion Prime Ministers left for London on the understanding that he had no authority to bind his Government to any new policy or to agree to any new commitments, economic or political."[17] Which prime minister? Even a casual observer of the six-week deliberations could have cracked the *Spectator's* code.

At London, then, King had in fact declared a kind of independence, but it was an independence from any unified and jointly crafted Commonwealth-wide stand against fascism, and from the collective-security mandate of an international organization that Canada had freely joined. Neither of these affirmations of autonomy fit neatly within the old Canadian-nationalist rallying cry that a haughty imperial England sought to coerce its subordinates into slavish obedience to the home country. Although King continued to frame his negotiations with the British along these lines, his actions at the conference were less a triumph for autonomy than the framework for a Canada that preferred isolation to a meaningful role in maintaining international concord and justice. Particularly given that Canada's own security could only be fully guaranteed through the protection offered by others, an internationalist option would seem to more clearly convey the stance of a mature, sovereign country acceding not to Downing Street but to the full responsibilities of nationhood. British officials, who had envisioned the conference as a public declaration of the Empire's readiness to stand as one against the mounting threats in Europe and Asia, got rather the opposite in the spring of 1937.[18]

In refusing to endorse collective action through the League of Nations, King may have missed a golden opportunity to strengthen domestic unity on the question of Canada's place in the world. Realigning foreign policymaking towards the mandates of a democratic international peacekeeping body like the League would have given real substance to the very message he sought to hammer home at the conference, and one fundamental to his appeal to Quebecers: Canada was not a toady of Empire, but a sovereign global state equal to all others. When that realignment eventually occurred, with post-war Canada taking a leading role in the United Nations, a large measure of French Canadians' opposition to internationalism evaporated. Of course, Francophones' embrace of globalism corresponded with the broader discrediting of isolationism inspired by the Second World War, but the League may have served as an early incubator of the internationalist ethos that would ultimately heal some of the cleavages between the nation's two solitudes. One component of King's (mis)calculations here was the overblown supposition that Francophones were unconditionally isolationist, not simply opposed to shoring up the British Empire. Another component was ideological.

Modern international-relations analysts have traditionally aggregated under two broad banners, realism and liberalism. Realists characterize both people and nations as inherently selfish, striving continuously to enrich themselves at the expense of others by any means at their disposal. Policing the anarchy endemic to an international order governed by such venality involves building up enough military strength, either on one's own or in alliance with other states, to dissuade attacks from predatory states and alliances. Successful implementation of this strategy results in an equilibrium known as the balance of power. Liberals, meanwhile, see humanity as essentially cooperative and altruistic; those who would breach the natural harmony of interstate relations are by definition outliers. But because these outliers can wreak havoc with the common interest, liberals maintain that the international order must be transformed in ways that would make obsolete the kind of unethical conduct among states that realists consider inevitable. And because of this conviction that progress in interstate relations is possible, that the right reforms could in fact completely eradicate interstate conflict, the term "idealism" has become more or less interchangeable with "liberalism" in the realm of foreign affairs. Mackenzie King's musings on labour relations and governance, which generally hold to this idealistic worldview and demonstrate an abiding faith in the essential goodness and perfectibility of humankind, mark him as a resolute, lifelong liberal.

During the 1920s, he acquired a good deal more company. Having suffered through an unprecedented bloodletting inaugurated under the system of alliances and (botched) power-balancing, politicians and thinkers of the interwar period were drawn to the promises of liberalism. Liberals differed, however, on the precise nature of the reforms needed to banish, or at least limit, future wars. Some, like US president Woodrow Wilson, called for radical structural adjustments to the international order. Upstanding states would need to band together to form international organizations powerful enough to establish and enforce rules that sustained the general interest and the peace – thus, collective security. Others, like Mackenzie King, held that progress would come through a change in values, that shared notions of ethical international conduct could be developed and enhanced through education and rational, good-faith dialogue.[19]

These latter liberals' rejection of fixed international laws and collective punishment for their violation put them in league with the realists, but for differing reasons. Where realists consider global regulations and organizations paper tigers easily circumvented by the mighty for their own ends, King and his ilk equated collectively enforced laws with impersonal machines, bound to isolate perceived violators and erase the human element from the art of diplomacy. Perhaps more importantly in King's mind, Wilson's plan to craft and implement joint solutions to international dilemmas would dilute the sovereignty of individual states and, in the case of Canada, could literally dismember the country. In essence, King's was a liberalism that preached universal brotherhood shorn of any mechanisms – save a rhetorical appeal to the higher self – to encourage cooperation and deter aggression. To be fair to King, this was also a gamble most governments of the twenties and thirties were prepared to make. The widespread unwillingness to give the League of Nations real teeth reflected the prevailing belief that national autonomy was sacrosanct, and that warring in the name of peace was as irrational as it was immoral. The soundness of Wilson's vision for a universal world body possessing regulatory and military power would only be widely appreciated after 1939.

Fresh off his presumed coup for Canadian autonomy and unity in London, for the liberalism of suasion rather than compulsion, King sustained the momentum gained in London when he had his initial, and fairly acidic, one-on-one with Nevile Henderson at the British embassy. King was further emboldened by the fact that the ambassador seemed a little sozzled – "evidently feeling free and easy after dinner," in the prime minister's more polite explanation. The booze-inspired looseness displayed by a man of this rank on such a significant occasion – King's own visit – left the latter "not altogether impressed," a reaction that bore a hint of the self-recrimination frequently evident in diary entries fretting over his own intake of alcohol and food. For instance, as international tensions rose in 1936 over the bellicose foreign moves of Italy, Japan, and Germany, an anxious King sought counsel first from his cabinet and later, at a table-rapping session, his dead father. "Please help me father," the prime minister entreated, "I am beginning to feel unequal to the tasks – help me to realize that there is power from beyond and above." As biographer Allan Levine recounted, "His father miraculously emanated from the Great Beyond to tell him to 'eat less, take no wine and pray.'"[20]

The bottle loomed especially large in King's imagination during his European visit the following year. Burdened by the enormity of the international challenges, and in particular the stress of handling Hitler properly, King sought solace in both celestial and worldly spirits. A handwritten diary entry from the London conference describes "several visions" warning against excessive drink, one in which appeared "bottles of whiskey it seemed, on a table" that King rightly rejected. "It clearly meant that I should abstain – I have kept away from liquor – no whiskey – no cocktails – or anything of the kind, but once or twice & instead of them have taken sherry, champagne or a little wine & a little port." Even these King felt should have been shunned: "I enjoyed the relief at the time," he confessed, but the drinks "caused me to have thoughts which I might have avoided." In a subsequent vision, he found himself lost and confused, accompanied by a strange woman of "indifferent character – seemed to belong to a bad gang." This apparition appeared after an Imperial Conference dinner during which he felt he had taken altogether too many liquids, which had once again "roused thoughts I should not have had – the vision was a revelation [about] the company & mistakes into which [alcohol] leads."[21] The precise nature of the troubling thoughts is a matter of speculation, although C.P. Stacey, the biographer prone to see repressed sexual cravings in nearly all of King's expressions of shame, would have little doubts. On this occasion at least, which blended intoxication with spectres of "bad" women, Stacey may indeed offer the most reasonable explanation.

Now standing before Henderson, however, King was sober. Feeling somewhat pious about this fact and recognizing the decided mental advantage it conferred, the prime minister, as he dictated to Pickering later that evening, "took to [Henderson] sharply." Pressed about the booking at the Hotel Adlon rather than the embassy and the fact that Henderson had to learn of the trip from the Germans, King pointed out that he was there at the invitation of his new friend Joachim von Ribbentrop, not the British Ambassador or any other British officials.[22] The instant sense of kinship with Ribbentrop had given King the confidence that he could also foster diplomatic communion with other leading Nazis, and most importantly, the Fuhrer himself.

Such a connection, on the other hand, was clearly absent as King and Henderson continued their conversation. Indeed, the tone of that encounter was continuing to worsen. King's clarification of precisely who had invited him segued into a general renunciation of any perception that his nation needed Britain's oversight in foreign matters: Canadians were, he reported brusquely, acutely sensitive of being "drawn into an Empire centralization scheme." The unfocused Henderson flubbed the point entirely, offering next to chaperone the PM to his appointment with Hitler. Here King, by his own account, dispensed with any semblance of diplomatic politesse. "I instantly resented it," reads the diary, "and showed how I felt. I said I did not wish him to come with me, and preferred to go alone ... I said some way or another, you people in the Old Land never seem to get an understanding of the point of view of the Dominions, or what is best in their own interests, in relations with other countries." Henderson responded, apparently calmly (or freely and easily), that demonstrating solidarity within the empire would go far in maintaining a strong hand for Britain on the continental matters presently causing such distress; he went on to explain that a French colleague had raised concerns that the dominions' reluctance to back the mother country would dampen Britain's appetite for facing down German demands in Eastern Europe.[23]

King countered this adroitly. A meeting *sans* Britain did not imply, he maintained, that Canada saw the problems then vexing Europe any differently than Britain, and the facts of this broad alignment on policy could be delivered to Hitler most convincingly without a representative of the Crown hanging over his shoulder, monitoring obedience.[24] King, however, was not being entirely forthcoming about the sum of his motives for a solely bilateral conversation. More importantly, this was to be *his* moment, *his* victory. His mission to Berlin (that King used the description repeatedly is *apropos* of the evangelical yearnings through which he framed it) was part of a providential plan for which his entire life to this point had merely been a grooming. If successful, Europe would be spared, Canada would gain unprecedented international regard as a sovereign actor, and King himself, world peacemaker, would fulfil his lifelong destiny.

5

The Holy Errand

"Destiny" is perhaps the best word to describe King's own perception of his reason for being. Biographer Allan Levine wrote that whatever his station or stage in life, "Urging him on was his overwhelming belief that his life was guided by God's will or the 'Hand of Destiny' as he deemed it." A portion of this calling was, in King's mind, hereditary. The grandson, via his mother's line, of Upper Canadian radical democrat and namesake William Lyon Mackenzie, the prime minister had long considered it his life's work to complete and thereby vindicate his grandfather's great cause. After leading the failed 1837 rebellion against Upper Canada's elitist Family Compact, the elder Mackenzie fled to the United States in disgrace before returning a decade later to resume a life in politics and journalism. On reading a biography of his grandfather in 1895, King wrote, in one of his earliest diary entries, "I can feel his inner life in myself. I have a greater desire to carry on the work he endeavoured to perform, to better the condition of the poor, denounce corruption, the tyranny of abused power and uphold right and honourable principles."[1]

The various strands of the noble family mission seemed to converge at the 1937 Imperial Conference, a meeting that King would – of course – recognize as being held on the centenary of his grandfather's freedom struggle. "It was a singular thing," he wrote after a day at the negotiating table, "that at the end of 100 years I was contending in the No. 10 Downing Street, for a policy that would preserve the Empire while preserving the national freedom of its parts, the very thing my grandfather was fighting for 100 years ago." Although most historians – and fiercely republican grandfather Mackenzie himself – would distance the 1837 Rebellion from any underlying desire to hold the empire together, in

King's mind personal, national, imperial, and global destinies were rounding into harmony, and were all held in his own hand.[2]

More phenomenological evidence also gave King confidence that he was the right emissary for this peace errand. As even detractors concede, the prime minister possessed considerable abilities as a negotiator and conciliator. While serving as Canada's first labour minister under Wilfrid Laurier from 1900 to 1907, King resolved over forty labour disputes through his combination of empathy for all factions involved (a sentiment rarely afforded the working class by nineteenth-century elites, but one increasingly championed by middle-class Progressive-era reformers like King) and a call for reasonableness and mutual respect among those around the negotiating table. Out of public office after an election loss in 1911, King was tasked by John D. Rockefeller Jr with placating employees of his corporation and salvaging the family name – and particularly Rockefeller's own – after company agents gunned down more than twenty striking Colorado miners in the notorious Ludlow Massacre of 1914. That King rose to the challenge of rebuilding Rockefeller Jr's reputation can be seen in the fact that Mary Harris "Mother" Jones, doyenne of radical labour and one of the more feared and fearsome enemies of corporate America, told the press that King's character resuscitation had "utterly changed her opinion" about the erstwhile personification of heartless monopoly capitalism, that she and other labour leaders had "misrepresented him terribly."[3]

These powers of conciliation and persuasion served King well as prime minister, in both domestic and foreign affairs. Fellow participants referred to him as "umpire of the conference" for his role in brokering a deal for greater dominion autonomy at the Imperial Conference of 1926. Once again, his starring role in the resolution confirmed that the fates had tapped him to midwife the gestation to full nationhood and complete the Mackenzie project. "We are certainly making history," he crowed with some justification in 1928 in reference to the "new Canada" he espied emerging under his watch. "I am convinced the period of my administration will live in this particular as an epoch in the history of Canada that was formative and memorable."[4] And now in 1937 there was the heroic stand against a unified resolution against fascism, this brokering of an agreement shorn of any guarantees to stand up to international aggression. The victory was a direct outgrowth of a lifelong apprenticeship in the art of the deal, and represented the vanquishing of those who, like sorry Prime Minister Savage, could not "express [themselves] in a manner to enable others to see any force in any of [their] arguments."

It was this faith in the power of logical and convincing argument –
and in his own capacity to deliver on it – that assured King that any
schemes for collective security could and should be dashed. He held
that conflict, regardless of the circumstance, could be forestalled
through frank, respectful, one-on-one discussions among men of influence. Since people were by nature peaceable and rational, if potential
aggressors were clearly shown the folly of using violence to achieve
their aims, they would choose other avenues to those aims. King's *Industry and Humanity* made clear the connections between his labour
conciliation techniques and international diplomacy. "The parallel between the enmities of rival states," he wrote, "fostered by and fostering
fear and suspicion, and the enmities of gigantic aggregations of Capital
and Labor, similarly begotten and fostered, is so plain that one wonders
how it can possibly be overlooked." The panacea for such enmities was
likewise aligned, as he argued in a speech just prior to the outbreak of
the First World War (whose pending belligerents, one must conclude,
were not listening). "Accustom men's minds in the industrial world to
remedy industrial wrongs by appealing to reason rather than force," he
maintained, "and you have helped to create a sentiment which will also
play its part in a much larger way in international affairs."[5] His mediation model was so consistent and central to his politics that it could
reasonably be termed the "King Doctrine."

This appeal to the natural rationality and peaceableness of humanity,
along with an acute sensitivity to the grievances of the German people,
the prime minister would later bring to the problem of Hitler. "It is
one of the first essentials in conciliation negotiations," he had written
as labour minister, "to let each party see clearly that you understand
all the things that have aggravated, angered and incensed them; that
you appreciate all the obstacles with which he has to contend, leaving to a secondary stage in the proceedings the weakest parts in his
position." The many successes realized through this all-purpose strategy provided King with the curriculum vitae to become leader of the
Liberal Party and prevail in election after election. He was certainly
not going to experiment with any other tactics in the most significant
face-to-face negotiation of his life. A short sentence from *Industry and
Humanity* serves as the aphorism that governed his entire public career:
"Ultimately, Force must give way to Reason."[6]

Private life was a rather different matter, for here, reason often took
a back seat to the unseen powers that, to King, guided all earthly phenomena. As in the material world, however, signs from the beyond

confirmed over and over King's singular destiny. The prime minister was hardly alone in his attempts to tap into the power of the paranormal; there existed something of a mania for innovative spiritualist experimentation in Victorian-era Britain and America. The vogue for all things mystical was driven by such factors as the waning of traditional religious belief, unease over the cold rationality of an increasingly scientific and technological approach to human affairs, and, for women, the esteem afforded by the belief that their superior reserves of emotion and empathy rendered them preferred conduits to the unmapped demesnes of the non-rational. The movement gained additional adherents following the Great War, as the trauma of unprecedented loss sparked interest in practices that promised a reconnection with the dead.[7] Even so, the depth and duration of King's fervour for mysticism was unusual, a truth reinforced by the great care he took to conceal his beliefs and practices from all but his most trusted confidants. His order that his diaries be destroyed was simply the final act of occlusion, as King was aware enough to understand that disclosure of his lifelong dedication to a mysticism of this intensity would tarnish his legacy and leave him open to derision. That prophecy, at least, proved correct.

Unusual, too, for a man of his education and accomplishments, was the seeming artlessness of King's spiritual practice. C.P. Stacey's judgment on the matter was particularly inhospitable. "It is the extraordinary crudity of the manifestations of spiritualism," he wrote in his biography of King, "the shattering naïveté of his judgments in these matters, that leave one with the ineradicable impression of limited intelligence. At times, it is simply impossible to take him seriously." *Globe and Mail* writer William French was scarcely more sympathetic in his review of Stacey's 1978 poison-pen biography. While relieved to discover that King apparently felt heterosexual urges – rumours abounded about the decidedly unmacho prime minister's inclinations – French concluded that the spiritual "aspects of his character put him right back among the eccentrics on the fringe of bananaland" (the loony manse also inhabited, it is clear from the reviewer's jibe, by gay men).[8]

As King's political career progressed he became more and more absorbed with spiritualism, and his only two true interests became increasingly bound up with one another: in politics, his success was facilitated by the succour offered by spiritualism, where the dead foretold and hailed his many political triumphs as a validation of his chosen-ness as humanity's benefactor. When his father interrupted his other-worldly, post-mortem undertakings to return to the living and predict a Liberal victory in the upcoming 1925 federal election, the corporeal King was delighted. "I believe it is all true," he wrote. "That the dear loved ones are round about it, that in this fight I am mostly an instrument to work out the will of God." Much later, as King contemplated retirement, both long- and recently-departed mentors Sir Wilfrid Laurier and Franklin Roosevelt stirred to action. FDR beseeched the seventy-three-year-old prime minister, "I beg of you at whatever cost to continue in public life ... I feel it is your duty not merely to your country but to the world to stay on."[9] Although he was moved by the pleas from these towering statesman, King's failing health precluded compliance.

If King were alive in our day, an age characterized by a thoroughgoing and some say excessive will to label any and all character traits and perceived abnormalities, he might well be diagnosed with pareidolia and/or apophenia. Those with the former exhibit a marked tendency to see distinct images in random and meaningless stimuli. A renowned example involved the 2005 internet purchase, for five thousand US dollars, of a grilled cheese sandwich purportedly showing the image of Mary, mother of Jesus. An apopheniac not only perceives the image detected by the pareidoliac, but deems it part of an ongoing stream of messages from the spiritual realm. He might also espy a cloud-shaped lion but further conclude that it had been made manifest specifically for him in order to provide guidance or succour. An apopheniac is also fixated on coincidences, perceiving and finding meaning in the interconnectedness of what others would consider a series of unrelated and unremarkable events – for instance, recurring images of lions, a concurrence that achieves a yet higher plane of significance when the observer's own middle name is a homophone for the creature. Individuals often exhibit both syndromes simultaneously. As literary theorist Karen Raber wrote, these conditions inspire "a kind of induced anthropocentric blindness to things as they are, rather than as we perceive them. Rocks, clouds, landscapes, the sun, electrical outlets, burnt toast all become merely projections of ourselves ... turning all things into us."[10]

Over time those demonstrating such behaviours can descend into paranoia or psychosis, but the symptoms have also been linked to increased creativity.[11] It also appears logical that a person who simply cannot help but make constant connections, who is bombarded with synchronized, repetitive, portentous signals, would be drawn to spiritualism; more than that, the traits associated with apophenia in particular *require* belief in the purposeful workings of unseen forces. Was King's obsession with the spirit world and propensity for perceiving signs and

associations – and to open his diary is to be besieged by them – enough
to render a diagnosis? More intriguingly, were these "gifts" a help or
hindrance to his ability to govern successfully? Any search for answers
here would exceed my purposes and grasp. However, future researchers with a greater insight into psychology may well find in King's
relentless and fertile pattern-recognition a key to his success, lending
him an uncanny ability to see and act on trends: to chart a course in
governance that draws dexterously on the lessons from past successes
and failures, for example, or to perceive the future ripple effects of a
particular policy decision. Perhaps, in other words, King's spirituality
is not merely a peripheral and derisible curiosity, but an essential ingre-
dient in the makeup of a political savant.

Back at the Imperial Conference and weighing his imminent call to
Nazi leaders, King found that the spectral despatches concerning his
destiny and ultimate success were landing with increased frequency
and focus. That such celestial revelations were extremely timely and
welcomed (and to the more jaundiced, stimulated by obsessive apprehensions about what he was getting himself into) can be established
by the fact that in weaker moments, the Canadian prime minister
confessed to a near-panic over meeting Hitler and the awful responsibility this implied. "The dread of what lies ahead is something very
real," wrote an uncharacteristically self-doubting King as the London
meetings wound down, "and something which must be overcome."[12]
The fates, however, were resolute in their assurances of guidance
and ultimate victory – that is, if their earthly instrument maintained
his single-mindedness and virtue. These obligations made the peri-
odic lapses regarding strong drink and "thoughts which I might have
avoided" particularly distressing to the prime minister. The diary entry
that disclosed the aforementioned dreamed liaison with a disreputa-
ble woman from a "bad gang," for instance, began with an admonition
from the hymn "One Thing I of the Lord Desire," by nineteenth-century
Scottish cleric Walter C. Smith:

Only as the heart is pure
Can larger vision still be mine
For mirrored in its depth are seen
The things divine.[13]

Then, after confessing to his diary the troubling vision of female
temptation, King wrote of another that provided "a deep sense of the

meaning of 'power' ordained of God – the power which is the secret of strength or failure," and challenged himself to "hold to the power [as] it all is for the right." A later dream found King on a winter ski trip with a group that included his sister and father, the latter "going somewhat ahead" and towards "a beautiful golden light shining on and about the horizon," proof of "guidance in some matters about to be undertaken." On his side trip to Scotland between his duties in London and Berlin, relatives had given him a blanket with the family colours; King wrote of being comforted by the "Mackenzie tartan" on nights before important and stressful duties throughout his trip, the empathetic fabric dependably and uncannily providing "just the right amount of warmth." "It was a very significant thing having this plaid put over my shoulders," he noted, reflecting on a gift that reinforced the sensation that "the whole Mackenzie clan were communicating in my diplomatic mission & telling me what to do." And the numbers and coincidences continued to pile up, for had it not been *thirty-seven* years ago that he, a young university student from Berlin, Ontario, had come to old-world Berlin to study? And here he was in 1937, the centenary of his grandfather's populist revolt. All in all, he noted while sailing for the Continent to take on his ultimate test, the "visit to the British Isles" had "been full of evidence of the invisible realities."[14]

During a four-day layover in Paris prior to setting out for Berlin, the auguries continued apace. King found in his hotel room a copy of *Lord Grey of the Reform Bill: The Life of Charles, Second Earl Grey* by British historian G.M. Trevelyan; the author was the era's preeminent practitioner of Whig history, a school whose faith in progress would be fatally undermined by two world wars and the Holocaust. Opening the book to page 195, King found a discussion of British relations with Russia that revealed "just the thoughts that seemed most appropriate" for his visit to Germany. He packed it in his luggage before departing for Germany on 26 June; the volume would join the tartan as a regular nighttime companion, as King found sleeping with the biography near his pillow a consistent source of comfort.[15] It is unclear whether the prime minister received permission to liberate the volume from his room, but given the task ahead it is doubtful that hotel managers would have denied King any talisman that might bolster his odds in Germany.

That same morning of his departure for Berlin, King could not help but notice a series of arresting coincidences: First, he read *London Times* coverage of a Neville Chamberlain address to Parliament urging the press and public to exercise restraint in commenting on European matters, lest their words increase international tensions. As he pondered this statement – "as significant," judged King "as any ever made by a Prime Minister in the British Parliament" – he was reminded of his March 1937 trip to Washington, DC. There, Franklin Roosevelt "gave me the mission to come to Europe, saying that I might be the means of keeping peace between the United States and Japan if I did so." On that very same visit, a certain "Mr. Root" gave a speech urging restraint in journalists' reports on international affairs – just as Chamberlain had now done. Despite what would appear to be an ordinary series of vaguely related and hardly uncommon official pronouncements on the dangers of public speculation, King found in them a further confirmation of his own life's purpose, "an amazing parallel and rounding out of the years," as he phrased it.[16] He continued:

> I have always believed that Divine intervention makes itself apparent and felt only when human agency has made clear its inability to cope with the existing situation. I believe that God looks to man to do all he can in the first instance; if he does that and has Faith, when the time comes for a greater power than man has disclosed, it will be revealed if the Faith of the man is strong enough ... Quite clearly, one is being used by powers beyond one's control.[17]

And the fact that the Canadian Pacific Railway was able to help coordinate his train travel from Paris to Berlin on short notice was plainly more evidence of an unseen hand; what's more, both of the high-ranking CPR agents involved in the booking had handled aspects of the PM's travels before, and one had even visited the prime minister at Kingsmere, his country retreat in the Gatineau foothills! King eulogized:

> Water running through so many waters returns in abundance after many years. Kindness done in many directions and kind thoughts and deeds bring their more than equal reward in the course of time. What I may be able to achieve in the healing of international strife, should I be able to accomplish anything, will be the fruit of early endeavours along industrial peace and the help given to those beloved ones who were at the time so greatly in need of help. By aiding, we are made strong; by leading the blind, our vision is increased. So is the law of God.[18]

All of life's rivers – family legacies, spiritual guidance, political experience, the fruits of good deeds offered and returned – were

converging in Berlin. Once King arrived in that city, a visit to the Pergamon Museum provided further proof. There, he viewed the "original"
heads of a Babylonian King and Queen dated to 1370 BC. The male
ruler was known, noted the PM, as "a 'reformer' King and who caused
the Worship of the Sun (light) over all other gods." The prime minister,
also a reformer King, "felt a strange sense of power come over me" as
he made the undeniable connection between his role as a bringer of
light and "those lives 3307 years ago."[19] Threes and sevens, enlightened
kings – these recurring signs were not arbitrary.

Moreover, as demonstrated by President Roosevelt's entreaty,
Mackenzie King was also being spurred on by living men of influence. It is not surprising that a range of public officials, having strug-
gled mightily to identify Hitler's ultimate aims and the appropriate
methods of confronting them, would endorse his planned venture to
Germany, particularly in off-the-record conversations with King himself. Other high-ranking figures, to be sure, had refused similar invitations as a matter of principle. Winston Churchill had initially been
willing to meet the relatively untested and still-in-opposition fascist
leader in 1932 (a get-together that, according to Churchill, the Nazis
abruptly cancelled after he raised the matter of Hitler's antisemitism),
but the litany of outrages that followed the Nazi seizure of power led
Churchill to decline repeated invitations from Ribbentrop between
1936 and 1938. And some who accepted faced scorn for sycophancy.
A visit by former British air force secretary Lord Londonderry a year
earlier, which saw him enthuse about the work done to reinvigorate
the nation and its economy, received condescension and disdain from
liberal British journalists and parliamentarians.[20]

Still, this effort by a long-serving, non-European head of state with
a reputation for fair play and brokering deals would certainly seem
worth a try, even if it provided a sheen of respectability to the German
regime. Despite these seemingly long odds against any significant private censure of his Berlin plans, King duly recorded endorsements of
the scheme in his diary. The newly crowned King George VI, wrote the
prime minister, told him the visit was "all to the good; that there was
nothing like meeting men personally." Likewise, both Chamberlain
and Anthony Eden "strongly approved of my going to Germany" on
account of Canada's relative detachment from current European quar-
rels, along with the perception that King was speaking for both his
country and the United States in declaring that German military aggression against Britain would not be accepted passively.[21]

After having British secretary of state for dominion affairs Malcolm MacDonald laud King for being "of the greatest possible assistance" at the Imperial Conference, the diary has MacDonald informing King, in unison with "many others," that "you can do more than anyone else[,] for Hitler will feel in talking with you that you are speaking not only for Canada" but also reflecting the feeling of Britain and the United States. "I believe this to be true to a certain extent," King confessed. "I felt in talking with Malcolm a sort of feeling as though this whole country was actually looking to me to help it." At a state dinner in Paris two days before King set out for Germany, Stephane Lauzanne, the editor of the arch-conservative daily *Le Matin*, expressed "delight" that King was bound for Germany, as this "was the right and necessary thing to do." (Lauzanne's grasp of appropriate behaviour was later disaffirmed by a French court, which in 1944 sentenced him to twenty years' hard labour for his steadfast support for Nazi occupiers and the collaborationist Vichy Regime.) At the same Paris event, French ambassador and historian Gabriel Hanotaux, by then eighty-three years old and a seasoned diplomatic participant and observer, flatly informed King that the visit "was the most fortunate thing which could happen at this time," the prime minister's diary reported, as "no one could do as much good in Europe today as I could by going to Germany."[22]

The consistent and suspiciously grandiloquent blandishments trumpeted in his diary ("*no one* could do as much good?" Not Roosevelt, a potential tie-breaker in any European confrontation?) must have been a balm to a prime minister who had earlier confronted critics and his own better judgment over the possibility of guesting with Nazis. Concerns about the optics of calling on Hitler had first arisen when King proposed a meeting in 1936. O.D. Skelton, the prime minister's under-secretary of state for external affairs (except for his last two years in office, King served as his own secretary on this most-significant file) had long expressed fear and revulsion towards fascism and Hitler. In a 1935 position paper drafted for foreign policy discussions in London, Skelton maintained that despite the fact that Europe was wracked with tension "in almost every corner," the "Nazi religion and its prophet" was without doubt the gravest source of danger on the continent.[23] There was little quarter in Skelton's opinion for the notions that other great powers shared much of the blame for tensions or that German grievances were mostly legitimate.

In his diary, King recorded the reaction of Skelton – the prime minister's most trusted foreign policy advisor – to the proposed 1936 visit. "On talking the matter over with Skelton, he still feels very strongly that it would be resented in Canada; that it would only be flattering Hitler by having him feel some more persons were coming to him; that he was so much of an anglo-maniac, that nothing could influence him." King heard similar warnings from British social reformer Violet Markham, with whom he had maintained regular correspondence since their 1905 meeting at the governor general's residence in Ottawa. When King mentioned the possibility of meeting with the Nazi leader, Markham reminded King that Hitler "is the head of a detestable system of force and persecution and real horrors go on in Germany today for which he is responsible"; she advised that should King go, he should guard, above all, against the Fuhrer's ability to "hypnotize you." King himself worried that "the Jingo press of Canada might misconstrue it all" and concluded in 1936 that "it might be better not to take the risk involved."[24]

Now, however, trusted world leaders – like the lions, numbers, coincidences, visions, as well as ancestors and other post-incarnate messengers – had clearly aligned behind the prime minister's peace agenda.

6

Sympathy for the Devil

Finally aligning, too, were Nevile Henderson and Mackenzie King, for they had moved their conversation away from the prickly topic of Canada's status in the Empire and into an area of mutual accord: the prudence of appeasing Hitler. The ambassador treated King to a protracted lesson on German fascism and foreign policy, issuing a series of declarations that differed little from key leitmotifs in *Mein Kampf* itself (a memoir the ambassador had just read and declared "a remarkable production"). Namely: that Soviet communism was the true threat to Europe; that the Nazi regime could not remain "aloof from countries which were populated largely by Germans" or from the alleged persecution of German minorities in other states; that the international community and the British in particular seemed intent on belittling these legitimate territorial claims (with Henderson recounting sympathetically Göring's charge that "if Germany stooped to pick a flower which was on the Eastern border, that England would not permit her"); that the German people had "a right to live under any system they wished"; that such a system had, in fact, much to teach an unjustifiably sanctimonious British populace; that the League of Nations and its collective security mandate was "a horror" that would only invite war; that Hitler was essentially an idealist who "had much at heart the people's welfare."[1]

Henderson was pushing against an open door, for King objected to none of these claims. The wisdom revealed in the British ambassador's estimation of Nazism and what it meant for Europe lifted King's opinion of Henderson considerably. The two parted amicably and the prime minister rounded the corner to the Hotel Adlon, all the more certain that his own approach to the German question was the right one.[2]

It was an auspicious time for those calling for sympathy for Germany's territorial claims. Britain's new prime minister Neville Chamberlain had signalled a greater openness to appeasement than his predecessor Stanley Baldwin, recognizing in the wake of the Imperial Conference that his nation's territory and interests could not be protected by the League of Nations when even his closest allies – the dominions – recoiled from the prospect of collective action. As an exasperated Chamberlain informed Parliament following the tumult of the Imperial Conference: "To those who think it is a simple matter to reach common under-standing, even amongst the dominions that go to make up the British Commonwealth of Nations, I say to them to have another look."[3]

Under these circumstances, Chamberlain could either go it alone in taking a tough stance against Hitler at a time when his war readiness lagged significantly behind that of Germany, or he could offer greater flexibility in addressing demands that ethnic Germans in neighbour-ing regions be absorbed by a redrawn map of Europe. While he would forever be synonymous with fecklessness, it was cold calculation, not credulous optimism, that drove Chamberlain's gamble. At best, his strategy would placate the Nazis. If, however, Hitler proved insatia-ble, the plodding to-and-fro diplomacy inherent to appeasement might provide badly needed time to rearm. The motivation was rather dif-ferent for Henderson and King, who viewed appeasement as both a sure-fire mechanism for averting war and a simple matter of justice for Germany. Both men were convinced that Hitler simply wanted to re-trieve lands severed by the Treaty of Versailles, an illusion the British Foreign Office had abandoned as early as 1933.[4]

That Henderson's smorgasbord of fascist-friendly prescriptions for handling Germany's grievances could find favour with the Canadian prime minister, a national leader who styled himself a democrat, a mod-erate, a bridge-builder, and a lover of peace, is not entirely unexpected on several counts. First, while King was clearly a sage as a political op-erative, he was not an overly sophisticated or consistent political logi-cian. In fact, scrutiny of King's speeches, letters, diary entries, and other written testaments to the workings of his mind reveals a clever tactician with an enviable memory and uncanny ability to draw associations, but not a particularly deep or original thinker. He had a habit, for instance, of describing his encounters with the world in vague, simple, and of-ten fawning language. An English estate boasted "the most beautiful country grounds that I have ever seen or ever expect to see" (no further description provided); the Belgian ambassador, like so many others described in his diaries, was "an extremely pleasant man"; an opera in Berlin "was exceptionally well performed; beautiful singing; excellent staging"; Canada's attitude towards Germany was "of the friendliest"; "Nothing could be more beautiful nor more impressive" than the statues bathed in electric light outside the Louvre on a summer evening; dinners, speeches, people, train rides, and a host of other phenomena are "exceedingly fine affairs," "most interesting," "most enjoyable," "most pleasing," "most agreeable," "most delightful" and so on.[5] The descriptions are at once awash in superlatives and, in their failure to provide any justification for these judgements, conspicuously empty. This was a mind best fitted for political strategizing, not for rigorous analysis or reflective insights.

Accordingly, King could articulate a range of seemingly contradictory ideological convictions. "Any attempt to make Mackenzie King's mind a unified and harmonious whole," wrote historian Reg Whitaker, "is akin to squaring a circle." To wit: King insisted time and again that he was simply an instrument of the Canadian people, the even-handed conduit of their will, yet he preferred to craft policy behind closed doors with the fewest and highest-ranking associates feasible. He detested the burgeoning fetish for governmental transparency, protesting, for instance, the idea that conference attendees issue public statements summarizing their deliberations – and even the idea of conferences themselves. "Conferences were dangerous things," he confided to US secretary of state Cordell Hull in the fall of 1937. The fractious imperial meetings in London that spring that were followed by his cloistered, constructive one-on-ones with top Nazis had provided further proof that "more good could be effected by the old fashioned diplomacy of nations dealing quietly with each other."[6] On this, King seemed not to appreciate the caveat furnished by the First World War, when the prevailing "quiet diplomacy" of secret agreements and private guarantees helped set the world ablaze. (King's persistent claim that "personal contacts" would generate the friendly atmosphere inimical to armed conflict likewise elided the glaring counterpoint of 1914: the chummy rapport between cousins Wilhelm II, Nicholas II, and George V proved little brake on the slide to war, and the monarchs then turned on one another with unholy vengeance.)

King reserved special scorn for the prying eyes of the press, in an age before opinion polling one of the few avenues to discerning the public mood. This posture points to yet another ideological inconsistency that the prime minister seemed not to think through: both he and his

revered rebel grandfather had begun their careers as journalists, deploying the press to expose and redress the abuses of the powerful.
Once King himself had joined those eminent ranks, however, he came
to fully disavow whatever feeble nods to rebelliousness he had entertained in youth, and his determined evasion of the fourth estate became
one of his more consistent (and unwelcomed) sources of exercise. When
interactions with reporters could simply not be avoided, he habitually
offered up some of the vaguest generalities in the history of Canadian
political discourse; the clear implication was that the public had no intrinsic right to monitor the inner workings of government. The mature
King's devotion to order, deference, and discretion would fate him to
a lifelong clash with the nosy and irreverent scribes who made their
living snooping about for a sensational scoop.[7]

And woe to those who would find fault with their leader. King biographer Joy Esberey summed up the prime minister's zero-sum approach to interpersonal relationships: "Those who were not for him
in everything were against him ... there was no room for half measures."[8] Thus the vitriol reserved for journalists who were simply doing
their jobs in holding government to account. King's certitude about his
own special destiny did him little favours here. Second-guessers were
simply accessories to the conspiracy to gum up the designs for which
Providence had anointed him, kindling in King a burning desire for
name-taking and score-settling that in spirit differed little from Richard
Nixon's infamous "enemies list." No surprise, then, that although he
personally shunned the temptations of tobacco, the proverbial smoke-
filled back room was King's atelier.

Similarly, the circle could not be squared when it came to King's motley characterizations of tyranny. In April 1937, Ontario's Liberal premier Mitchell Hepburn ran roughshod over the rights of striking auto
workers in Oshawa, a strike that ended the day before King sailed for
the Imperial Conference but one he continued to seethe over throughout his trip. From London King wrote in his diary that Hepburn was
undoubtedly "a Fascist leader," an autocrat whom King feared would
round up his leftist enemies "into Communist camps." In the very
next sentence, the prime minister pivoted to his conversation with real
fascists who built real camps for leftists and other enemies, reporting
without a trace of irony his "most pleasant" phone call with Joachim
Ribbentrop regarding Hitler's enthusiasm for the prime minister's impending visit. (In fairness, King was not alone in smearing Hepburn
as a crypto-fascist for his assault on labour: reporting on the prime

6.1 The prime minister and the tyrant: King chats with Ontario Liberal leader Mitchell Hepburn in 1934, the year Hepburn was elected premier. Their later falling-out was absolute. (Library and Archives Canada, C-087863)

minister's consultations in Germany, *Saturday Night* magazine's Hal Frank quipped that King's "experience in interviewing Mr. Hitler will probably stand him in good stead when he comes to have his talk with Mr. Hepburn.")[9]

As was the case with non-deferential journalists, King's classification of Mitchell Hepburn was not uncharacteristic of the ways the prime minister described rival politicians. He had a habit of referring to his domestic political foes in ways far more suited to the foreign autocrats he treated so respectfully in person and diary. Both Hepburn and Quebec premier Maurice Duplessis were "incipient dictators," in

King's reckoning. Forced into opposition during Conservative R.B. Bennett's 1930–35 tenure as Canadian prime minister, King wrote that at the1932 Remembrance Day ceremonies in Ottawa, Bennett "looked like a butcher, a tyrant and bully which he is." Bennett was detestable, King continued, for "the extremes to which he is apt to go ... The extreme man is always more or less dangerous, but nowhere more so than politics." After smiting this tyrant and his minions in the 1935 federal election, King gave an acceptance speech that dished on, as he described in his diaries, "the dangers that threatened responsible government – the dangers of dictatorship – the dangers of economic nationalism and imperialism ... and above all the need for a Christian spirit and not materialism and selfishness as a guide in national affairs."[10] Here again, the foil for King's more democratic, munificent, and compassionate governance was not the glaringly obvious counter-examples provided by Hitler, Stalin, or Mussolini, but Bennett and his suppression of alleged communists.

In September 1939, by which point King's ardour for the Fuhrer was (at last) in full retreat, the prime minister christened Premier Duplessis "little Hitler" for opposing Canada's participation in "big" Hitler's war. While it is true that Duplessis, Bennett, and Hepburn shared dishonourable records of repressing civil liberties and those on the political left, King's own legacy on these matters was little better, particularly after his government imposed the draconian War Measures Act to reign in alleged subversion during the Second World War. The self-styled consummator of grandfather Mackenzie's vision of egalitarian liberalism had to be schooled in the House of Commons by John Diefenbaker, leader of the "jingo-tory-militarist" Conservative Party, on the fundamentals of *habeas corpus* and civil liberties.[11]

That wartime hounding of leftists points to one of the more consistent traits of King's political praxis, and a second reason that he and Henderson could regard Nazism with such positivity. Although genuinely moved by the plight of the working class and a proponent of progressive social welfare legislation, King saw far greater danger on the political left than the right. This disposition he shared with many in the Depression-era chancelleries of the West, and it fed logically into the tactic of cozying up to the left's most determined adversaries: fascists. The European "difficulties would soon adjust themselves," King wrote while at the Imperial Conference, if only "Russia were out of the picture." Meeting exiled Queen Victoria Eugenie of Spain ("an exceedingly interesting woman; very pleasant to talk with") and one of her

6.2 The ex-prime minister and the tyrant: with R.B. Bennett in 1933, when King was opposition leader to the Conservative prime minister he called "a butcher." (Library and Archives Canada, PA-148532)

daughters ("also ... very pleasant") while in Britain in early June of that year, King was treated to the aristocratic explication of the civil war then engulfing their country. Although the fighting began when right-wing Nationalist generals rebelled against a democratically elected, popular-front Republican government comprised of centrists and leftists, the queen informed the prime minister that "the trouble had been stirred up from Moscow."[12]

While it was certainly true that the besieged Republicans accepted Soviet military assistance, the exiled noblewomen insisted that Stalin was the ultimate puppet master of the operations, that this was all part of the Soviet master plan to get "the World pretty much aflame." And despite the widespread and vitriolic international condemnation that followed the aerial bombing of the Republican town of Guernica just weeks before, the royals spoke only of the brutality of the "Reds" – King himself, they maintained, would be shot immediately on account of his posh dinner jacket – and declared that fascist general and Nationalist leader Francisco Franco "was anything but a dictator." Not mentioned was the systematic killing of Franco's Republican opponents that outnumbered by roughly five times the corresponding executions of right-wing Nationalists, or the military and financial support provided by fascist Germany, Italy, and Portugal to Franco, a "mild sort of man who simply wanted to keep order," as the Queen's daughter described him to King. Many Canadians disagreed with that characterization. Nearly seventeen hundred volunteered to fight for the Republican cause, despite legislation banning participation that the King Liberals rushed through the House of Commons two weeks after the prime minister returned from Germany. The prime minister feared that Canadian veterans of the conflict would come home hardened revolutionaries intent on sparking their own leftist revolution in the dominion.[13]

The wider world was well aware that it was the German and Italian air forces that had razed Guernica on 26 April in support of Franco's cause; here was Europe's first experience of the strategy of "terror bombing" – deliberate aerial bombardment of civilians. The tactic would soon be adopted by all major belligerents in the Second World War, despite the expressions of horror emanating from all corners of the globe following the Guernica assault. Although that attack was front-page news in Britain for a full week in late April to early May (when newspaper aficionado King was in London), the prime minister's diary does not refer to it until 5 May, when newly crowned King George VI broached the subject in private conversation with the visiting Canadian leader. The British sovereign was profoundly disturbed by the attack – a consequence, he feared, of various countries' obsession with testing their newly developed weaponry in advance of future and more extensive campaigns. George VI was correct. The Nazis, by their own reckoning, carried out this gross violation of international law not only to beat back international communism, but also to train and test the Luftwaffe in preparation for comparable attacks against any who would resist their quest for *Lebensraum*.[14]

That King's diary records no objection or qualification to the Spanish royals' wholly partisan synopsis of the civil war is notable, given the very recent global outrage over Guernica. Instead, the conversation with Victoria Eugenie and her daughter led King to ponder how best to blunt the appeal of leftist solidarity and activism, the ultimate cause, both he and the Spanish regents believed, of the troubles plaguing their country and continent. His thoughts turned to his graduate days at the University of Chicago studying "revolutionary movements," insurrections unnecessarily egged on, in his reckoning, by heavy-handed corporate and government repression of labour.[15] Consequently, he saw great danger in the violent repression of strikes.

One such incident had occurred just before the prime minister departed for the Imperial Conference. "Incipient dictator" Mitchell Hepburn, outraged by King's refusal to deliver the RCMP to break up the aforementioned Oshawa auto strike, mustered a private army (dubbed "Sons of Mitches" by strikers) to intimidate a workforce Hepburn considered communist inspired. Another example of how not to defeat socialist sentiments took place just a week before King's evening with Spanish royalty – Chicago's Memorial Day Massacre, when ten striking steelworkers, labelled "reds" in media accounts, were killed and more than a hundred injured by police bullets and clubs. "That is the way civil war is brought on," wrote King in reference to both incidents; in other words, this suppression of labour was the very thing that grew the appeal of socialist revolution. Even as he surveyed the worrying relations between European states first hand in the summer of 1937, he concluded that the clear and present threat to peace lay within, not beyond, national borders – that "greatest fear, I think, today, is with the classes of industry." His views on this had changed little since the November 1918 publication of *Industry and Humanity*. Writing in the midst of the most appalling technological killing the world had yet known, he argued that "the horrors of international war pale before the possibilities of civil conflicts begotten of class hatreds."[16]

It is here that we can gain further understanding of the prime minister's considerable forbearance for fascism. That ideology was at once anti-communist and, in its efforts to elevate the status of farmers and factory workers vis-à-vis the moneyed and aristocracy, an approach that sought to ameliorate the tensions between capital and labour so conspicuous in other capitalist countries of the era – tensions that could easily metastasize into the leftist revolt that King ultimately dreaded.

Germany's labour harmony had, to be sure, been realized through a ban on all unions aside from the Nazis' own Deutsche Arbeitsfront (DAF) and the arrest of independent union leaders, part of a wider climate of terror and intimidation that muted dissent in Hitler's Reich. But coercion was only part of this story. Ideologically, fascists loathed the international working-class solidarity championed by communists, as this required linking hands with racial inferiors across the border ("Workers of the world, unite!," implored Marx and Engels). To fascists, such a transnational approach sapped the vigour of race and nation alike. Practically, fascism took pains to undermine the call of domestic leftism by making workers feel valued through initiatives like the Kraft durch Freude (KdF, Strength through Joy), an organization that subsidized travel and leisure opportunities for the working class. A sister organization Schönheit der Arbeit (SdA, Beauty of Work) combatted the drudgery and danger of industrial labour by cleaning up factories, making them quieter and better lit, and bedecking their walls with posters exalting hygiene, teamwork, the dignity of labour, and of course, the *Vaterland* and its Fuhrer.[17]

Nevile Henderson had this focus on worker well-being in mind when he told King that "there is a lot that England can learn from Germany in treatment of the masses of the people."[18] Throughout his trip the prime minister, too, repeatedly hailed the Nazis' efforts to valorize labour as an analogue to his own life's work as an industrial peacemaker. Unlike the police raids against strikers witnessed back home, this was a variety of anti-communism that appeared not to contain an inbuilt, self-defeating advertisement for communism. The gaping hole in such a rationale for saluting the Reich's labour program lay not only in the coercion behind it. The "masses" extolled by Hitler were not truly the masses, but only those deemed physically able and of Aryan descent; indeed, the devotion to the state, party, and DAF incubated under Nazism was deepened by the sense of superiority even the lowliest Aryan labourers were instructed to brandish over their racially inferior neighbours. Henderson and King, in praising the Reich's efforts to erase class tensions, had themselves completely erased the issue of race.

King had witnessed, and hailed, aspects of the fascist curriculum before, on a 1928 voyage to Europe to add his name to the (then) widely hailed Kellogg-Briand Pact outlawing war as an instrument of foreign policy. Following the signing ceremony in Paris, the prime minister called on Italian dictator Benito Mussolini in Rome. King was "enthused," he wrote, by Mussolini's transformation of the city: "when one hears how he came with his blackshirts," he continued, "offered his services to clean up the government and the House of Representatives filled with communists ... cleaned the streets of beggars and the houses of harlots, one becomes filled with admiration." On departing, King "wished him well and the necessary strength to carry on his work," and observed that "there were evidences of sadness and tenderness as well as great decision in his countenance. His hand was much softer than I expected to find it."[19] While still devoid of analytical complexity, the prime minister's diaries demonstrate a consistent striving to capture the appearance and mannerisms of people of influence as a means of grasping their character and inner workings.

The thrill of mingling with elites like *Il Duce* never grew stale for King, even after decades of personal encounters with the globe's most powerful figures. This fondness for the moneyed, titled, and famous provides further insight into his capacity to engage with top Nazi officials in a manner that was completely out of proportion with the blood already on their hands. As a bourgeois, small-town boy from a clan of some disrepute, "King derived tremendous personal satisfaction," observed Levine, "whenever he was permitted to enter the puffed-up world" of the rich and powerful. He was, for instance, simultaneously a stubborn and effectual Canadian nationalist and a lifelong enthusiast for the House of Windsor. At the Imperial Conference, it was King who suggested that the legations from the dominions commission a painting of the coronation to present to the newly crowned but hardly needy royals in "recognition of all the hospitality which had been extended to us while we were here"; he had Pickering draft a letter ("in very good form," noted King, in a rare tribute to the labours of subordinates) informing George VI of the gift in advance so that it could be duly heralded in the newspapers before the Canadian prime minister left London.[20]

Conversations with British lords also gave King a special charge, and while in London preparing for his German jaunt, he paid close heed to the counsel offered by English aristocrats with personal ties to Nazi Germany – the so-called fellow-travellers of the right predisposed to German fascism. At a reception on 10 May he chatted with Lord Lothian (Henry Kerr), a leading member of the Ribbentrop-founded Anglo-German Fellowship who had taken his own visit to the Reich two years earlier. Lord Lothian promised to furnish a detailed summary of his impressions, and the following day, King received a ten-page letter marked "confidential" that synopsized those 1935 meetings with Hitler, Göring, and Reichsbank president Hjalmar Schacht.[21]

The European situation, Lothian's letter began, was "both more dangerous and more soluble than I thought." Dangerous because Britain was scandalously unsympathetic to Germany; soluble because a simple volte-face on the matter would end any possibility of a clash between

Europe's two leading powers. Nazis held their fellow-Nordic Britons
in high esteem, wrote the lord, and conflict between them "could
only result in the triumph of the less civilized races." Cooperation, on
the other hand (including gifting the Reich a few insignificant colonies, "say in Central West Africa") would be mutually advantageous,
maintaining not only the peace but the proper ordering of the world.
"Jawaharlal Nehru," warned Lothian, "is openly awaiting the next
world war to let loose revolution in India. It would probably end, as
Hitler says, in the ruin of both Germany and the British Empire and the
triumph of the 'lesser breeds.'"[22] The "better-bred" Britons' energetic
campaign for cooperation was clearly more than just a plea for peace;
on many fundamental issues, there was little distance between German
Nazis and British peers.

At the completion of the Imperial Conference, King made a final
visit to the newly crowned British sovereign to inform him that "we
all had to thank both him and the Queen more than anyone else" for a
new spirit of unity throughout the empire; the PM added, as his diary
records, "that I hoped he would not think I was saying that just because I was speaking to his face but that I found it difficult to discover
words to tell him how greatly I admired and how greatly everyone admired the manner in which he and the Queen had met every situation,"
and on and on. Whether George VI, like British High Commissioner
Floud's wife, yearned for a bath after such an ingratiating homage is
not recorded, but nearly every other aspect of this mere thirty-minute
encounter with his sovereign was, in a diary entry that filled five typewritten pages. ("I bowed," King's dictation to Pickering began, "and
then the King who was standing some 10 feet away, advanced forward
and shook hands ... We talked for a few moments facing each other
standing, and then the King beckoned me to sit on the chair to the right
of the fire-place as one faced it, and he took the chair on the side opposite. There was no fire ..."). As historian Christopher Dummit wrote,
when the British monarchs arrived in Canada two years later for a royal
visit, the prime minister's "diary showed Mackenzie King pedantically
battling with the governor general about who would greet 'His Majesties' first." When his chance came, King pledged to His Majesties "that
I was prepared to lay my life at their feet in helping to further great
causes which they had at heart."[23]

And now in Berlin, King, a devotee of pomp and the powerful, was
an honoured guest in the Nazi Reich – a regime at the very centre of
global intrigue – holding private talks with, and being feted by, its most

powerful officials. He was pleased to learn that "von Ribbentrop had sent for [Hewel] to fly all the way to Munich to meet Hitler and himself with regard to my visit, and to receive from them instructions as to giving me the fullest information about everything." Party officials of all ranks referred to him as "Your Excellency"; his diary entries made meticulous reference to encounters with eminent sites. At the Olympic Stadium sporting exhibition King noted with satisfaction that he was "given the seat Hitler himself occupied at the Olympic Games"; later, he enjoyed "tea in [the] room Hitler meets his friends in," and at the opera "was given the seat in the center where the Emperors used to sit and where Hitler sits when he attends the Opera. As we went to our seats," King enthused, "word seemed to go quickly around the audience for nearly everybody turned and looked toward the box."[24]

In short, recognition mattered to a surprising degree for a man of the prime minister's rank and achievement, and his Nazi hosts delivered. Pleased by the unprecedented visit from a Western leader and the opportunity to charm a statesman who enjoyed the ear of the imperious and uncooperative English, Reich officials treated King to a litany of lavish teas, dinners, and cultural and sporting events. Topping it off were the confidential sessions with men who, as we now know, were carving time out of their preparations for European conquest in order to entertain the PM in meetings that, as King pointed out with evident pride, typically went longer than planned. Conversely, in domestic affairs, lack of deference to the prime minister and his agenda, such as that mandated by being a member of the Official Opposition, rankled King to no end; thus the persistent and utterly disproportionate venom aimed at domestic political opponents. It was also the case that King had a tendency to empathize most pointedly with those he met one-on-one, rarely challenging even in his private musings their opinions unless they directly contradicted his own or showed him in a bad light. Similarly, the King diary provides repeated testimony that his "personal" opinions on a given issue were highly susceptible to those of the individual to whom he last spoke. All of this would shape King's conduct while in Germany and his reflections on the visit in the days and weeks following his departure.

All in all, day one of the holy errand had featured an impressive catalogue of inimitable experiences, new and promising relationships, and auspicious signs: rejuvenated Berlin, hospitable Hewel, the youth camp, the trip through the bucolic German countryside, the athletic exhibition at the majestic Olympic Stadium, and the extended tête-à-tête with

Henderson that had begun with such strain and that King had steered towards greater harmony and a greater appreciation for Canada's autonomy. King's dictation to Pickering of the day's events wrapped up around midnight with a concise summation of the optimism the PM had gained through these first encounters. "I am more convinced than ever I have done the right thing in the interests of Canada and the Empire in coming to Berlin at this time."[25]

After dismissing Pickering for the evening, King, alone in his suite at the Adlon, added a handwritten postscript to the day's log expressing appreciation for the succour provided by unseen forces: the lions, the numerological coincidences, and the celestial "cloud of witnesses who are helping today. Tonight's talk with the Ambassador," he wrote, "was the first round – I think I scored standing on my own under guidance from beyond." He walked out onto his balcony overlooking Pariser Platz for a last look at the collection of international flags on display, banners surrounded by those bearing the Nazi swastika, and reflected on the magnitude of, and his personal aptitude for, "this mission." By 1 a.m., he was finally settled enough to attempt sleep. He placed the biography of Lord Grey on his nightstand, but uncharacteristically forsook the Mackenzie tartan in favour of the Adlon Hotel's double blankets.[26]

7

Haunted Berlin

Pariser Platz, the square visible from King's room at the Adlon, was the grandest of its kind in the city. At its western limit stood the Brandenburger Tor (Brandenburg Gate), a commanding, twelve-columned, Athenian-inspired passageway that marked the beginning of the westbound road to Brandenburg, the original seat of the House of Hohenzollern. Built in the late eighteenth century as a monument to peace and in the neoclassical style that would come to dominate prominent nineteenth-century Berlin architectural projects, the structure took on the metaphorical and literal scars of the tumultuous two centuries that followed. Napoleon marched his victorious Grande Armée through the gate after defeating Prussian troops in 1806, and completed the humiliation by unbolting the massive, four-horse quadriga from the top of the structure, a statue whose chariot carried Greek goddess of peace Eirene, and carting it back to Paris to mingle with his vast collection of war booty. (How vast? When Citizen Wicar, just one of the officers Napoleon assigned to the portfolio of art confiscation, died in 1843, he bequeathed to his hometown over one thousand artworks seized following victorious battles – this after he had sold off the majority of his stolen treasures during his lifetime.) For this act of imperial vandalism, Prussians christened the hated French Emperor the "horse thief of Berlin."[1]

Vengeance was served quickly. The Prussian occupation of Paris following Napoleon's defeat in 1814 prompted the quadriga's triumphant return, along with the transformation of this symbol of peace into one of righteous belligerence. Eirene was rechristened Victoria, goddess of victory, and made to hold a staff topped with an eagle and iron cross, symbols of the Prussian monarchy and military, respectively. The square itself, to this point officially nameless, became Pariser Platz in honour of the retaliatory routing and occupation of the French capitol.

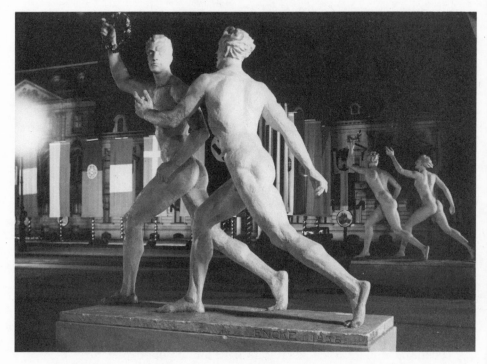

7.1 Pariser Platz dressed for the 1936 Olympics. The international flags were still flying when King visited the following summer. (Bundesarchiv, B 145 Bild-P017100)

This fierce tug of war for the monument symbolized the wider battle for hegemony on the Continent, and only augmented the centuries-old myth that the newborns of France and Germany came into the world bearing a genetic loathing – a so-called hereditary enmity – for one another. When Chancellor Otto von Bismarck's drive for German unity was sealed in 1871 by victory in the Franco-Prussian War, no one had to ask about the location of the party for the returning conquerors; when Germans marched once more towards France in 1914, the gate again served as the site for enthusiastic send-off festivities. Because it was meant to dazzle the citizens of Berlin, the quadriga faced east towards the city, but this had the happy consequence of directing the horses' buttocks permanently towards Germany's "intrinsic" foe.[2]

The Nazis, of course, had no quarrel with either the militaristic transformation of the monument or its implicit debasement of the French, and celebrated Hitler's January 1933 appointment as chancellor with a torchlight march through the gate by approximately sixty thousand brownshirts. The procession was organized by chief Nazi propagandist Joseph Goebbels and broadcast live on German state radio, with exultant commentary provided by Hermann Göring, future head of the Luftwaffe and Hitler's handpicked successor. When the Olympic Games came to Berlin, massive Nazi flags interspersed with banners featuring the five-ring Olympic symbol hung between the gate's six sets of double columns, and the structure was flanked on both sides by flagpoles installed to fly the colours of participating Olympic nations. This ode to international camaraderie was still on display when Mackenzie King looked out from his hotel balcony in the summer of 1937.[3]

The paean to brotherhood would in short order figuratively and literally crumble. During the Second World War, most structures in the vicinity of Pariser Platz were ground into rubble by Allied bombs, but the gate, though badly damaged, was still standing at war's end. In a rare display of cooperation, the mid-1950s governments of East and West Berlin signed an agreement to stabilize the structure (the East's task) and rebuild the quadriga (the West's). After West Berlin artisans dropped off the restored quadriga at the foot of the gate in 1958, their counterparts from the east promptly sawed off both the Prussian eagle and the iron cross, the latter banned in the communist Deutsche Demokratische Republik (DDR) for its association with Prussian militarism. The claim that this surgery had restored the structure to its status as a symbol of peace was, however, muddied by the fact that DDR officials would soon seal off the gate and make it a component of the Berlin Wall. From 1961 to 1989 the monument overlooked the border's notorious "death strip" and a forlorn Pariser Platz denuded of its stylish palaces, embassies, galleries, and hotels.[4]

The gate once again served as a site of revelry when the Berlin Wall fell, but reunification revived old and bitter arguments over the proposed refurbishment of the quadriga. Mostly, it appears, because they had been removed by the DDR, the eagle and iron cross were restored, although not without vigorous protests against latent militarism from those on both sides of the old Cold War divide. Urban historian Brian Ladd noted that owing to its turbulent past, "the much-restored but never removed Brandenburg Gate, with its thrice removed and twice reconstructed quadriga, is as authentic a symbol as Berlin can offer."[5] Little wonder that the Brandenburger Tor vies with the DDR television tower that dominates the skyline for the position of foremost emblem of Berlin.

7.2 Pariser Platz and Brandenburger Tor in June 1945. The square's proximity to Berlin's Government District, where the Fuhrer cowered underground in the closing months of the war, ensured that it would be subjected to relentless aerial bombardment and some of the heaviest ground fighting in the spring 1945 Battle of Berlin. (Bundesarchiv, B 145 Bild-P054320, Weinrother, Carl)

Just to the east, at the other end of Pariser Platz, lay the Hotel Adlon. Opened in 1907, the restrained classical structure with neo-baroque ornamentation was Berlin's answer to the luxurious, multi-use hotels that had sprung up in major European and American cities around the turn of the century. It was the first address on Unter den Linden, the magnificent boulevard leading eastward to the Stadtschloss, primary residence of the Hohenzollerns. The Adlon soon developed into a hub for Prussian aristocrats and Berlin socialites and the preferred location for visiting dignitaries. It remained thus after the ascent of the Nazis,

7.3 From 1945 to 1990, the Brandenburger Tor and Pariser Platz lay in East
Berlin. The presence today of a Starbucks cafe (not shown) and various costumed
figures whose connection to German history is not immediately apparent (but
who for a small fee are willing to pose with visitors for a photograph) provides
one reply to the question of who won the Cold War. (Author photograph, 2011)

whose top brass booked the hotel's rooms overlooking Pariser Platz to
observe the procession of torch-bearing brownshirts in January 1933.[6]

The war those same fascist apparatchiks initiated inspired hotel management to add a well-appointed bomb shelter, as well as a thick wall
completely encircling the ground floor to protect diners and revellers
from bomb debris and shrapnel. These measures appeared to reassure
the grandees in and around Berlin, as the Adlon's business remained
brisk throughout the war despite recurrent bombing raids against the
city. "Everyone seemed to come to the Adlon," recalled American war
correspondent Joseph Harsh, who as a hotel guest in the early 1940s

7.4 The Hotel Adlon in 1926, looking southeast from Pariser Platz.
(Bundesarchiv, Bild 102-13848F)

encountered journalists from around the globe, cagey foreign operatives of unspecified portfolio, and Hohenzollern Crown Prince Wilhelm,
who spent most of his days up the street at the Stadtschloss waiting in
vain for Hitler to restore the monarchy.[7]

The party would not last. In the last months of the war, the Adlon's
basement barbershop was converted into a makeshift operating
room, and the bodies of those that doctors could not save were piled
in the once-splendid Goethe Garden behind the hotel. In late April, as
Hitler and his most fanatical loyalists huddled in the Fuhrerbunker
two blocks to the south, Adlon management decided to clear out
their 250,000-bottle wine collection rather than relinquish it to the
approaching Soviet troops. Tuxedo-clad waiters tiptoed through
the debris to serve patrons oblivious of or indifferent to the dead
in the garden, but the wine cellar's holdings proved too vast. The

7.5 The Adlon following the war, looking southeast. After Allied bomber squadrons began targeting the German capital in the early 1940s, hotel owners added the protective brick cladding surrounding the first floor to protect guests from flying debris. The makeshift railroad tracks in the foreground are post-war additions installed to facilitate the transfer of rubble, some of which has been loaded into hopper cars, to the outskirts of Berlin. (Bundesarchiv, Bild 183-S93249)

Soviets arrived in time to finish off first the wine and then the Adlon itself, in early May setting a fire that would destroy much of the structure. Apparently because they confused his title of "general-director" for a military rank, Red Army officials arrested the hotel's proprietor Louis Adlon, who died in their custody under mysterious circumstances. East German officials, anxious to utilize anything left standing, later reinforced the Adlon's small surviving rear wing and used it as a hotel and then a residence before levelling the remains in the mid-1980s.[8]

7.6 *"Platt historistisch"*?: The New Adlon, opened in 1997, looking southeast. (Author photograph, 2017)

A new Adlon opened at the same location in 1997, an edifice that assumed the same footprint and general, though simplified, aesthetic of the original. This was an unfortunate decision according to the French foreign minister, who called the facsimile "stiff and tasteless." German critics concurred, disparaging the resurrected Adlon as *"platt histor-istisch,"* or vulgar historicism and, more lyrically, as "the superficial evocation of deluded dreams."[9] At least, and at last, the "hereditary" foes had outgrown their habit of perpetual discord.

The fracas over the new Adlon reveals one of the myriad dilemmas for a nation ruined by a conflict brought on by their own, reprehensible regime. Should reconstruction efforts focus on restoring the pre-Nazi built environment, the one that harkens back to the era of the Hohen-zollerns? Cities like Munich and Dresden answered in the affirmative, preserving their inner-city street grids and carefully recreating struc-tures dating from the medieval through the Weimar eras; Dresden's comprehensive and meticulous restoration program continues to this day. Yet how satisfying can it be for a modern, democratic, and diverse community to ground its identity in contemporary replicas of structures born in the age of monarchs? Other cities – Frankfurt and Hamburg, for instance – focused on a modern reinvention of their annihilated cores, yet here the danger lies in eradicating many of the cultural lodestones of the past, leaving post-war citizens unmoored among unfamiliar and often hastily constructed and characterless streetscapes. And neither approach offers an intrinsic response to the imperative of remembering the crimes of the Third Reich – in fact, without care, both can have the effect of simply erasing any vestige of that evil. Under these circumstances, which remnants of the Nazi past should be preserved, and which eliminated? Will preservation gratify neo-Nazis? Will elimination lead to amnesia? Should commemorative monuments and practices impugn Germans as a whole for Nazi atrocities, or only those who were direct perpetrators? At what point, if ever, can the debts to the past and its victims be considered paid, and Germany become a "normal" nation?

Answers do not come easily, but it should be noted that Hotel Adlon, Mark II, confronts and reflects the burden of history to a greater degree than was recognized by those who dismissed it as vulgar historicism: designers added modern components that clearly, though perhaps inadvertently, invoked the painful ghosts of its violent past: bullet-proof windows and – for those willing to pay – a handful of steel-plated rooms.[10]

8

Arbeit Macht Frei

Something was wrong on Mackenzie King's first night in Berlin. He woke at 5 a.m. after just a few hours' sleep, too hot under the Hotel Adlon's double comforters. He got out of bed and checked the clock (no numerical or angular portents tendered, or at least recorded), regarded once again the flags in Pariser Platz, then retrieved the Mackenzie tartan and returned to bed for another attempt at sleep.[1]

The revered fabric once again worked its magic, and King was soon slumbering and receiving otherworldly callers. Great-grandmother and Grandmother Mackenzie dropped by to deliver a letter that seemed to portend the establishment of a Canadian embassy in Berlin (no more dust-ups with Henderson over accommodations!) and to assure the PM that, as he recorded, "the whole Mackenzie clan were communicating in my diplomatic mission and telling me what to do. I was wrapped in the tartan," King continued, "when Nicol came to wake me."[2]

Nicol? The narrator can be forgiven for overlooking the presence in Berlin of King's long-time valet until deep into the story, for Nicol faithfully discharged his duties in a manner commensurate with the very model of a traditional manservant: while frequently described as "omnipresent," he was also called "sober," "expressionless," and "inscrutable," an intensely loyal and unobtrusive aid who never, it seems, revealed details of King's private life or, more remarkably, raised the PM's ire. He was practically, and by personal intent, a phantasm. (Nicol also faithfully cleaved to the manservant stereotype in that nobody seemed to know his first name.) Indeed, King only referred to the valet on two other occasions in a scrupulous account of the German tour that runs to thirty typed pages, or nearly eight for each day: there is a brief reference to a satchel Nicol purchased for his boss, and, after the prime minister met Hitler, to the valet's admiration for King's diplomatic feats in Berlin.[3] By contrast, King invokes Pickering on multiple occasions in his descriptions of various sites, events, and meetings, and even affords him occasional speaking parts. Nicol, unlike Pickering, does not appear in any photographs from the visit, and it is likely that he spent his days in Berlin alone, awaiting his liege's return to the Adlon.

Now, however, Nicol had to get King up and running, as Herr Hewel was to arrive at the hotel at 9:30 a.m. to shepherd King and Pickering through a second day of carefully choreographed Third Reich sightseeing. First stop was the Berlin headquarters of the Reichsarbeitsdienst (RAD, Reich Labour Service), situated in a monumental, baronial building erected near Grunewald Forest to symbolize the RAD's commitment to tradition, nature, and the outdoors. Here the prime minister was introduced to the organization's director, Konstantin Hierl. Balding, mustachioed, and diminutive (in photos, the 5' 9"/175 cm Hitler towers over him), Hierl was, at sixty-two, one of the older members of the Fuhrer's inner circle. Like many of the other early Nazi Party sympathizers, Hierl was a Great War veteran and career soldier who became a leading figure among the right-wing paramilitary street thugs who called themselves the Freikorps, a citizen militia that harassed, fought, and killed thousands of communists and Weimar Republic supporters alike in the first years after the war; that there were many Jews among the ranks of their enemies clearly vitalized the bloodletting.[4]

As early as 1923, Hierl was agitating for the creation of a labour program that would "overcome the class system, Marxism, and democracy," as he wrote in a memo to his boss, the Reich Chief of the Army Command. Hitler's solidarity with Hierl's recipe for German greatness led to the latter's appointment as head of the RAD, and in 1945 to his receipt of the *Deutscher Orden* (German Order). This was the highest award in the Nazi Reich and one given to just eleven men; Hierl was one of only two living recipients of the honour. An American denazification tribunal later found him guilty of "major offences" and gave him a modest five-year sentence – aptly, in a labour camp. However, Hierl was granted the kind of mercy anathema to his fascist brethren and dogma and excused from serving time on account of his advanced age. He died in 1955 after dedicating the last years of his life to trying to rehabilitate his name and contribution to nation-building.[5] The RAD chief apparently made little impression on Mackenzie King, as the PM did not comment on their brief meeting in his diary. The RAD camp at

Werbellinsee, a large lake seventy kilometres northeast of Berlin that was the next stop on the agenda, left a much more vivid mark.

By the time of King's visit, a six-month term with the labour organization, previously voluntary, was compulsory for all German men (and soon, women) aged eighteen to twenty-five, a kind of finishing school for the fledgling fascists groomed by the Hitler Youth. Those prohibited from serving in the RAD reveal how the Nazis defined both German-ness and manhood: Jews and other non-Aryans, men married to Jews and other non-Aryans, the disabled, "asocial," and "hereditary ill," as well as those convicted of crimes or "dishonouring actions" or otherwise covered by the blanket and nebulous category of "enemies of the regime," were, through exclusion from the Labour Service, effectively denied standing as either men or citizens. Cultural sociologist Orlando Patterson coined the term "social death" to describe the status of individuals and groups similarly dehumanized and erased from the public sphere; his work described the process as it relates to the history of slavery. In Nazi Germany, this figurative killing conditioned the future perpetrators of genocide for the literal and systematic murder of those marked by the same "dishonourable" classifications.[6]

Even before the work term became compulsory, foreign governments raised objections that the regimented, uniformed, and drilled men of the RAD were engaged in a thinly veiled form of military conscription, a measure prohibited by the Treaty of Versailles. As that same agreement capped membership in the German armed forces at 100,000 and by 1934 the RAD alone employed 230,000, confirmation of the essentially martial character of the organization would constitute a double violation of the treaty. The Nazis themselves rendered the issue moot by introducing straightforward conscription in 1935. The decade-long educational and physical fitness regimen required for each German male was now complete: from Hitler Youth to Labour Service to Armed Forces.[7] Comprehensive *Gleichschaltung* demanded nothing less.

Along with securing free labour for the massive infrastructure projects dreamt up by Hitler and other Reich officials, the RAD was instrumental – in conjunction with conscription and the erasure of women and Jews from official labour records – in lowering unemployment figures, thereby burnishing the myth of a Nazi "economic miracle" that had delivered Germans from the ravages of the Depression. More importantly, RAD service constituted a vital cog in the mass ideological distortion of the cohort expected to expand the frontiers of the thousand-year Reich. In fact, the focus on traditional, pre-industrial labour techniques (shovels rather than bulldozers, for instance) intentionally hamstrung the productivity of the Labour Service, suggesting indoctrination as the foremost objective. As one official stated, "The goal of the total registration of the young members of the Volk by the national labour service is to train a national-socialist attitude toward the community and toward work."[8]

German historian Peter Dudeck called compulsory labour service "the most extreme form of collective disciplining" among the Nazis' many civilian training programs, as participants were shipped off to isolated rural environs that foreclosed any contact with school, church, family, or other formative institutions. The camps' program of total, collectivized regimentation eliminated distinctions between work, leisure, and individual relationships; cooperative manual labour, ideological instruction, and rituals like flag raising and marching in formation sought to implant complete deference to authority, intensive male bonding, and unquestioning loyalty to the community.[9] The ultimate purpose in imbuing such qualities in an entire generation of young men is not difficult to deduce.

Yet King was far from troubled by what he saw at the Werbellinsee camp. This despite the fact that he must have been aware of the controversy surrounding the RAD, as the prohibition of compulsory labour organizations issued at the Geneva Disarmament Conference of 1933 constituted one of the many grievances that led to Germany's simultaneous withdrawal from both the conference and the League of Nations, moves that shocked and alarmed the international community. Throughout the 1930s, the foreign press continued to raise alarms about the program. A November 1934 investigative report from the *London Spectator*, for instance, concluded that the labour camps' core mandate was to ensure that young German men were "ready to obey the call to arms unhesitatingly ... ready both in body and mind to face the field of battle."[10]

In King's defence, it must also be assumed that the military features of the camp were toned down for his review. At least one camp, in Hamburg, was designated as a showpiece for foreign visitors and accordingly shorn of its more extreme military trappings, suggesting the Nazis were fully cognizant of, and took pains to modulate, the more provocative aspects of the work programs' reputation. After his own visit to Germany in 1939, Cambridge economist C.W.

Guillebaud wrongly concluded that "the real significance of the compulsory Labour Service in Germany is essentially social rather than military," for he had constructed a false binary: socialization was both central to the RAD's mandate *and* fundamentally militaristic in nature. Although other camp visitors reported concerns similar to those voiced about the Hitler Youth about the robotic conformity they witnessed, Guillebaud, like King, can be excused for failing to grasp the full extent of the camps' military purposes given the degree of Potemkinism involved in the guided tours. In large part owing to these careful manipulations, Guillebaud was correct on at least one point, writing: "Of all the institutions in Nazi Germany the compulsory Labour Service is the one which has received the widest measure of approval from foreign visitors."[11]

That being said, it does not seem unreasonable to expect at least a trace of apprehension over a program involving hundreds of thousands of uniformed, military-aged men who were required to undergo physical and mental conditioning by a hyper-nationalistic, dictatorial regime, one whose increasingly bellicose rhetoric and action had stimulated widespread dread of another world war. If King harboured any such reservations, he did not record them. Following his own tour that Monday morning, King wrote admiringly of witnessing men "of all classes" camped out in a pastoral setting alongside a lake, "the whole resembling to an Elizabethan village," and engaged in a "very simple regimen of work in the morning, with rest and teaching in the afternoon." King's economical conclusion? "One gets the impression that Germany is paying much attention to further development of the people. We had some noodle soup for lunch at this camp."[12]

Along with the soup, camp director Hermann Müller-Brandenburg, whose lengthy career as a propagandist for right-wing nationalist causes began before the First World War, also gave the prime minister copies of his annual summary of RAD activities, *Jahrbuch des Reichsarbeitsdienstes* (Yearbook of the German Labour Service). King also received a copy of what he referred to as "Shoulder Spades," likely a recording of the RAD theme song *Spaten und Wehr – Deutschland Voran!* (Spade and Defence – Germany Forward!).[13] The song's chorus expressed sentiments that most Germans of any era could get behind:

We love freedom, we love peace,
We want to forge the future of the Fatherland.
Germany forward!

The grey columns of the Labour Service have been termed the "Army with Spades", and no better designation could be found, for it is in reality an army equipped with spades and dedicated to the task of conquering German soil. It resembles the army only in one respect the strict order and discipline with which every member must comply.

8.1 The obvious military overtones of the Reichsarbeitsdienst, or German Labour Service, seemed not to strike Mackenzie King. He was, however, captivated by the government-issue spades. Many other foreign observers found reassurances like the one from the photo caption in this 1936 Nazi propaganda pictorial unpersuasive. (From Richter, Carstensen, and Hitzer, *Germany*, n.p.)

The third and fourth verses, however, openly declare the more ominous objectives undergirding the RAD:

> Tomorrow, we'll be standing next to you, a man
> in the ranks of the youngest soldiers;
> We put on the field-gray honour dress, and we
> shoulder rifles instead of spades.
> Once the drum is stirred to appeal, Comrade,
> bridle your horse, and get on it!
> There is no hesitation, the weakling loses,
> male courage is measured in the field.[14]

In other words, Treaty of Versailles and Geneva Disarmament Conference be damned. Whether at any point King listened to or understood *Spaten und Wehr*, he was impressed by the actual spades used at the camp, and asked his hosts if he might have one as a memento, for personal use at his Kingsmere estate. RAD officials promised to mail one to Canada; three months after returning home, the prime minister received a letter from Hermann Müller-Brandenburg that addressed King as "Your Excellency" and informed him that "the standardized tools used by the Reich Labour Service" had been shipped.[15] One month after that, King unwrapped a package holding an entire RAD labourer's toolkit, coveted spade included. His written response to Müller-Brandenburg ran to three full pages, and was quintessential King:

> I have seldom, if ever, had a more delightful surprise than that which came, a few weeks ago, when I received your letter [stating that the tools were on their way]. This surprise was only surpassed when, a few weeks later, I received ... a complete set of the tools ... I confess that I am at a loss to know how to thank you ... Perhaps I cannot do better than to say quite frankly that, in the course of my public life, no expression of personal remembrance, or of international good-will, has touched me more deeply. To have received the tools as a gift from your country is an honour which I prize more highly than words can express.[16]

Following the war, indoctrination continued to be the order of the day at Camp Werbellinsee. As with many former Hitler Youth and Labour Service sites, DDR officials converted the facility into a summer camp for the regime's Junge Pioniere (Young Pioneers). These scarf-wearing nascent Stalinists would vanquish the legacy of fascism by pledging their fidelity to another variant of authoritarianism. Today the camp is in private hands but still serves as a youth education camp, one that teaches German to international students aged ten to seventeen. The structures built by RAD labour for "teaching in the afternoon" are at long last serving a redeeming pedagogical purpose.[17]

After they returned to the Adlon in the early afternoon, Hewel gave King what the latter called, with typically vagueness, "an interesting book on Germany." Titled simply *Germany*, this was the English-language version of a 1936 large-format pictorial that exalted the landscapes, built environment, and (relentlessly overjoyed) Aryan peoples of the Reich. King's copy of this homage to fascist Eden, a book published in support of the wider Olympic-year global con job, is now held by Library and Archives Canada. King repaid Hewel's gesture by offering a biography of himself, a hagiographic piece of propaganda originally penned for the 1925 federal election by John Lewis, a journalist hired by the prime minister. The version given to Hewel was the second edition, revised for the 1935 campaign by law professor and soon-to-be Liberal cabinet minister Norman Robertson (assisted by significant written and design input from King himself). Hewel, King, and Pickering then enjoyed a second lunch and a rest before driving to the headquarters of the Deutsche Arbeitsfront; here they were treated to a 5 p.m. tea and a presentation on the Nazi labour organization's enlightened revolution in industrial relations.[18]

The showpiece and cornerstone of this transformation was the organization Kraft durch Freude (KdF, Strength through Joy), a subsidiary of the DAF that sought to manufacture a cheerful citizenry via state-sponsored opportunities for leisure. The vacations, civic beautification campaigns, sports and arts clubs, and subsidies for cultural events offered by the KdF shared a number of overlapping goals: as with the Hitler Youth and labour programs, to unify Aryan Germans of different classes and regions, strengthen their bodies, and build their devotion to the state; to distract the populace from the more ruthless components of the Nazi reinvention of Germany; to mute potential hostility over the elimination of traditional unions and the increased production demanded by a state gearing up for continent-wide war; to truly inspire widespread happiness – a goal, wrote historian Julia Timpe, that "was intrinsically linked to the Nazi dream of purifying and strengthening the German *Volksgemeinschaft* or 'racial community,' for the intention was that this should be a happy community."[19] Surely the master race had every right to relish its own existence.

8.2 Photograph from *Germany* (1936), the propaganda pictorial assembled for the Berlin Olympics. King's copy, a gift from Walther Hewel, is now held by Library and Archives Canada. (From Richter, Carstensen, and Hitzer, *Germany*, n.p.)

8.3 German women enjoying a summer retreat sponsored by the Kraft durch Freude organization. (From Richter, Carstensen, and Hitzer, *Germany,* n.p.)

Scholars remain divided as to whether this the top-down attempt to infuse bliss actually made much difference. Colonel H.G.D. Crerar, the gloomy philosopher Martin to King's Professor Pangloss, conducted his own investigation of the KdF program and arrived at some unflattering conclusions. "It is supported by party funds," he reported to Canadian officials, "though facilities for its members appear to be sometimes obtained by methods which, in this country, would be considered coercive. Needless to add, the various forms of 'Joy,' so cheaply provided, are thoroughly exploited for Nazi ends." "Adults as well as children," he continued, "have their spare time so thoroughly organized that there seems some justification for the joke that the only time a good Nazi family ever meet collectively is at the Annual Party rally." Hitler, Crerar was told, was the "driving force behind" these efforts to regulate even the leisure time of his Aryan flock, as the Fuhrer fretted that unscripted free time encouraged "dangerous thinking, with possible undesirable results."[20]

King's diary made brief and affirming reference to the happiness project, and, as in the case of the visit to the All-German Sports Competitions the day before, none at all to DAF head Robert Ley. If Ley was present at DAF headquarters, King may have been put off by the fact that the embezzling, womanizing, extraordinarily antisemitic labour chief operated in a constant state of full-blown inebriation; if Ley was absent, it was likely for the same reason. The DAF chief went on to play a significant role in the wartime deployment of slave labour and would have undoubtedly been hanged at Nuremberg had he not fashioned his own noose from the towel in his cell before his trial began.[21]

What we can be certain of is that King greatly admired the Nazis' economic *Gleichschaltung* initiatives, including the ban on all labour organizations except the DAF. Here again, the violence and disregard for workers' rights that accompanied the "coordination" – including arrests and beatings of union leaders and their internment in concentration camps, as well as confiscation of union property and funds – was widely reported and condemned in the international media. Olympic boycott proponents made much of it, as did British and North American unions and religious groups behind the wider Nazi-boycott movement that emerged almost immediately after Hitler's seizure of power and that continued throughout the 1930s.[22] As we have seen, King himself was wont to frame heavy-handed responses to trade unionism as an invitation to civil strife and leftist revolution, and had little appetite for any form of state-directed violence. Seemingly incongruous, then, is his approving synopsis of the Nazis' forced synchronization of labour:

> The most significant thing of all is the change that has come over the organization of German industry, whereby trade unions have been abolished as being an antagonism to employers, and brought into one organization, and all parts having a share in government of industry. This is virtually advocated in [King's book] "Industry and Humanity"; the State appoints referees and strikes, in this way, are ended. I confess that what one sees here of the Socialist State causes one to see many merits in the system.[23]

King's equation of Nazi labour ideals with his own was self-flattery in his mind, and a cringing correlation to later readers of his diary. The linkage was also fitting, to a point. Rather than unfettered competition, both he and the Nazis embraced a form of corporatism whereby labour disputes and the dreaded spectre of revolution would be dissipated through employers' commitment to worker well-being, not simply profits. Both feared grass-roots unions and what King derisively called "labour democracy" as intrinsically volatile and uninformed, and fa- voured instead paternalistic "labour" organizations created under the auspices of government and industry.[24] Both abhorred strikes and any meaningful structural alteration to the economic status quo. Yet (mer- cifully) King's economic philosophy differed in marked ways from Hitler's. Nazi corporatism was manufactured at the barrel of a gun, with the overriding purpose of serving and empowering a racist and murderous state. King's liberal corporatism was built on an appeal for employer benevolence and labour submissiveness, with the goal of serving the greater good through the elimination of conflict in relations between classes, states, and races.

King's approach had evolved following a brief, youthful flirtation with socialism. Like many of his background in the Progressive era, he was galled by the vast gulf between the titans of industry and the work- ing poor, a gulf that encompassed not just income but access to health care, education, safety, infrastructure, and the seats of political power. Socialism's emphasis on materialist forces as the driver of historical change rendered it "strange and obscure" to a religious believer like King, and in its promise of state-guaranteed economic equality he saw an invitation to idleness. The writings of nineteenth-century British economic historian Arnold Toynbee (the elder) struck the right note, as Toynbee advocated a free-marked capitalism tamed by a Christian responsibility to eradicate exploitation.[25]

King embraced this attitude in word and deed, heading off to the University of Chicago to study political economy and to volunteer at Hull House, the settlement agency for new immigrants founded by renowned reformer Jane Addams. At university he was transfixed by a course taught by Thorstein Veblen, one of the Progressive era's foremost critics of laissez-faire economics and self-absorbed bourgeois avarice. Before entering politics, the future prime minister worked as a muckraking journalist in Toronto, exposing the miserable working conditions in the city's sweatshops. The distance between his liberal corporatism grounded in Christian idealism and social conscience and the hate-based tenets of fascist corporatism could hardly be overstated.[26]

That said, King's labour relations' schema was not without its flaws. We have already touched upon the fact that his prescription for growing economic harmony and equity aligned closely with his methods of building international accord, and was equally credulous: (1) in areas of seemingly competing interests, the path of universal mutual benefit could be clearly mapped; (2) all parties involved, once shown the map, would naturally embrace the path of universal mutual benefit. In considering the dilemmas of capital and labour, King assumed that the basic architecture of free-market liberalism was sound, but that humankind's competitiveness and self-interest – concepts any student of free-market liberalism would understand as foundational to the system – would have to go. *Industry and Humanity* stated it plainly: "An industrial system characterized by antagonism, coercion, and resistance must yield to a new order based upon mutual confidence, real justice, and constructive good will."[27]

How would the system yield? As with international relations, industrial peace and stability would be fostered not by re-examining the systems that had facilitated discord and inequality (in international affairs, replacing power politics with a rules-based order enforced through the principle of collective security; in economic affairs, recognizing unions organized by workers themselves and the right to bargain collectively and strike). Rather, reconciliation would come through the mediation of enlightened men who would lead previously conflicting factions to a higher level of consciousness. Wrote King: "the habit of mind which resolves its problems sectionally, in terms of class, or even of country, must be abandoned, and its place taken by a world outlook ... an [sic] universally accepted faith in human brotherhood." The heart, rather than the relations of economic production, must be transformed; because humans were inherently rational, clear communication of the "facts" underlying labour conflicts would bring about the change of heart. The resulting empathy would at last prove to the human race that the notion of competing interests itself was a fallacy – that what was best for my neighbour was, in truth, also best for me. Put most plainly, employer and employee must come to "mutual recognition of common as contrasted with opposed interests."[28]

King's commitment to this approach never wavered. While touring a Scottish linoleum factory one week before his excursion to Nazi Germany, the prime minister was sincerely distressed by the plight of the "many girls at machines." Despite "good factory conditions," the work struck him as "sort of slavery." Distressing, too, was the vast disparity witnessed on the same trip between the British upper classes and the "masses of people on the sidewalks at the time of the Coronation," as he revealed in conversation with Canadian ambassador to London Vincent Massey. Yet here again, King held that these dilemmas could be rectified not by any systemic reforms or schemes for economic redistribution, but by a simple alteration in personal priorities among men of means: "the whole struggle was between materialism of the day and Christianity," he informed Massey, "Christian life of the simple type which puts its emphasis on service for the love of service." The plight of the dispossessed, in other words, would be ameliorated through the paternalistic largesse of the mighty, an approach for which history offers a most miserly catalogue of precedents. As King made clear to John D. Rockefeller Jr while serving as the tarnished entrepreneur's PR point man, "men of power or position, however attained, have a special obligation to secure justice to the many who were in a relatively weak position."[29]

There is more than a little self-interest in play here, for middle-class reformers like King – situated as they were between wealthy industrialists and the labouring masses – presented themselves as the indispensable instruments of class conciliation, the heroic fixers on whom public adulation would be bestowed. Grass-roots organizers lacked the capacity and disinterestedness to elevate the lot of the lower classes; paternalistic intervention by skilled intermediaries from the ranks of their social superiors was necessary. In industrial relations, King wrote, "machinery is nothing, personality is everything." When in 1898 two letters arrived in King's mailbox on the same day, one from socialist American labour leader Eugene Debs and the other from an affluent Canadian, King felt a certain validation. "A labour agitator and a millionaire," his diary records. "To know both and understand their interests, sympathies and points of view. This is well."[30]

The central problem of this personality-driven mode of mediation, of course, is that it is ad hoc and voluntary rather than institutionalized and binding: it holds that conflict will be avoided only if altruistic and capable individuals bent on taming the inner beasts of humanity materialize at each time and place of potential crisis; moreover, that they have the ear of all involved; moreover, that all parties will agree upon definitions of the common good; moreover, that all parties crave the common good and resolve to uphold it. (This constellation of assumptions sums up King's Hitler strategy in a nutshell.) "Co-operation," King had written in his formative years, "has in it all the virtues claimed for Socialism, with none of its defects; it is individualistic, all self help, self initiative, and self dependence, no government protection."[31]

Regulations and laws, in other words, were both anathema to liberty and unnecessary. And as historian Reg Whitaker observed, King's co-operative model failed to grasp that his "neutral" conciliators were not truly neutral at all: since the overriding objective of his corporatist mediation efforts was to keep the gears of the industrial machine turning at any cost, capital always held the upper hand in clashes with labour, for the job would always get done. Only access to the workers' most powerful weapon – the ability to halt production and profits – would give labour real leverage at the negotiating table. Several writers have argued that rather than resolve the many labour disputes he mediated at the Ministry of Labour, King had simply applied a band-aid, as the labour peace he helped fashion ignored workers' underlying demands for greater bargaining power and union recognition. In this view, these deferred grievances provided the powder for the eruption of labour militancy that dominated Canadian industrial relations in the decade following the First World War.[32]

Though he would have chafed at the label, King's liberal corporatism resonated with a long tradition of Canadian toryism. This worldview, inherited from British thinkers like Edmund Burke, described the ideal society as an organic, ordered, and cooperative whole managed by selfless political, corporate, and religious elites. Revolution was the greatest danger to this natural order; change would be effected, when necessary, through incremental reforms introduced by a wise and compassionate leadership.[33]

To King's credit, his was a timely update to the tory tradition. Where previous regimes had focused the state's energies primarily on tempering Canada's French-English divide, King widened the scope to include the plight of labour. And when confronted with the greatest crisis capitalism had yet generated, King overcame his qualms about state intervention in the market, bringing relief to Depression-era Canadians through social welfare legislation that became a fixture of the assumed responsibilities of governance. This responsiveness to the free market's inherent inequities helped to blunt the appeal of leftist panaceas for the dilemma of the Depression, thus maintaining the centrality of liberalism within Canadian statecraft; these moves likewise transformed the Liberal Party into an organization suited to the modern, industrialized, multi-ethnic nation that King's Canada had become, and did much to make the Liberals Canada's "natural" governing party in the decades to follow.[34] And once again, we can quibble with the prime minister's inconsistency, paternalism, and overconfidence in the better angels of human nature and still acknowledge that his was a *Weltanschauung* grounded in a lifelong, humanistic concern for what he considered the general welfare.

Little surprise, then, that portions of *Industry and Humanity* read like direct indictments of the kind of power politics and blood-and-soil fanaticism at the heart of fascism. King had originally penned his polemic amidst the twin shockwaves of the Great War and the Bolshevik Revolution, and his plea for class amity cited both events as the logical consequences of unrestrained economic competition and an indifference to those it left behind. With fascism dragging the world once again towards the abyss, his warnings were just as timely in 1937 as they had been two decades earlier. "Humanity," his treatise maintained repeatedly, "has rights superior to those of Industry or of Nationality." He denounced both "the iron heel of Militarism" and "the competitive arming between nations" as harbingers of international conflict, and railed against those who "foster prejudice, in order to gain power." He held that the ultimate cause of war was "the blindness with which we all are afflicted in regard to the feelings of creatures and peoples different from ourselves." This blindness, he continued "lies at the root of all our intolerance, social, religious, and political."[35] Although King's gift for augury could best be described as mercurial, his 1918 sketch of the evolution of a tyrant reads like a psychiatric diagnosis of the Fuhrer himself:

Some men become hardened, arrogant, and despotic; the significance of other lives ceases to have a meaning for them. All human life may lose its value through the lust for power. Men of the type described come in time to ignore every principle of just and humane relations. It matters not whether the incentive be pride or prejudice, a mistaken zeal or a vile hate – to such men, once powerful enough, class, and race, and nationality become but instruments for the outworking of fanatical or devilish wills. In some abstract theory which furthers their own greed or ambition, they find grounds for the elimination of all human considerations. The purer the instincts, the nobler the purposes of other lives, the more they prey upon these virtues to selfish ends. To other men and to other nations, they attribute their own desires and rapacity. And so, ever imagining new means of destruction, they force nations to be constantly ready for the battlefield; and once entering upon violent conquest, compel those who

would rid mankind of the scourges that beset it, to rise regardless of sacrifice, and defend *the Law of Peace, Work and Health* against *the Law of Blood
and of Death*.[36]

In the summer of 1937 King was walking in a land gripped by the
vilest embodiment of such a monster, and yet seemed entirely at ease
on his journey. Following his tour of DAF headquarters, however, he
expressed trepidations, for the first time since setting foot in Germany,
about potential pitfalls ahead. After confessing "that what one sees here
of the Socialist State causes one to see many merits in the system," he
offered this caveat: "Of course, back of everything is Government imposing its own will on the people; so long as that will is wise, all may
go well, but an organization may swing everything into the opposite
direction."[37] What could King possibly mean here? That without Hitler
at the helm, Nazi Germany might devolve from a fair, sensible, and efficient regime into one that sabotages the "many merits in the system"
he described? What would "swing[ing] everything into the opposite
direction" from the course embarked upon since 1933 look like? Could
it not but be an advance towards the very notion of humanity King
claimed to revere?

Once again the overriding question must be posed: How could King
be so oblivious, given the yawning chasm between his own lifelong
and deeply held convictions and the disturbing realities he had read of
in four years of press coverage and was now witnessing first hand? We
can reiterate the rationalizations, but they cannot, alone or in concert,
completely satisfy: In no particular order, the prime minister was:

- treated to a sanitized presentation of Nazism;
- charmed by his hosts' calculated blandishments and, in general,
  swayed by personal encounters;
- deeply alarmed by socialism, labour militancy, and revolution;
- admiring of efforts to enhance worker well-being;
- not always discerning or consistent in his political reckonings;
- wowed by Germany's (overestimated) economic rebound;
- intoxicated by the gravity of his mission and his opportunity to save
  civilization;
- conditioned by his experience as a mediator to convey empathy;
- sensitive to Germany's rough treatment at Versailles;
- something of a Teutonophile, a product of his affiliations with two
  Berlins.

No such inventory, based as it is on conscious and unconscious traits, sensibilities, and biases – on assumptions and beliefs acknowledged and (as the ego proscribes an absolute self-honesty) unacknowledged – can ever be considered exhaustive or precise. It is a rough estimate based on the totality of King's life and thought, as well as his private ruminations about what he had seen thus far in Hitler's Reich. There is, however, another source of the prime minister's openness to his hosts' program, one that falls into the overlapping categories of the unconfessed and the unconscious. That King has not once referred to the issue thus far in his ruminations on the visit, despite its centrality to both Nazism and its opponents' censure of the movement, confirms that it belongs on the list. This is the simple fact of the prime minister's antisemitism.

9

Whither the Jews?

Canadians like to think of their country as a multicultural meritoc-
racy, a land of tolerance and opportunity mercifully free of the bitter
racial animus that has tainted the history of their southern neighbour.
Swedish intellectual Gunnar Myrdal famously called the United States'
struggles over race an "American dilemma," and smug Canadians
would appreciate the respect racism apparently affords international
borders under this definition.[1] These Canadians would also be sorely
mistaken. Racist beliefs, practices, and legislation, much of it patterned
directly on the more infamous American practices, have a lower profile
in the Canadian story primarily because the storytellers were too often
unwilling or unable to see it.

More recent interrogations of Canada's past have made this uncomfortable truth plain, putting paid to the widespread and self-
congratulatory national mythologies surrounding racial harmony. The
seventeenth-century Europeans who began relocating to what would
become Canada inaugurated a centuries-long campaign to variously
kill, relocate, and assimilate the Indigenous population, a campaign
current generations are still struggling to acknowledge and reconcile.
While long denied in the historical record, slavery did indeed exist in
Canada, until an 1834 British statute forbade it. An assortment of laws
and practices preventing or discouraging non-WASP immigration, citizenship, integration, voting, business and labour competition, and social mobility were not challenged in the courts until after the Second
World War. The country had its own Rosa Parks in Viola Desmond, a
black Nova Scotian who in 1946 was fined for refusing to give up her
theatre seat, but whose story remained excluded from the public school
curriculum until the 1990s. Some African Canadian children in Ontario

and Nova Scotia continued to attend separate, and distinctly inferior, public schools well into the 1960s; in fact, an 1849 Ontario statue authorizing segregation in public education was not overturned until 1964, ten years after the landmark Brown v. Board of Education ruling in the United States.[2]

Unlike people of colour in the United States, who could fight for their country in both world wars if they joined segregated military units, many of their Canadian counterparts were simply told they were not wanted. Ethnic minorities were denied access to some Canadian institutions of higher learning and professional training programs until the 1960s. From the late eighteenth to the late twentieth century, sporadic incidents of mob violence broke out against minority groups and their property in cities from Vancouver to Halifax.[3] This is just a sampling of the story of Canadian bigotry, and does not take into account the innumerable personal exclusions, insults, and acts of violence faced on a day-to-day basis by those deemed inferior by "mainstream" Canadians.

King was just such a Canadian. No cloven-hoofed racist firebrand like those that populated the Nazi hierarchy, he nonetheless shared the chauvinisms of those of his background and era. Foremost among these was an inclination to see race and racial hierarchies everywhere. In an age when nations dominated by Anglo-Saxons seemed invincible, English-speaking Protestants the world over equated their vast territorial holdings and advanced industrial economies with their status as the elect. "Many men in the United States, Great Britain, and the English-speaking dominions," wrote historian Edward Kohn, "held the notion that loyalty to the race existed on a higher plane than loyalty to one's nation. Such a union would serve to ensure the peace of the world and the onward march of civilization and Christianity." Even Canada's francophones and anglophones, today lumped together as generic whites or Caucasians who happen to use different words, were to King and his ilk separate "stock" – with little question about which was superior. After reading a flattering biography of Scottish grandfather Mackenzie in 1895, the younger King wrote: "I have become a greater admirer of his than ever, prouder of my own mother and the race from which I am sprung."[4]

King's political philosophy reflected these biological assumptions. His attitude towards immigration – that dilution of Canada's WASP majority would destroy the character of the country – never changed. As deputy minister at the Department of Labour he was tasked with investigating the 1907 anti-Asian race riots in Vancouver, and convinced the Laurier government that the surest way to limit white violence against Asians was to limit the number of Asians admitted to Canada. As prime minister, he implemented the 1923 Chinese Exclusion Act, a measure whose assortment of restrictions was so rigorous that in the twenty-one years the law held sway, Canada "welcomed" exactly fifteen Chinese nationals.[5]

King's Liberals also mimicked FDR's executive order interning citizens and residents of Japanese descent for the duration of the Second World War, divesting more than twenty thousand of their homes, belongings, and livelihood. Importantly for our purposes, a politician prepared to consider such measures would be disinclined to raise strenuous objections to camps built by other states for their own internal enemies. Moreover, King had been a loyal Liberal public servant when the British established abysmal concentration camps for their enemies in the Boer War, and the Canadian troops sent to assist the British had helped to fill them.[6] Internment predicated on race and guilt by association was hardly anathema to the prime minister.

The treatment of Canada's Indigenous peoples provides additional parallels. Did the Third Reich's ban on Jews in the military, restrictions on where they could live, and denial of their rights as citizens strike King, man of ceaseless and fertile associations, as strangely familiar? The congruencies between the experiences of German Jews and Canada's First Peoples would certainly undercut any moral objections to race-based proscriptions the prime minister might have raised with Hitler and other Nazi officials, who were known to cite the example provided by the European settlers of the Americas to justify their own racial policies and program of *Lebensraum*.[7]

The prime minister's policies on race and immigration were, it must be noted, applauded widely in Canada; here, he lived up to his reputation as a proxy rather than bellwether of public opinion. And while King was proud of "the race from which I am sprung," he had little trouble extending his admiration to other European "races." When world-renowned pilot and soon-to-be Nazi apologist Charles Lindberg flew to Ottawa to take part in Canada's sixtieth birthday celebration, King's depiction of the visiting Nordic eugenicist was virtually erotic: "A more beautiful character I have never seen. He was like a young god who had appeared from the sky in human form – all that could be desired in youthful appearance, in manner, in charm, in character, as noble a type of the highest manhood as I have ever seen."[8] (Cue C.P. Stacey ...)

And then there were the Jews. Even as a university-educated adult, King believed ghastly medieval legends about their need for Christian blood, generally from newborns, for a variety of rituals; he confided in a 1906 diary entry that "there is something in a Jew's nature which is detestable. The sucking of blood." Whether or not he ascribed to these myths throughout his life, he continued to single out Jews for special mistreatment; the presence of Jews on the rolls of domestic and international leftist organizations and in Franklin Roosevelt's unnervingly socialist administration simply redoubled King's intolerance towards the group. At a 1935 dinner with medium Helen Lambert and her son Barron, talk turned "to the efforts at World conquest by the Jews – and their hold to this end on the present administration at Washington," as King wrote casually in his diary. In the 1930s he purchased a Kingsmere neighbour's property for three times its appraised value in order to, in his words, "prevent Jews or other undesirable people from getting in."[9]

That decade was an especially ugly one for Jews of many nations. While the Depression helped to frame all "outsiders" as unwanted labour competition, commonly held delusions that the Jews controlled, and by extension sabotaged, international finance led demagogues to smear them with increased savagery. Fascists in Europe and North America fed and rode this wave of bile; in Canada, nativist premiers like Alberta's William Aberhart and Quebec's Maurice Duplessis lambasted Jews as a sinister threat to economic recovery. Such prejudice was no "top-down" ailment, as an antisemitism unprecedented in its fervour proliferated in all Canadian classes and regions during the thirties. This hatred found expression in new or reinvigorated practices of discrimination in housing, education, hiring, and access to public space, as well as in the steady growth of Canadian branches of the Ku Klux Klan.[10]

Even in this context of intensified antisemitism for Jews throughout Christendom, however, the vulgarity of the Third Reich's proscriptions alarmed. Reflecting in a 1936 diary entry on the near-universal condemnation of Nazi racial policies, the prime minister offered the remarkably weak endorsement that "there are good as well as bad Jews and it is wrong to indict a nation or race;" that such a statement need even be said *to oneself* says a great deal about the writer's desultory opinions on the matter. Canada's most significant act of redress to the outrages committed against German Jews would have been to allow them entry into Canada. However, King and his cabinet, fully aware of the depth of his country's antisemitism, knew this would invoke a public outcry from anglophone and francophone alike and thus did nothing, despite a personal appeal from US president Franklin Roosevelt. This was racism married to political calculation: Canada's Depression-era Jewish population, at 170,000 only about 1.7 per cent of the total, meant relatively little to the electoral fortunes of any national party, while a more humane immigration policy could cost the Liberals both Protestant and Catholic votes. The prime minister wrote: "my own feeling is that nothing is to be gained by creating an internal problem in an effort to meet an international one." His government's virtual ban on Jewish immigration rendered Canada the least welcoming Western nation for Jewish refugees fleeing Nazism; of the eight hundred thousand Jews who escaped from Nazi-held territory between 1933 and 1945, Canada accepted less than five thousand.[11]

French theorist of nationalism Ernst Renan wrote that because national unity forges kinship via the rejection of those deemed dissimilar, it "is always effected by means of brutality."[12] Canada's domestic history provides numerous examples of that brutality expressed towards First Nations peoples, the Métis, and non-European immigrants; here we find an internationalization of that dictum. To keep the country together, Canada would permit the perpetuation of a brutality against European Jews that the nation had at least some ability to temper.

Of course, this dismal response to Jewish suffering was not confined to Canadian borders. Other countries may have done better than Canada in resettling Jews, but that was a very low bar to surpass. Leaders the world over stubbornly refused to increase their quotas for Jewish immigrants, even after *Kristallnacht*. The fact that government officials habitually foregrounded the national interest and their own political fortunes in their response to international humanitarian crises does not mean, however, that the record of all world leaders on the matter was identical. In *FDR and the Jews*, historians Richard Breitman and Allen Lichtman reveal an American president initially aloof about the plight of the Jews and focused on domestic economic recover rather than efforts to rescue victims of Nazism. By the middle 1930s, however, his thinking began to evolve, and Roosevelt came to act "more decisively to Nazi crimes against Jews than did any other world leader of his time." The transformation in Roosevelt's thinking is partially attributable to the importance of Jewish support to his New Deal Democratic Party coalition (the percentage of Americans who identified as Jewish was more than twice that of Canada, and most voted Democrat). But it was his ongoing dialogue with Jewish leaders about the predicament of their German kin that nurtured in the president a deep sympathy and a re-evaluation of his own responsibilities towards this astounding violation of human dignity.[13] As he did on the idea that the United States needed to play a central role in the war against fascism, Roosevelt sought to enlighten and transform, not merely reflect, public opinion.

To Mackenzie King, the American president's movement on the issue was simply further proof that his administration was in the clutches of Jewish influence. For all intents and purposes, the prime minister and many of his compatriots deemed Nazi persecution of Jews none of Canada's business. It may have been a troubling practice, but that did not lead them to conclude that it should interfere with the vital work of building international goodwill and a healthy bilateral trading relationship.[14] Today many governments speak of "constructive engagement" with regimes that flout human rights and international law, arguing that such connections can inspire better behaviour. Critics rightly point out that this often amounts to little more than lip service in the name of maintaining profitable financial and strategic relationships, but in the case of Canada and Nazi Germany, the engagement came with no strings attached, no words of warning, no incentives for improved conduct.

It is a measure of the depth of King's own racial assumptions that revelations of the death camps seemed not to unseat his views of either Jews or the wider fallacy that human behaviour was programmed by ethnicity. When in 1946 Russian defector Igor Gouzenko revealed that a handful of Canadians had provided information to the Soviet Union (at a time, it should be noted, when the country was allied with Canada in the fight against Hitler), King fixated on the fact that five of the twenty accused were of Jewish descent. In his diary entries, he mused repeatedly on an apparently genetic affinity among Jews for leftist sedition, concluding that "in a large percentage of the race there are tendencies and trends which are dangerous indeed." When the US government did not pursue with expected vigour the allegations against Americans caught up in the same spy investigation, King thought he knew why. "I am coming to feel," he wrote in a reprisal of his earlier suspicions, "that the democratic party have allowed themselves to be too greatly controlled by the Jews and the Jewish influence."[15]

Similar accusations of Jewish cunning, of secret cabals of treasonous Zionists clandestinely manipulating the levers of power, peppered the drivel from far-right agitators prior to the war; sadly, King appeared unable to amend the kind of assumptions about race that would not have appeared out of place on a Nazi propaganda poster. But once again, he must be viewed as a spokesperson for "middle Canada" on the matter. An opinion poll from 1946 found that, given the opportunity to ban specific "nationalities" from immigrating to Canada, 49 per cent of respondents chose Jews, second only to the 60 per cent who named those from recent wartime enemy Japan. Aggregate percentages for those on the unwelcome list exceeded 200, as respondents could cite as many foreign undesirables as they wished; just 18 per cent of those asked declined to blacklist anyone on the basis of nationality. Nearly one-third also voted to prohibit "Negroes"; as in the case of Jews, this demonstrated that nationality served as a euphemism for race in the eyes of many.[16] Like their prime minister, many Canadians stubbornly resisted facing up to some of the war's more urgent lessons.

This does not mean that King simply could not abide Jews or did not treat the ones he encountered with civility, even respect. Near the end of the 1937 Imperial Conference, he wandered into London's Museum Bookstore and discovered a painting of Quebec produced in 1837 for Lord Durham, governor general of Canada. The momentous date inevitably caught his eye, and he approached the shop owner to enquire about the "exceedingly interesting" work that he decided "should be secured for Canada." The proprietor, whom King simply called "Kasner," struck the PM as "an extremely interesting man. He is a Jew, extremely well read; has a multitude of books round about." Further conversation revealed Kasner to be a dabbler in the paranormal, and the bookseller suggested that he and King call on a similarly inclined friend later that evening. The PM jumped at the chance.[17]

Once assembled, the cabalistic threesome enjoyed, in King's words, "a very interesting evening's conversation," one "closely in touch with reality and truth." Against long odds, the prime minister's fondness for Kasner deepened. "Although a Jew," King wrote, "he is one of the most interesting men I have yet met; has a fine philosophy of life." Kasner's friend, apparently something of an oracle, brought glad tidings: King would govern until age eighty-four, live to ninety-three, and enjoy, as King reported, "health and strength all my life. It will be amazing to see what becomes of this kind of prediction."[18]

Not much, as it turned out. King would step down as prime minister in 1948 at age seventy-three and die two years later, plagued by a

As different as the landscape of the various German provinces
are the features of the peoples which inhabit them

9.1 Diversity, Nazi-style. In praising Hitler for giving "every man the same opportunities" while remaining silent on National Socialism's persecution of ethnic minorities, Mackenzie King, too, was making the assumption that only Aryans were true Germans. (From Richter, Carstensen, and Hitzer, *Germany*, n.p.)

variety of debilitating ailments in his final years. But once again, we see the dependable formula for gaining King's admiration: a face-to-face encounter, kindness, flattery, a partiality for the mystical. King also stuck to script by tossing off bland and unsupported superlatives, and by seeming to completely forget the plight of fine men like his two new friends once he was in the company of those with an altogether differing outlook.

Such was the setting two weeks later when King toured the world capital of antisemitism. Given his lifelong racialist worldview, it comes as no great bombshell that the Nazis' treatment of Jews and other "impure" Germans was not top of mind for the prime minister. There is no evidence that King initiated any talk regarding the persecution of Jews, or of their absence from the youth and work camps, track meets, bureaucratic offices, and the community at large, where racially targeted harassment, firings, vandalism, and prohibitive legislation had provoked suicides and a mass exodus. What the prime minister saw instead in his examinations of the Nazi conditioning curricula was a spirit of inclusion and universal betterment, concluding that what Hitler "is striving most for is to give *every man* the same opportunities as others have in matters of physical development, industrial development, enjoyment, leisure, beauty, etc." He matter-of-factly dictated to Pickering Hewel's explanation that Hitler's "talks about the race" had been misrepresented by "the outside world" – that the Fuhrer's aim was simply "to keep the blood of the people pure."[19]

Specific reference to the "Jewish question" did not appear in King's diary until the last of his four days in the city – and only because Germany's foreign minister Baron Konstantin von Neurath broached the subject, boasting of the ongoing purge of Berlin Jews that would see their numbers reduced from one hundred sixty thousand in 1933 to eighty thousand in 1939. "He said to me," King dictated to Pickering that evening, "that I would have loathed living in Berlin with the Jews ... He said there was no pleasure in going to a theatre which was filled with them ... They were getting control of all the business, the finance ... It was necessary to get them out to have the German people really control their own City and affairs."[20] The man who had paid a considerable price to keep Jews out of his own neighbourhood offered in conversation or diary no rebuttal to these views.

10

The Uses and Abuses
of Mackenzie King

Day two of King's visit had been a busy one. The long drive to and from the labour camp, the presentations, discussions, lunches, and teas had left little time for rest. Now, King's entourage was heading to an 8 p.m. dinner that, though described by his hosts as informal, would nonetheless require King to maintain the kind of conversation and comport worthy of a visiting head of state.[1] Doubtless, the sixty-two-year-old prime minister, who frequently chastised himself over his weight, eating habits, and inability to sleep, was weary. Nonetheless, it was to be a long night.

The evening's reception took place at the headquarters of the Deutsch-Englische Gesellschaft (DEG, German-English Fellowship). Founded by Ribbentrop in 1935, this ostensibly independent friendship society had by the spring of 1937 been purged of all non-Nazis. Its aim was to build bilateral accord, a full appreciation for the threat posed by Bolshevism, and an admiration for Hitler's regime in concert with its London-based sister organization, the Anglo-German Fellowship (AGF). As a leading DEG official stated frankly, the lobby's task involved convincing their "influential English friends," the conservative and often pro-Nazi British aristocrats, industrialists, and media magnates that made up the AGF, to "undertake intensive propaganda for Germany." The familial ties between members of the German and British aristocracy clearly abetted this effort to cloak the Nazi wolf in the garb of a lamb, and party officials believed they had witnessed a marked improvement in the relationship by the time of King's visit. Unbeknownst to German officials, both British and Soviet agents, including notorious Cambridge Spy Ring communist moles Guy Burgess and Kim Philby, also joined the AGF in order to monitor British-German contacts; the latter became editor of the group's newsletter.[2]

Walther Hewel's command of the English language, network of international contacts, and surfeit of *Gemütlichkeit* made him a key figure in the DEG and its first treasurer. Joining him for dinner with King that evening were German diplomats who had served in London and Washington, including Prince Otto Christian Archibald von Bismarck, grandson of the revered German nation-builder Otto von Bismarck. Unlike his grandfather, Bismarck the younger lacked a coherent vision for Germany, but he certainly inherited the Iron Chancellor's legendary guile and survival instincts, opportunistically hopping aboard whatever political train offered the greatest prospects for personal advancement. He began his shape-shifting career in partisan politics in 1924 as a member of parliament for the right-wing Deutschnationale Volkspartei (DNVP, German National People's Party), a group whose embrace of expansionism, antisemitism, the "stab-in-the-back" myth that German politicians rather than soldiers lost the First World War, and eventually Hitler himself, rendered it a key partner in Nazism's ascent.[3]

After four years in the Reichstag, Bismarck was appointed German ambassador to London. Here he reported on the mounting apprehension among some British officials over the German electorate's growing affections for Hitler following the 1930 elections, when the number of National Socialist representatives in the Reichstag rose from 12 to 107. When the DNVP dissolved in 1933, redundant now under a likeminded regime, Bismarck wasted little time in becoming a dues-paying Nazi and one of the most important DEG members. Following the war, he flirted briefly with German liberals before running for the conservative Christian Democratic Union and sitting in the federal Bundesstadt for twelve years; the prince also served concurrently in the Parliamentary Assembly of the Council of Europe, rising to the position of vice president. Like too many among the Nazi hierarchy, Bismarck escaped post-war retribution for his crimes, despite his central role, while ambassador to Rome, in pressuring the Italians to hand over Jewish refugees in occupied Croatia for "dispersion and elimination."[4]

Despite Reich officials' confidence that their friendship campaign was bearing fruit, British officials never had much use for either of the bilateral fellowship clubs. Just prior to King's Berlin trip, UK Foreign Office undersecretary Robert Vansittart had successfully lobbied his colleagues in government to cease all further contact with the diplomatic dilettantes, calling them "silly." "We must put a stop to this eternal butting in of amateurs," wrote Vansittart in a memo, as their ham-fisted efforts "render impossible the task of diplomacy." Mackenzie King, by contrast, was rather well disposed towards those he met during dinner at DEG headquarters, judging them all "exceedingly interesting men."[5]

The headquarters itself was located at a rather odd address for a bilateral fellowship society: 30 Bendlerstrasse, just south of Tiergarten, was part of an extensive complex of buildings known as the Bendlerblock that served as the headquarters of the Wehrmacht. King likely noted, given his sensitivity to associations, coincidences, and destiny's song, that he was now enjoying his meal just a stone's throw from his German billet in 1900. Far more significantly, the block would become the setting for one of the Second World War's most intriguing "what if's." It was at the Bendlerbock in a building directly opposite DEG headquarters that Operation Valkyrie was plotted; this was the 20 June 1944 effort to kill Hitler by detonating a bomb at the Wolfsschanze (Wolf's Lair), the eastern headquarters where the Fuhrer commanded much of the war against the Soviets. A successful assassination would have led to immediate negotiations with the Allies, possibly sparing the tens of millions of deaths and the decimation of countless German cities in the ten-plus months of fighting that followed the botched scheme. Believing their plot had succeeded, the conspirators began moving to assume command of the military and the state from their redoubt at the Bendlerblock, leaving little doubt as to their involvement when a wounded Hitler began making furious phone calls. Several coup participants were arrested that same day, and just after midnight, plot leaders General Friedrich Olbricht, Major General Henning von Tresckow, and Claus von Stauffenberg were executed in the main courtyard of the Bendlerblock. In the ensuing weeks, nearly five thousand Germans believed to be associated with the plot, however remotely, met a similar fate.[6]

Today the former Bendlerstrasse is called Stauffenbergstrasse, renamed by West German officials in 1955 for the conspirator who planted the bomb. Wartime aerial bombs pulverized Bendlerstrasse 30 and surrounding structures, and at present a sprawling and architecturally uninspiring hotel owned by the German Maritim chain of resorts monopolizes the entire city block where the men of the DEG once assembled. In 1968, a portion of the original Bendlerblock opposite number 30 was transformed into the Gedenkstätte Deutscher Widerstand (German Resistance Memorial), a museum commemorating Germans who took a stand against Nazism. The building's courtyard features plaques and interpretive panels dedicated to those who were executed there on 20 June 1944, along with a statue of a bronze figure with bound hands. Honoured along with the bomb plotters in the exhibits inside are

10.1 Courtyard of the Gedenkstätte Deutscher Widerstand. The statue with bound hands commemorates those who defied Hitler's regime. (Author photograph, 2017)

Germans who from 1933 onward were wise enough to see the regime as humanity's enemy, and courageous enough to act on that knowledge.[7]

These commemorative efforts faced intensive scrutiny – clearly a leitmotif in our story. In this instance, the inescapable controversies that follow any proposed Nazi-era memorials proved especially thorny. We can easily dismiss critics (mostly from an earlier generation) who called Stauffenberg and his associates traitors, although the persistence of such sentiments among a populace fully cognizant of Nazi crimes is admittedly confounding. More complicated questions arose over whether aristocratic military officers who were contemptuous of democracy, and who offered scant resistance to Hitler until Germany's defeat was certain, should be eulogized as heroes. Detractors also feared the exhibit would overstate the significance of the other scattered and ineffectual acts of anti-Nazi resistance. This could leave an overall impression not of collective guilt but, as a museum brochure from 1972 argued, of a reassurance "that the entire German people was not stricken with the disease of totalitarianism and that in Germany, too, the tradition of inalienable human rights could not be destroyed." The fact that – along with Jews – socialists and communists were among the regime's most determined opponents was a prickly issue in the Cold War and beyond, made more so by the exhibit's homage to leftist resistors who went on to found the repressive DDR.[8] Very little, it should be abundantly clear by now, is straightforward in post-war Germany.

Mackenzie King had finished his dinner at Bendlerstrasse 30, but his night was still not over. Instead of returning him to the Adlon, Hewel drove the PM around Tiergarten, and the two had what King described as "an interesting talk." Hitler's confidant spoke of his leader's contempt for British foreign secretary Anthony Eden, who "had got under Hitler's skin" by equating Nazism with communism. (Here was a slight that was, to the communist-loathing Fuhrer, somewhere on the order of Mao's calling Khrushchev a capitalist in the late 1950s – "and not very smart," Mao had added for good measure.) The Nazi movement, Hewel insisted, was *saving* Europe from the scourge of communism, and Britain was not only sitting idly while Hitler tried to rescue Spain, but was rebuffing any attempts to partner in the broader and exigent international struggle against Marxism-Leninism. The Fuhrer had had enough, and would make no further efforts to curry favour with the *naïfs* in London.[9]

This was not what King wanted to hear. Anglo-German rapprochement and cooperation served as the very cornerstone of his strategy for global peace and stability. As Hewel spoke the prime minister interjected repeatedly to make it clear that Britain's recently appointed prime minister, Neville Chamberlain, would pursue a policy of greater sympathy towards Germany. Hewel was listening. "Each time I spoke of Chamberlain being friendly," King reported, "Hewel seemed to receive the statement with genuine satisfaction and urged me to assure Hitler of this fact." Hewel then declared that Hitler would have invited them to his own house for the next day's meeting had it not been for some unspecified obligations to the Congress of the International Chamber of Commerce on the same day, a statement King recorded with obvious pride. Given that the Fuhrer ruled with an iron fist, this scheduling conflict seemed like a blatant dodge; if so, the prime minister did not pick up on it. (Berlin social columnist Bella Fromm attended the ICC reception at the Stadtschloss the following day, and did not find Hitler in attendance.)[10]

Hewel's receptiveness to the prime minister's message about Chamberlain raises a key question: just what did the Nazis hope to gain by hosting King? Clearly, any visit by a democratic leader could be used to enhance legitimacy at home and abroad, but what about more specific diplomatic or strategic objectives? Of what use was King to Hitler at this juncture in his war preparations? As we have seen, in King's estimation the trip was an expression of goodwill on behalf of both Canada and the British Empire, and a manifestation of his faith that personal connections and rational discourse would rebuild Anglo-German friendship.

There is little to suggest that, by 1937 at least, Third Reich officials shared these objectives. It is true that Hitler had appointed Ribbentrop as ambassador to the United Kingdom in 1936 with the goal of securing a formal alliance with Aryan Germany's nearly-as-evolved Anglo-Saxon cousins, whose military strength and international influence could be a potential asset or threat to Nazi plans for expansion. The Fuhrer, however, could hardly have made a shoddier appointment. Ribbentrop turned off his hosts immediately with his gratuitous and seemingly uncontrollable Nazi saluting at official functions, his ignorance of international relations and the workings of British politics, his general stupidity, and his spectacular pomposity.[11] (Keep in mind that, because he clung to the illusion that the aristocracy still wielded the real power in Britain, Ribbentrop had appalled a class of men not generally put off by "airs.")

The German ambassador had initially expressed confidence that he could seal the alliance, believing not without cause that King Edward VIII was at heart a Germanophile and antisemite, and preposterously, that the British sovereign ultimately dictated his country's foreign affairs. Edward's abdication in December 1936 was deemed by both Ribbentrop and his boss (and with typical unimaginativeness) the work of a secret cabal of Jews, freemasons, and other German-haters, and the changing of the guards left the ambassador with little hope of bringing Britain into an anti-Comintern pact.[12] Ribbentrop's innumerable gaffes and breaches of protocol made for great copy in the British press, and long before he was laughed out of town towards the end of 1937 he had developed a burning hatred for all things British. An Italian official's diary entry from the period observed that the once-Anglophilic German diplomat had turned on his hosts with the "fury of a woman scorned." Ribbentrop shared his plaintive tale of rejection and pain with the Fuhrer, who had himself grown increasingly irate over London's unreceptiveness and whose attitude to Britain, too, "had come to resemble that of a lover spurned," according to biographer Ian Kershaw.[13]

By the summer of 1937, then, the jilted Reich statesmen had dispensed with any illusions of a possible Anglo-German rapprochement. Instead, they had shifted their policy towards shoring up alliances with fellow Anglophobes (Italy) and had begun considering new alliances with states previously regarded as mortal enemies (the Soviets). Solid evidence for the turn away from Britain was furnished six days before King arrived in Berlin, when Hitler abruptly cancelled a planned visit to London by German foreign minister Neurath. The pretext given was that the British were refusing to punish loyalist Spain for (trumped-up) acts of aggression against German ships in Spanish waters, a violation of a multiparty non-intervention agreement to which Britain was a party. The specific incident involved an alleged, unsuccessful torpedo attack against the German cruiser *Leipzig*. Nevile Henderson surmised, quite correctly, that the Germans – themselves serial violators of the non-intervention pact – were simply casting about for an excuse to torpedo any further hopes for an improved Anglo-German relationship. Henderson also concluded that the humiliated Ribbentrop was instrumental to the cancellation, having beseeched Hitler not to send a higher-ranking official to draw attention to, and seek to clean up, the mess the ambassador had made in London. Here again, Henderson was spot on.[14]

Hitler, in other words, was fed up with grasping vainly at bilateral amity, turning his focus instead to isolating, outmanoeuvring, and punishing his British rivals. Enter Mackenzie King, fresh off a conference that included newly appointed British prime minister Neville Chamberlain, whose leadership Nazi officials had not yet fully sized up in the thirty days since he assumed power. Time and again, to Hewel, Ribbentrop, Göring, Hess, Neurath, and Hitler himself, the Canadian prime minister repeated the same refrain. Chamberlain was a friend, a lover of peace and hater of militarism, a man sympathetic to Germany's valid grievances, and one who was disinclined to "interfere in the particular policies of other countries." King also interjected wherever he could that, having now attended three Imperial Conferences, he "never knew the attitude toward Germany to be as friendly as it was this year." Every time he made such remarks, King's diary reported, his German hosts appeared to perk up, "pleased to hear what I had said about Chamberlain."[15] The prime minister's mission was making headway.

11

Canada Makes Headlines!

Mackenzie King had a habit of overstating the significance of his sundry political undertakings, but there can be little argument that his current initiative was a portentous one. The Nazis were feeling snubbed and cornered, Europeans dreaded war, alliances were in flux, British opinion roiled over the appropriate response to the Third Reich, and Hitler's foreign aims were the subject of intensive and conflicting speculation. All of these delicate matters could be better understood and perhaps influenced, for better or worse, by the prime minister's interactions with German officials. What's more, the exceptionality of a visit by a democratic head of state was likely to raise both the ire and hope of various leaders and citizens wrestling over the correct response to the German problem. Little surprise, then, that daily journalistic despatches on King's negotiations with Germany's leaders made headlines in that country, in Britain and throughout Europe, in the United States, and of course in Canada.[1]

King had, as we have seen, a rather low view of the fourth estate and its role in the democratic process, counting press coverage as little more than a spanner thrown into in the complex machinery of policy formulation and implementation. The delicate and arcane task of governing, to his mind, ought to be captained by informed, judicious public servants like himself without the prying eyes of the media. His persistent reporter-phobia provides yet another explanation for the prime minister's willingness to break bread with NSDAP officials: he suspected that much of the negative international reporting on Germany was simply false, a product of journalists' jingoism, overwrought anxieties, and ignorance. He went so far as to consider newspapers the ultimate threat to European concord. "The one danger to all countries is the Press," he mused in a typical diary entry while in Berlin, citing fears that "through its misrepresentations and persistent propaganda, some incidents will arise which will occasion conflict. If that comes, however, it will be, I believe, because of the interests behind the Press, not because it is the wish either of Governments or of the people."[2]

Journalists might rightly protest that they were keepers of the interests of the government (many newspapers of the era were consistent and candid advocates for particular political parties, including, as King well knew, the pro-Liberal *Toronto Star*) and the interests of the people.[3] Was King's talk of "interests" pointing to the overriding objective to sell papers rather than report facts, or something more menacing? The phrase "interests behind the Press" smacks of the kind of language frequently employed to describe the control International Jewry supposedly exerted over the affairs of Christendom. The prime minister's ruminations on Jews' "dangerous tendencies," as well as his assumptions about the true puppet masters behind the US Democratic Party, brings such a hypothesis into the realm of the possible.

While King decided not to call on Hitler in 1936 because he was sure that coverage by the "Jingo press of Canada" would warp his intent and undermine his mission, he needn't have fretted. When he overcame his qualms and added Berlin to his itinerary following the 1937 Imperial Conference in London, mainstream Canadian press reactions ran from cautiously supportive to fawning. Both French- and English-language newspapers posted factual, dispassionate Canadian Press reports on King's activities that read as if this were a foreign trip like any other, despite the inclusion of some disturbing details and juxtapositions in the reportage. "Nazi Swastikas and Union Jacks Greet Premier's Arrival in Berlin," reported one *Globe and Mail* headline, explaining that King's was a noble mission aimed at "promoting international understanding"; further down the same front page another story reported that twelve "Nazi pastors" were at that very moment facing trial for defying the regime.[4]

By the mid-1930s, Hitler realized that at least some of Germany's Christian churches would remained stubborn obstacles to his centralizing *Gleichschaltung* initiatives. Independent-minded religious sects, he insisted, were little more than usurpers of his rightful authority, breeding grounds for a potential allegiance to God, clerics, fellow congregants, individual conscience, and humanity that undermined absolute devotion to "One People, One Reich, One Fuhrer." While largely successful, efforts to muzzle political commentary from Catholic priests and to force disparate Protestant congregations into a unified "Reich Church" had generated determined resistance among a handful of churches and a simmering public feud. Open persecution of unruly clerics, toned down for the 1936 Olympics, was on the rise again in 1937. In April, propaganda chief Goebbels organized "immorality trials" against Catholic leaders, bringing trumped-up charges of sexual abuse against priests and nuns who ran religious schools, and of rampant homosexuality in various religious orders.[5]

By the summer, a roundup of Protestant pastors associated with the "Confessing" or "Confessional Church," an association of the (comparatively few) congregations that declared ultimate allegiance to their sects' confession of faith rather than state diktat, was in full swing. On the Sunday morning of King's arrival in Berlin, Lutheran pastor Martin Niemöller, one of the founders of the Confessing Church, was in the Berlin suburb of Dahlem giving what turned out to be his final sermon before eight years in custody, mostly in the Sachsenhausen and Dachau concentration camps. "No more are we ready to keep silent at man's behest when God commands us to speak," he proclaimed to his congregation that morning. Niemöller was arrested on 1 July, the day King departed Germany, part of a wave of detentions surrounding the prime minister's stay. (The pastor would gain international renown with his post-war poem on persecution, "First They Came ...")[6]

Despite his own deep religiosity and lifelong membership in the Presbyterian Church, a sect also classified as confessional, the prime minister did not express public or private reservations about the arrests. A year earlier he had applauded the principled stand taken by the German Confessing Church, writing: "The best thing I have heard in these times was the open defiance of the Nazis by the Protestant Church in Germany on the score of [Nazism's] materialism and agnosticism. It is a brave move." King's diary entries from Berlin suggested that he now accepted Hewel's claim that the churches were positively thriving under the Nazis. Hitler's faithful henchman informed the prime minister that despite the friction with the churches, the Fuhrer was in fact "deeply religious," and "believe[d] strongly in God; as a matter of fact, more congregations had been established in Germany in the last few years than in many years proceeding; that the trouble with the Church had been a political trouble, their interference with politics."[7]

This was simply an Orwellian truth reversal: in the fall of 1933 pro-Nazi Protestants had demanded that the National Socialists' "Aryan paragraph," which barred Jews from the civil service, be adopted by German churches as well. As a result, many Christian clergymen of Jewish ancestry were driven from their posts. *Toronto Star* reporter Matthew Halton quipped that "even God had been *gleichschaltet*," or brought into synchronization. The Reich Church initiative was a further affront. It was these blatant – and outside Germany, universally condemned – political intrusions into matters of faith that had spawned the Confessing Church.[8]

Like King, Canadian journalists covering his trip seemed unwilling to connect the dots between the various headlines emerging from Germany. Two days after reporting on the arrest of the "Nazi pastors," the *Globe* wrote that King sought only "to see something of modern Germany for himself and learn something of her rulers' viewpoints"; the plight of the insubordinate clerics apparently placed no obligations on the prime minister, and indeed, was no longer news. Montreal's *La Presse* focused on the economic basis and benefits of the trip, stating that King was meeting "avec les chefs des gouvernements français, belge et allemande" in order to bolster trade with a range of seemingly comparable foreign administrations. The following day, the same paper included a story on the quickening of ecclesiastical persecution, citing a roundup of 102 German pastors. Again, however, no connection was made between this Gestapo sweep and the prime minister's concurrent communications with the Nazis.[9]

The disturbing and yet unexamined juxtapositions continued. An article in Ottawa's *Le Droit* noted blithely (and wrongly) that King "a visité un camp de concentration" (while such camps were indeed holding enemies of the regime from 1933 on, this was a reference to the prime minister's tour of the Hitler Youth camps). *Le Droit* editors then praised the mission without qualification, writing, "Il est bon que les chefs de gouvernements visitent de temps in temps les autres pays" (It is good that government leaders visit other countries from time to time). Canadian Press correspondent George Hambleton, citing as proof the bilateral trade agreement so disparaged by Liberal parliamentarian Samuel Factor, and sounding much like Mackenzie King, noted proudly that "Canada's relations with Germany are of the friendliest." Even the *Winnipeg Free Press* and *Toronto Star*, Nazi Germany's most consistent and acerbic critics among mainstream Canadian media outlets, refrained from condemnation in their matter-of-fact reports on the meetings. The *Star's* restraint owed something to the fact that its publisher, Joe Atkinson, was one of the few members of the media that King considered a supporter.[10]

The *Ottawa Citizen* was the most steadfastly non-judgmental of Germany and impartial regarding European tensions, informing readers that the discord in Europe was purely economic in origin, and therefore easily resolved: "The German people," editors wrote, "refuse to accept [the] sentence of economic servitude or of national inferiority." The *Citizen* maintained that if only Britain would exhibit more flexibility regarding Germany's commercial interests (acknowledging the hypocrisy of denying Germany colonies, for example), London, like Prime Minister King, would grasp "the possibility of leadership along new economic paths away from war." To the paper, failure to recognize the fundamentally economic basis of European friction meant that "public opinion is confused with arguments about race, religion, politics, Socialism, Fascism, and a multiplicity of side issues." The *Citizen* maintained that Hitler was supporting the fascist Franco regime in the escalating Spanish Civil War, for instance, not out of any ideological consonance or aggressive agenda but simply because Germany needed Spanish ore.[11]

The silence from other media outlets on "side issues" like race, religion, and human rights seemed to confirm the *Citizen's* stance: the Nuremberg Laws, censorship, rearmament, religious persecution, concentration camps, the violations of civil rights and international treaties – these were ephemera unworthy of derailing the conversations in Berlin. To the few in Canada who may have harboured such concerns, the *Globe and Mail* argued that the visit "does not require, as some imply, any justification with the public at home." To the journalists covering his trip, King himself stated only that he was impressed by Germany's post-war recovery and that his talks were "most interesting," "most informative," and "extraordinarily frank."[12]

Here again, the matter of forbearance must be raised. How can we bridge the considerable chasm between what was known of Nazism on the one hand, and the public acclaim for King's initiative – abetted by the Canadian media's refusal to mention Nazi transgressions in their coverage of the visit – on the other? After all, the liberal British press had shown Lord Londonderry no mercy a year earlier when he, like King, took up Ribbentrop's invitation and afterward extolled the "Nazi miracle" in public statements.[13]

The antisemitic currents in Canadian policy and practice discussed earlier certainly provide one explanation of the salutatory news coverage. It is inconceivable that, had the Nazis subjected British or French nationals to four years of odious legal restrictions, state-sanctioned and -coordinated theft, and systematic mob violence, Canadian journalists would be cabling home upbeat despatches on the prime minister's daily adventures. But with reporters now witnessing harassment of their Catholic and Protestant co-religionists, it is impossible to attribute all leniency towards fascist initiatives to simple racism or indifference to racism, if any such distinction exists.

The nature of the reporting itself points to another factor in the collective affirmation of the trip: namely, the perennial desire for greater Canadian international prestige. Easily overlooked internationally and keen to demonstrate independence from both British and American policymakers, newly autonomous Canada was now presented with an opportunity to take centre stage, perhaps even alter the plot, in the momentous drama that was interwar Europe. As we have seen, this impulse was certainly central to the prime minister. Criticism of his foreign venture could embarrass both King and the country he represented, a variant of the "politics-stops-at-the-water's-edge" dictum that held a powerful appeal for citizens of a young and insecure international player like Canada.

Saturday Night magazine editors reflected this tendency – and had no way of knowing how precise their analysis of King's mindset was – in summarizing the prime minister's negotiations with European leaders: "We believe, and we are confident that Mr. King believes, that he has never been nearer to being a Man of Destiny than at the present moment. The hour is critical." The "Jingo press of Canada" was alive and well, although it was assuming a perspective different from the one the prime minister initially feared. Rather than castigating King for cavorting with Nazis, journalists were, like the prime minister, framing the visit as Canada's international coming-out party. Coverage along these lines was so pervasive that *Saturday Night's* "Rideau Banks" (a.k.a. Norman MacLeod) was entirely justified in satirizing the Canadian reporters who hailed King's visit as the dawn of their nation's global eminence and a resetting of European relations. In an article titled "Not Settling the World," MacLeod provided a sampling of the press hype surrounding the trip and lampooned the collective message that "the peace of the world has been placed in King's hand." It was patently absurd, he countered, to think "that British statesmanship has confessed defeat and abdicated in favour of the Prime Minister of one of the Dominions."[14]

Criticisms of the Canada-centric coverage aside, it must be granted that a certain measure of the positive press reporting and attendant diffidence regarding Nazi wrongs was understandable, even prudent: Canadian observers sought to avoid interfering with and perhaps sabotaging potentially delicate negotiations that could lessen the prospect of war. On this, the overall atmosphere in interwar Canada, the United States, and Europe was undeniable: citizens and governments alike were prepared to go to extraordinary lengths to avoid a return to the bloodletting of the Great War, a conflict viewed as singularly horrific – and more and more, in the collective post-mortems of the twenties and thirties, one sparked by relatively petty grievances and that had settled little. While Hitler's domestic abuses were well documented by the mid-thirties, his foreign agenda was still widely debated and subject to a broad range of contradictory interpretations and international approaches. By 1936, King reflected these tensions, as he was both open to treating Germany as a favoured trading partner and expressed alarm in his diary "that Hitler has been permitted to go to the lengths he has."[15] Now, a year later, personal inspection of those "lengths" had replaced that alarm with relief.

12

Atavistic Beasts:
Der Dicke and His Bison

As a rule, to peer beneath the surface of even the most outwardly innoc-
uous Nazi initiative is to find oneself immersed in depravity. Take the
plan to replenish herds of bison and other big game in the Białowieża
Forest. Hitler's second-in-command Hermann Göring charged zoolo-
gist Lutz Heck with the task of bringing back the "primeval German
game" that had once roamed the woodlands. From here the malevolent twists to a seemingly benign story of habitat renewal begin to pile
up in quick succession: this was but a component of the Nazi fantasy
of recreating the romanticized Germany of yore, before the poisons of
modernity and non-Aryan immigration fouled the Teutonic paradise;
the restoration project relied on the application of the Nazis' notorious human eugenics theories and experiments to the animal kingdom,
as living descendants of ancient species like aurochs – enormous,
horned cattle extinct since the early seventeenth century – would
be "back-bred" to produce a kind of devolution to earlier forms; the
Białowieża Forest was, for the moment at least, in Poland; the forest,
with an area of more than three thousand square kilometres, was home
to thousands of Slavic, Jewish, Roma, and other non-Aryans who were
to be "cleared" by the Wehrmacht and Einsatzgruppen death squads
after German forces had cleared Poland from the map of Europe.[1]

While unaware of the scheme's myriad cruelties and the crackpot
science behind it, Canadian officials were a junior partner in the project.
Worried that the European variant of bison, called wisent, were nearing extinction, Lutz Heck travelled to Canada in 1935 to arrange for
the importation of some two dozen North American specimens, which
possessed, he believed, "immense reproductive energy." A few of these
Canadian expatriates were put on display at the Berlin Zoo, and King

was delighted to meet both the creatures and Dr Heck himself, now the zoo's director, on his first day in the city. Even more delightful was the placard at the bison pen thanking the Canadian prime minister for the gift (tacked onto the fence specifically for his visit?).[2]

On the morning of Tuesday, 29 June, day three of his stay in Germany, King was in the office of the man who had set it all in motion. "General Göring," as King called him, began the conversation by thanking the prime minister for the animals. King thanked Göring for the "personal acknowledgement and inscription at the zoo," and assured the general that Canada had plenty of bison should the general need more. The prime minister was in good spirits, if a little apprehensive: this was the "Day of Interview with Herr Hitler," as he titled his handwritten diary entry, underlining the heading for emphasis.[3] King never included titles for his diary entries – not for election wins, the beginning or end of world wars, or the death of family members. This was a day like no other.

The previous day had been a long one. Following their late-night talk during the leisurely drive around Tiergarten, Hewel returned King to the Adlon around midnight. With the momentous interview looming, the prime minister didn't trifle with the Adlon blankets, covering up instead with the Mackenzie tartan after placing the Lord Grey biography by his side. This time he slept soundly. He awoke at 8:15 a.m., giving him enough time for a morning devotional focused on scriptural readings that spoke of God's protection and guidance. "Put on the whole armour of God," he read, transcribing the beginning of Ephesians 6:11 in his diary to indicate one passage studied, but stopping short of writing out the complete verse: "that ye may be able to stand against the wiles of the devil." The next two verses, also not transcribed but surely read since they round out the Apostle Paul's lesson, summed up the day's formidable challenge as well as any in the Bible: "For we wrestle not against flesh and blood, but against principalities, against powers, against the rulers of the darkness of this world, against spiritual wickedness in high places. Wherefore take unto you the whole armour of God, that ye may be able to withstand in the evil day, and having done all, to stand."[4] Did King choose the passage because he had a darker view of Hitler and Nazism than he was willing to admit to others and himself? Or were European leaders, journalists, and other opinion makers as a whole responsible for "the darkness of this world," the "spiritual wickedness" that augured war? Or did the passage choose King?

Now, at 10:30 a.m., he was shaking hands with Göring. If King had possessed a greater curiosity for matters beyond politics, mystical signs

12.1 Two photographs, spliced together rather inelegantly, were required to accommodate the colossal Reichsluftfahrtministerium headquarters in an image assembled shortly after its completion in 1936. The photographer faces southwest, capturing the intersection of Wilhelmstrasse (left) and Leipziger Strasse. (Bundesarchiv, Bild 183-H28407)

and wonders, and himself, and if he commanded greater powers of description, he would have provided a more comprehensive portrait of his surroundings. What the prime minister called "a spacious office overlooking a garden" was Europe's largest office building, the recently completed headquarters for the Reichsluftfahrtministerium (RLM, Reich Ministry of Aviation) headed by Göring. Located on Wilhelmstrasse five blocks south of the Adlon Hotel and British Embassy, the fortress-like seven-story RLM headquarters took up the entire block and featured nearly three thousand rooms and seven kilometres of corridors. Its architect Ernst Sagebiel had also designed Templehof Airport, and both structures shared the massive, unadorned neoclassical facades characteristic of Nazi construction, labelled "National Socialist intimidation architecture" by a later German author. Göring's visitors were typically, and by design, "overawed" by the building's stark, muscular grandeur.[5]

The monstrosity had certainly produced the desired effect on the always observant and wary Colonel Crerar two weeks earlier. He was not reassured by the enormous resources poured into the air force headquarters, writing with obvious trepidation that the building's scale "makes one think." Informed of the sheer number of rooms, the career army officer trained in military intelligence noted soberly: "An idea of the size of the Air Ministry staff can thus be obtained."[6]

Like all prominent Berlin structures that survived the war, the aviation building has a story to tell. Despite its size, function, central location, and proximity to the most significant government buildings in Nazi Berlin, it somehow escaped major damage from Allied air assaults (insert conspiracy theory here). Although it was at the very centre of Nazi war planning and operations, the virtual absence following the war of any other usable structure in the government quarter proscribed demolition of this crime site. During the Cold War the former RLM headquarters became the most important administrative building in East Berlin, used first by the hated Soviet occupiers and later by the mostly hated DDR as its de facto seat of government, now renamed the Haus der Ministerien (House of Ministries). It was here that the DDR was officially founded in 1949, and it was here four years later that Soviet tanks fired at striking workers protesting increased production quotas and demanding that same government's resignation while East German officials cowered inside. Some of the dozens killed in what became known as the Berlin Uprising of 1953 fell in the building's forecourt, within sight of an insipid mural dedicated to the joys of socialist brotherhood that was added to the north façade to commemorate the founding of the DDR. Forty-one years after the workers' revolt and five years after the collapse of East Germany, a plaque honouring the uprising was affixed to the same facade, and a huge photograph of strikers, locked arm in arm as they marched towards the House of Ministries, was inserted into the sidewalk in front of the socialist mural. A proposal to add a plaque commemorating the victims of the terror bombing campaigns directed from within these walls stalled in the planning stages.[7]

As if the building did not have enough history to digest, its association with terror and callous bureaucratic machinations continued after the Cold War. The structure's immensity and functionality saved it once again from demolition following reunification, despite its official post-reunification designation as a historically "burdened building." In the early 1990s, Göring's erstwhile citadel served as the headquarters of the agency responsible for privatizing the DDR's state-owned assets. Hundreds of thousands of government employees lost their jobs as a result, and left-wing terrorists exacted their vengeance by assassinating

12.2 A photograph of striking East Berlin workers now interrupts the sidewalk along Leipziger Strasse on the north side of the former aviation headquarters. Some of the protestors were killed here, within sight of the DDR mural (at rear) celebrating the workers' paradise ushered in by communism. (Author photograph, 2011)

the head of the privatization program. Today the building is known as Detlev-Rohwedder-Haus in honour of the slain bureaucrat.[8]

At the time of Mackenzie King's visit, large sculptures of the Nazi *Hoheitszeichen* (national emblem), an eagle perched on a swastika, topped the columns of the fence surrounding the aviation building. A giant relief of the same served as the focal point in the Ehrensaall (Hall of Honour), the grand reception room that was the centrepiece of visitors' tours and, in 1949, the very spot where Hitler's great nightmare – a communist Germany – would be proclaimed.[9]

When the prime minister was shown to Göring's office, he found the Reichsminister at his desk, clad in the white military uniform he favoured in warmer weather. The office was, like its inhabitant, outsized, with Göring's desk at one end and at the other an ensemble of sofa and chairs large enough to accommodate the two statesman, Hewel, Pickering, and Paul-Otto Schmidt, chief interpreter for the German government and Hitler's personal translator.[10]

Schmidt was no Nazi zealot, having gained his post under the previous Weimar regime and not joining the NSDAP until 1943. He would, however, become a primary conduit for Nazi schemes and crimes, serving as interpreter at the Munich Conference and at wartime meetings between Hitler and foreign allies. During several of these consultations the Fuhrer provided, via Schmidt, candid descriptions of his plans for eastern Europe, and demanded collaboration in the roundup of Jews. After facilitating Nazi officials' conversations with Mackenzie King, Schmidt's next discussions involving Canadians took place in the wake of the disastrous 1942 Dieppe Raid, where he served as the chief interrogator of the thousands of captured Canadian infantrymen. Following the war, Schmidt convinced Allied prosecutors that those in his position were simply "moderate career diplomats," and was made a witness, rather than defendant, at Nuremberg. Those hoping for a similar "moderate career" marked by intrigue, complicity in high crimes, and highly contentious clemency had only to enrol in the Sprachen & Dolmetscher Institut München (Language and Interpreters Institute, Munich), founded in 1952 under the directorship of Hitler's chief translator and accepting applicants to this day.[11]

While King felt he had much in common with some of the other German officials he met, he and Göring were a study in opposites. The forty-four-year-old aviation minister was born to an aristocratic military family and gained national prominence during the First World War as a decorated fighter pilot. Dashing, womanizing, and handsome – at least in his youth – war hero Göring brought prestige and glamour to the fledgling Nazi Party when he joined in 1922. While he, like King, grew increasingly plump as he aged, "der Dicke" (the fat one), as he was known, gained his corpulence from a lifetime of cheerful surrender to the call of food and drink; he counted neither abstinence nor any attempts to curb excesses at table or bar as virtues.[12]

Despite his girth, Göring was an active outdoorsman who cultivated a macho persona. He loved to hunt, sail, drive fast cars, throw debauched parties, and collect exotic animal species – including pet lions – which he kept on his sprawling country estate. He was loud, quick-witted, gregarious and, despite his refined background, often shockingly vulgar. His buffoonish ostentation in manner and dress – medieval hunting outfit one moment, full-length gown, makeup, and foppish hat the next – was renowned, and frequently lampooned in the foreign press. Göring was also a drug addict. Shot in the groin during the Beer Hall Putsch, he developed a decades-long dependence on the painkiller morphine that was only overcome during his detention while awaiting trial at Nuremberg, where no morphine was on offer. Somehow cyanide was, however, which allowed Air Minister Göring to die by his own hand rather than face the hanging assigned by the Nuremberg court, which called his guilt "unique in its enormity."[13]

None of this portends a potential meeting of the minds at the aviation headquarters. Yet the extroverted and outlandish general and the repressed and puritanical prime minister appear to have gotten on rather well. A month after their meeting King was writing "my dear General Göring" to extend an invitation to hunt big game in Canada. It is unclear whether the prime minister was proposing that they go together. It is difficult to picture the exceedingly citified, fastidious, animal-loving King mucking through the forest with the bombastic aviation minister and firing in the general direction of an innocent creature. But Göring seems to have caught his fancy. Others who dealt with Nazi officials had a similar reaction, declaring him the "good Nazi," at least in the sense of the one whose company they most enjoyed. Nevile Henderson had no doubts that Göring was instrumental in the Reichstag fire, the Rohm purge, and other acts of treachery and ruthlessness, but confided, even as war raged in 1941, that the general "had certain attractive qualities: and I must frankly say that I had a real personal liking for him." Henderson's affections were sadly evident to socialite and columnist Bella Fromm. "The Englishman," reads a diary entry from May 1937, "seems to see only the brilliantly entertaining side of this barbarian's game."[14]

After their ice-breaking chat about the Canadian bison, King treated Göring to the usual spiel about how growing up in Berlin, Ontario, surrounded by ethnic Germans gave him a special connection with his host's land and people – "To get under way with friendly feeling," as King later dictated to Pickering. Göring moved briskly to bilateral commercial opportunities, pressing King about which German manufactured goods might be in demand in Canada. The prime minister willingly acknowledged that he was no expert on the intricacies of trade, "that this lay a little outside my special field of larger political

12.3 Machismo unbound: Hermann Göring unloads at a shooting range before enthralled minions in this undated photograph. Despite widely divergent backgrounds, tastes, and sensibilities, King and Göring appeared to hit it off. (Bundesarchiv, Bild 146-1979-190-05A)

questions."[15] The journalists who had insisted King's visit was primarily commercial in nature had gotten it wrong; these matters seemed the furthest from his mind.

For Göring, on the other hand, commercial interactions were of the highest priority. The massive Nazi rearmament program, now four years in, was threatening to ruin the German economy and give the lie to the "Nazi miracle." Decreasing living standards could abrade the sheen from the Fuhrer cult and threaten the very existence of the regime; short of reigning in military spending (anathema to a leader set on war), a reinvigoration of the economy was essential. By the summer of 1936 the fiscal crisis had progressed to the point where Hitler reluctantly pivoted from his fixation on German expansion and the elimination of its enemies to issue an economic memorandum that out-lined a rather vague but ominously worded "programme for the final solution of our vital need." Hitler then dumped the file onto Göring's lap, anointing him "Reich Plenipotentiary of the Four Year Plan" (it was one of eleven major military and civil offices that Göring headed con-currently by the early 1940s).[16]

Plenipotentiary Göring pushed in several directions at once in order to prime the fiscal pump, intimidating private corporations into increas-ing production and thereby enhancing the nation's autarky, establish-ing a vast bureaucracy to intensify *Gleichschaltung* among the various sectors of the economy, and bolstering the program of "aryanization," which amounted to seizing Jewish businesses and assets and turning them over to Nazi-friendly interests. Ultimately, however, German offi-cials concluded that their economy would be sustainable only through the raw materials and productive capacity gained via territorial expan-sion. A sizeable increase in exports could provide a short-term buffer against financial collapse until the Wehrmacht was fully equipped to initiate the next phase of economic growth.[17]

The dilemma here lay in the fact that Germany's trade with the world's largest economies was in serious remission. In 1935, the United States placed Germany on its trade blacklist, removing previ-ous tariff concessions from German imports as punishment for what the Americans considered unfair trading practices (although a vocal "Boycott Germany" movement continued throughout the 1930s, only a few American companies refused trade with the Reich on moral grounds). While Germany's capacity to produce goods for export and buy foreign products increased substantially between 1929 and 1939, the volume of American-German trade fell by 50 per cent over the same period. And at the 1932 Imperial Economic Conference, hosted in Ottawa, members of the British Empire agreed to lower tariffs between themselves and raise tariffs on all other nations. While King's Liberal government, under pressure from the United States, had by 1935 aban-doned this practice of "imperial preference," the British variant was still in effect when King visited Germany. The German-Canadian trade deal ratified in the spring of 1937 was thus an important component of the wider war-preparation scheme, one that also sought to expand Ger-many's commercial ties with Latin America and southeastern Europe.[18]

While King could offer Göring little of substance on commercial mat-ters, he promised to hand over further negotiations on this file to "our trade experts." Göring then questioned whether such a discussion would be profitable, wondering whether Canada had the capacity to act independently of London on trade and other foreign matters given that the nation conducted its business with Germany through the British Embassy. The discussion had moved into King's wheelhouse. He explained that Canada was a newcomer to the international arena (via the 1931 Statute of Westminster). Reliance on the British Embassy as a channel for German-Canadian relations was a temporary state of affairs, King assured, pointing out that he was personally responsible for establishing permanent foreign legations and had chosen Washington, Tokyo, and Paris first based on strategic needs and the availability of "the right men." Berliners, he promised, could anticipate a Canadian embassy in short order (events would conspire to extend the wait to sixty-eight years).[19]

The prime minister then clarified that the newly won autonomy of the dominions within the Empire had actually improved imperial ties and cohesion. Since their foreign policies were not set by Britain, the dominions now felt like valued partners, and had thus freely chosen to coordinate policy with the mother country based on a common "inheritance of freedom which we were determined to preserve." King made clear what this preservation entailed: the Canadian public "would almost certainly" come to Britain's defence if that country was imperilled by aggression. Accordingly, and despite his preference for peace, his government had increased defence spending on account of the growing friction in Europe. Göring probed further. Would this marvellous spirit of imperial camaraderie compel Canadians to "follow Britain *in everything*?" King said no – that as a rule, "We made our own decisions in the light of questions raised."[20]

The conversation was quickly heading into cat-and-mouse territory. Göring offered up a specific example of "questions raised." Suppose, he hypothesized, that peoples of the same race living under separate flags chose to unite; he offered up the not-so-random example of Germany and Austria. If Britain took steps to prevent such a union, would Canada "back up Britain?" The gist of King's response would have been no surprise to the domestic political opponents and journalists who had, for decades and mostly in vain, laboured to get a straight answer from the virtuoso waffler. "I said: our attitude in this matter would be the same as for all other possible questions which might arise, we would wish to examine all the circumstances surrounding the matter, and would take our decision in light of the facts as existing at the time, and all the circumstances considered." This, King "clarified," was the "Canadian position" on all international matters; it could also be described as the manner in which humans in general tend to select any course of action.

To this study in emptiness Göring responded that King had demonstrated "a very reasonable attitude." At the very least, the prime minister had not presented Canadian support for Britain as automatic (or so it seemed from his meandering jumble of contingencies). The cat then continued to toy with the mouse, and the mouse continued to deliver a master class in political dithering. Göring assured King that "because I have put the question in this way, I do not wish you to think that there is going to be any attempt to take possession of Austria."[21]

By 1937, no one in the Reich, not even the Fuhrer, was pushing harder for the annexation of Austria than Hermann Göring, and the coveting did not appear a secret to H.D.G. Crerar during his visit earlier in the month. "From various conversations," Crerar wrote in his post-visit brief, "I judged that the absorption of Austria by Germany, in one way or another, is regarded as a closely approaching event." The annexation had long been on Hitler's agenda, of course, with the imprisoned Nazi leader spelling out his rationale in *Mein Kampf*: "German-Austria must return to the great German motherland, and not because of economic considerations of any sort. No, no: even if from the economic point of view this union were unimportant, indeed, if it were harmful, it ought nevertheless to be brought about. Common blood belongs in a common Reich."[22] For Hitler, this was a simple question of blood-and-soil destiny.

Conversely, Göring's primary calculus for absorbing Austria involved the "economic considerations" the Fuhrer deemed irrelevant to the matter of *Anschluss*, or union with Austria. The Reich Plenipotentiary of the Four Year Plan coveted his neighbour's raw materials, especially its vast iron ore deposits, as a means of achieving the benchmarks outlined in his economic brief. Accordingly, Göring became the most aggressive lobbyist for "an early and radical solution to 'the Austrian question.'"[23] It was all of a piece: trade deals, access to resources, successful absorption of territory, and the uniting of Germanic peoples would stabilize the economy, burnish Hitler's image and Nazi authority, and add the soldiers and resources required to achieve *Lebensraum* and purge the undesirable races from the Greater German Reich. All economic considerations were at once political and military, and vice versa; Göring's simultaneous heading of portfolios in politics, economics, forestry, and the military was a logical reflection of this single-minded, harmonized schema for German dominance.

Britain was the greatest wild card in these calculations. Would this leading European power broker, whose dominions constituted a permanent (if not always enthusiastic) stable of allies and resources, and whose worldwide territorial possessions provided millions of potential soldiers, stand in the way? Göring continued to gauge King on the matter. The general accused the British of overreacting to perceived snubs – namely, the cancellation of Neurath's visit in light of the *Leipzig* incident – and more generally of "trying to control Germany's actions." King countered that England had no particular animus for Germany. Rather, Britain's close watch over continental affairs was grounded simply in the desire to maintain European stability. Germany should, in truth, be grateful: Britain's special genius for mediating disputes made it an indispensable arbiter in matters that had the potential to "set the whole of Europe aflame." The prime minister then repeated his refrain about the unprecedented level of goodwill towards Germany he perceived at the Imperial Conference, and about his certainty that Chamberlain in particular would prove to be a friend. He added for good measure that the recently crowned king, whom German officials feared would not be as kind to Nazism as his zealously fascist predecessor, was likewise "understanding in his attitude." Upon hearing this, Göring, the prime minister reported, "was pleased." King, keen student of both the English and German "mind," was convinced that he was nurturing the kind of mutual, cross-cultural understanding that formed the crux of his conciliation method, and upon which lay the fate of nations.[24]

It was now noon. The talk had gone on for ninety minutes, despite the fact, noted the prime minister with obvious satisfaction, that "it was quite clear the General had many other engagements which he was letting slip by." Before parting, King invited Göring to visit Canada. The general seemed moved, noting that the prime minister "was the first one to extend an invitation of the kind."[25] In fact, Göring was still seething over the uproar in Britain the previous month after the press learnt he might attend the coronation of George VI. In response, Göring had pouted to Lord Londonderry, the man who had invited him, that he would not set foot in a country whose citizens were "calling me all kinds of names, and sending me many offensive telegrams." While grateful for King's invitation, Göring doubted that he could take up the offer, as his myriad duties made him "very busy." All the more reason, responded King, to take a little time away. Göring conceded that he would fancy some rest and relaxation in the wilderness "for a few days' shooting of big game, elk or bear." King promised to make the arrangements. Now, however, he had to run – his appointment with the Fuhrer began in forty-five minutes.[26]

13

Baiting Godwin's Law

In 1990, American attorney and technology commentator Mike Godwin proposed a theorem that became known as "Godwin's Law." Observing the trajectory of online discussions on a fledgling new communications system called the Internet, Godwin proposed the following: "As an online discussion grows longer, the probability of a comparison involving Nazis or Hitler approaches one." The law's creator had a simple message: "I wanted folks who glibly compared someone else to Hitler to think a bit harder about the Holocaust."[1]

Although the Internet encouraged the flourishing of such facile comparisons to Nazis, the phenomenon was hardly new. Since the Second World War, politicians, journalists, historians, and a host of other well-positioned voices have employed Nazi analogies as a cudgel to vanquish critics – so much so that, already by the early 1950s, political theorist Leo Strauss had coined a term for the cheap debating ploy: *Reductio ad Hitlerum*. In the realm of international affairs, *Reductio ad Hitlerum* became a favourite discursive strategy among those endorsing toughness, red lines, and military responses to threats to peace and stability – and belittling anything that hinted at "appeasement" (i.e., negotiation, compromise, de-escalation). From the perspective of the West, the list of tyrants who allegedly took up where the Fuhrer left off is a long one. A very abridged inventory includes Joseph Stalin (multiple nominations), Egyptian president Gamal Abdel Nasser (by British PM Anthony Eden), Saddam Hussein (President Bushes I and II), Mahmoud Ahmadinejad (Bush II), Bush II (American liberals), Barack Obama (American conservatives), Osama bin Laden (multiple), Donald Trump (ibid.), and Vladimir Putin (ibid.). The call to stand firm against these neo-Hitlers typically includes some reference to Munich, 1938, and a general libelling of the statesmen who attempted to talk their way out of the increasing volatility of the 1930s.[2]

With the benefit of hindsight, it is easy to scoff at those who advocated appeasement (notably, a term worn proudly by its proponents prior to the war). It must be acknowledged, however, that the approach was favoured in the interwar period because it had a solid track record. Any number of European diplomatic initiatives that offered concessions in the name of averting war in the century of relative peace between Napoleon and the Great War, for instance, involved some level of appeasement of an aggrieved party's complaints. Not all factions were fully satisfied by the diplomatic solutions hammered out, and simmering resentments often provided a rallying cry when later conflicts did emerge, but on the whole, deals forged under the "Concert of Europe," as the post-Napoleonic system was called, had mostly prevented the type of savage altercations between great powers all too common to earlier centuries.

When the concert collapsed in 1914, the world was given a stark lesson in the costs of forsaking diplomacy in an age of industrialized "total" warfare, an experience so traumatizing that post-war leaders were urged to avoid the resort to combat at all costs. In the 1930s those leaders sought to collaborate in this task with a regime whose anger and provocations could be contextualized – if not excused – by the alleged vindictiveness of the Treaty of Versailles (to its critics, the very antithesis of appeasement), and whose wanton treachery and cruelty was only fully grasped after it was too late. The modern era had not seen a head of state quite like Hitler before, nor a mass movement so methodically and utterly indoctrinated in cold-blooded, dehumanizing hatred as Nazism. In assuming the old models of give and take would work, the appeasers got it wrong, but we ought to be frank: they possessed no template for handling the Third Reich.

Appealing to the example of Hitler as a means of formulating an appropriate response to subsequent international threats and despots is, under these circumstances, to dishonour the singular horrors and suffering of Nazism's victims. It is also, by extension, bad policy. Aligning national and international strategies for maintaining peace and stability around the prospect of confronting the "next Hitler" follows the same logic as remaining indoors lest one be struck by a meteor. It draws not on the preponderance of evidence gathered over millennia, but on a catastrophic aberration – in the case of Nazism, one fuelled by the collective descent into barbarity within a state possessing the military power to seize an entire continent. To model conduct on aberration is also to deliberately diminish one's own quality of life: by refusing to go outside in one instance, by profligate spending on weapons and overreliance on military responses to complex social and political dilemmas in the other. Proponents of the protracted and inconclusive wars in Korea, Vietnam, Iraq, and Afghanistan habitually invoked the "lessons of Munich" to gain public assent. By and large, the world became a more dangerous place in the wake of each of these repudiations of "appeasement."[3]

This is not to say that there is nothing to learn from the international war against fascism, that the very exceptionality of Nazism proscribes applicable lessons. That humankind has borne witness to the annihilation such extremisms bring – to both nations and the very essence of what it means to be human – makes the prospects of a worldview of commensurate evil taking control of a modern, industrialized nation-state possessing the military capacity to swallow up its neighbours all the more remote. In polities blessed by the prosperity and stability that such military capability implies, the percentage of rational people conscious of the outcome of blood-and-soil fanaticism is simply too great to permit the metastasization of an analogous nationwide cult of death. Even those members of the human race not horrified by any potential association with Nazis have seen the ultimate fate that awaits such plays for continental or regional hegemony.

To those who would counter by pointing to modern examples such as the emergence of the white supremacist "alt-right" in the United States, some basic statistics are in order. In the 1920s, anywhere from two to five million Americans joined the Ku Klux Klan, or as much as 5 per cent of the total population, and when thirty thousand hooded clansmen marched through Washington, DC, in 1925 they were warmly welcomed. As Linda Gordon argued in a recent history of the organization, "The K.K.K. may actually have enunciated values with which a majority of 1920s Americans agreed." Estimates for 2017 Klan membership figures range from five thousand to eight thousand (less than 0.003 per cent of the population). Marches by current devotees to white supremacy inspire near-universal opposition, even in the Deep South that was once their base, as well as condemnation from every politician with a conscience and rudimentary understanding of history.[4] Awareness of the Holocaust will do that to a movement.

Of course, savage dictators bent on the violent elimination of internal and external state enemies have not been banished from the modern world, but they are typically the bane of nations marked by poverty, hopelessness, and a history of perceived humiliation. Those post-Nazi autocrats who have succeeded in seizing control of countries powerful enough to wreak havoc with global stability (read: Joseph Stalin) have secured their power primarily through terror rather than public adulation, severely constraining their prospects for inspiring a robotic march to collective suicide. As military historian Jeffrey Record observed, "given the rarity of genuine Hitlerian threats – agendas of regional, even global, conquest married to the military superiority to act on them – the Munich analogy has been misused far more often than used accurately to depict a security threat."[5]

What's more, we have made structural changes to global governance that preclude a return to anything like a Nazi empire. Today we are more attuned to the conditions that breed nativist ethnic nationalisms. While, sadly, hate-based political movements and parties continue to draw adherents, members of the global community are warier of conducting "business as usual" with anti-democratic and human-rights-abusing governments; morality, while not the only criteria upon which foreign affairs decisions are made, now has a place in the international relations calculus. Collective sanctions against rogue states have, on notable occasions, fulfilled their goal of reducing tensions and amending aggressive behaviour. Human rights themselves have been codified in a United Nations declaration that all members must adopt. Collective security and the obligations that go with it, exercised through the UN, NATO, and other alliances, is considered foundational to the maintenance of peace. International law has been refined and enhanced. We have negotiated arms-control and-reduction agreements that have actually held.[6] States have also acknowledged their "responsibility to protect" the lives and rights of people whose own governments are unwilling or unable to do so. These are all direct legacies of the Second World War. They are also, as with all mechanisms aimed at regulating human affairs, imperfect instruments when applied, and frequently ignored when inconvenient. But the world has changed, and by some measures drastically. Wars between states, to cite one example, are almost unheard of in our age.

All the more reason, then, to avoid flippant Nazi analogies. Under the current international system and climate of opinion, the prospect of a modern dictator pulling out of the United Nations, cancelling all foreign debt payments, confiscating bordering lands through intimidation and brinksmanship, brazenly violating arms-control treaties, setting up camps to house those ideological and ethnic undesirables not summarily executed, *and being treated like a normal head of state, with all the respect and rights that implies*, is unthinkable. That being the case, that same dictator's ability to move on to the next litany of horrors – territorial appropriation through warfare and the establishment of direct or collaborationist rule over multiple formerly sovereign states, the enslavement of millions of the conquered and the mass murder of millions of others in numerous killing factories – appears well beyond the realm of possibility. The prospect of a successful coordinated program of racial purification and substantial expansion of living space has been relegated to history. There is only one Hitler.

All of the above throat-clearing about the folly of Nazi analogies serves to put in context and very carefully circumscribe what follows: a meditation on the commonalities between Adolf Hitler and Mackenzie King. Given the foregoing, it should be clear that this task is undertaken with serious caveats. Foremost among them is the fact that the preponderance of the two leaders' character traits, methods, goals, and worldviews are diametrically at odds; the ensuing comparisons should by no means be construed as an exercise in moral equivalence. King was a steadfast democrat, a deeply committed man of faith who constantly sought self-betterment based on the dictates of the golden rule and felt horribly guilty when he believed he had wronged his fellow man (or beast). He was a hater of war and all forms of violence, a humanist capable of deep empathy who displayed a lifelong willingness to listen to others and, on occasion, concede the error of his ways. That said, we need to come to grips with why the prime minister was so taken by the Fuhrer. At least part of the explanation lay in the similarities King sensed between himself and his opposite number. It is a simple fact that in Hitler, the prime minister perceived something of a kindred spirit.

We know that Mackenzie King was nothing if not a very dexterous political operator. His record at the polls and, once in power, his ability to outmanoeuvre rivals and maintain popular support, serve as a testament to these immense talents. He also possessed an abiding hunger for public adulation, although here his record is decidedly spottier. By the time King visited Germany in the summer of 1937, the burgeoning Fuhrer cult had rendered Hitler among the most popular national leaders in the world – perhaps *the* most. This apparent mastery over the domestic political landscape captivated King; here was a compatriot in the art of governance, a success story whose career arc mirrored the prime minister's own rise from small-town nobody to head of state.

Bearing in mind the "limited opportunities in [Hitler's] early life, his imprisonment, etc.," King wrote in his diary, "it is truly marvellous what he has attained unto himself through his self education."[7]

Those marvellous achievements arose in some measure from Hitler's complete absorption in politics, an inclination that King, too, shared. Neither man had much time or feeling for anything else, and both made for rather dreary dinner companions when the conversation moved on to other matters (unless, of course, King was in the company of a trusted fellow mystic). The seriousness with which they approached their jobs was an extension of how seriously they took themselves; neither exhibited the faintest ability to laugh at themselves or to truly enjoy "frivolities" like social events that were unconnected to political affairs. Hitler's renowned abstemiousness – his forswearing of luxury, meat, and alcohol – was also a trait King could admire, if not fully imitate, and one which the prime minister equated with a monk-like dedication to public service. "He is a teetotaller and also a vegetarian," King wrote admiringly in his diary, "abstemist [sic] in all his habits and ways." Not surprisingly, neither of these sombre and single-minded political operatives had many friends.[8]

And fewer girlfriends. Both Hitler and King were tremendously unnerved over the prospect of a romantic relationship. The younger King made a few desultory attempts at courtship, which ended as a result of his own bungling or sudden loss of interest. Although his diaries still have him holding out hope for marriage into middle age, he made virtually no efforts on this front and eventually resigned himself to a life alone; thoughts of sexual intimacy seemed to mobilize him only when he had been drinking. Likewise, Hitler's dating record, according to Ian Kershaw, was essentially "a void." While he was sometimes linked romantically to various women as he rose through the political ranks, "none of his liaisons, it seems, had been more than superficial," Kershaw noted. "No deep feelings were stirred." Although by the mid-1930s the Fuhrer had developed a (rather distant) relationship with Eva Braun, the public did not know of it until after the war. When King called on Hitler, the former perceived a man completely given over to service to his nation, one for whom a mate would be but a distraction from his great calling. King often referred to his own lot in similar terms, having apparently convinced himself that his solitude was the product of a principled denial of the flesh rather than romantic gaucherie.[9]

At the risk of bodging psychoanalytic theory, it does not appear a stretch to surmise that a portion of this legacy of romantic uninterest and incompetence lay in each man's idealization of his mother – to an extent that other women could simply not live up to the standards established at home. King's Pantagruelian adoration for Isabel Grace Mackenzie is frequently cited, and derided, as foundational to his personal development. No other woman, his Oedipal-hued diary entries repeatedly make plain, could approach her beauty or virtue. "I have met no woman so true and lovely a woman in every way as my mother," he wrote at age twenty-five, a statement he never found cause to amend. Isabel's opinion counted most, both before and after her death, whenever King needed to make any important decisions; the lightbulb over her portrait at the prime minister's residence was never switched off; during times of stress, King was wont to stroke the lock of her hair he kept near the portrait.[10]

The young Hitler's love for his mother Klara, meanwhile, "was his most striking feature," recalled Klara's doctor, who stated flatly that he had "never witnessed a closer attachment." When Adolf was eighteen, Klara died, and the same physician reported, "I have never seen anyone so prostrate with grief as Adolf Hitler." The Fuhrer had made similar declarations of affection in *Mein Kampf*, and King was well aware of them. Such devotion, he concluded, was a clear measure of Hitler's essential nobility. Shortly after returning to Canada, King wrote in his diary that Hitler's "Mother's spirit is I am certain his guide and no one who does not understand this relationship – the worship of the highest purity in a mother can understand the power to be derived there from – or the guidance."[11]

Their consistent struggles with interpersonal relationships did not extend to all species. In lieu of affection from humans, King and Hitler developed profoundly heartfelt attachments to their pets. The prime minister's companion, an Irish terrier named Pat, received far more ink in the King diaries than long-time valet Nicol and many other staff members – as well as far more respect. One entry from 1939 called Pat "a god-sent little angel in the guise of a dog ... a dear little saviour, that is what he is in his faithfulness ... asking only to be near one and to share the companionship of perfect trust." In July 1941, as Hitler's armies drove deep into Soviet territory in a dramatic escalation of the war, King rescheduled a cabinet war committee meeting to minister to an ailing Pat, determined not to repeat the mistake of not being at his mother's side when she died. His companion's ensuing demise devastated the prime minister, who sang the hymn "Safe in the Arms of Jesus" to speed the terrier's soul on its journey to "the beyond" (whence King would summon it in later seances).[12]

Pat's replacement, Pat II, proved equally inspirational. King told a 1944 radio audience that his "little friend" had kept him on the path of righteousness. "If I have been true to some of the great causes that I have sought to remain true to," King revealed, "it's been the example of that little fellow that has helped in many, many ways." Pat II's successor Pat III survived the prime minister and was willed to relatives of personal secretary Handy.[13]

Hitler, too, seemed far more engaged by beast than man. As a corporal in the Great War, he adopted a white terrier he named Foxl, whose disappearance late in the war distressed him far more than the death of any human comrade. Twenty-five years later, Hitler made plain that the pain from Foxl's loss was eternal, remarking that "the swine who took him from me doesn't know what he did to me." Later, as Nazi defeats mounted following their surrender at Stalingrad, the Fuhrer lashed out in all directions over the betrayal and cowardice that surrounded him, insisting that his only true friends were Eva Braun and his German Shepherd Blondi.[14]

While Hitler helped his newly betrothed Eva end her own life as the Soviets drew near in April 1945, he could not do the same for Blondi, charging his subordinates with the task while he waited in an adjacent room. When he entered to view the lifeless canine, he became inconsolable. Once again, the point here is not to draw prosaic links between the two men for amusement's sake or suggest they were essentially similar, but to excavate some of the foundations of King's admiration for Hitler. Walther Hewel took pains to convey to King the Fuhrer's fondness for animals and nature, which the prime minister duly noted with admiration. This was a consistent feature of Nazi propaganda meant to humanize Hitler, and a fondness for which the prime minister had a deep respect.[15]

No single attribute, however, impressed King more than a keenness for the mystical. Many leading Nazis shared these affinities, interweaving theories of race supremacy with ancient pagan legends of Norse gods Wotan and Thor and rekindling interest in medieval Germanic symbols, rites, and shrines. Hitler himself would have none of it. Beginning in 1938, he took direct aim at the neo-pagan impulses in the Nazi movement, delivering speeches that emphasized the folly and distraction inherent to this pre-scientific drivel. "What nonsense!" he exclaimed in a private conversation about SS chief Heinrich Himmler's obsession with the occult and ancestor worship. "Here we have at last reached an age that has left all mysticism behind it, and now he wants to start that all over again. We might just as well have stayed with the church. At least it had tradition. To think that I may some day be turned into an SS saint! Can you imagine it? I would turn over in my grave."[16]

King, however, had heard and believed reports that Hitler was a mystic. This the prime minister disclosed to Lady Aberdeen, wife of Canadian governor general Vincent Massey, during a break from the Imperial Conference deliberations. Although he stuck to down-to-earth diplomatic rationales when vetting his planned approach to the Fuhrer with the British cabinet, to Lady Aberdeen King confided his "higher purpose." Nineteenth-century British prime minister William Gladstone had materialized from "the beyond" to implore King "to have a heart-to-heart talk with Hitler," just the latest in a litany of living and spectral humans to nominate the prime minister for the task. Because the Fuhrer belonged to the "elect" who understood the role of unseen forces, he must, King reasoned, be a man of integrity and goodwill.[17]

On this the prime minister was partially correct. At least since the failed Beer Hall Putsch, and despite his tirades against spiritualism, Hitler had harboured an "almost mystical faith in himself as walking with destiny." Despite his hostility towards Christianity, the Fuhrer spoke repeatedly of a "mission," that would fulfil "the work of the Lord." "I go with the certainty of a sleepwalker along the path laid out for me by Providence," he declared at a 1936 rally in Munich.[18] That certainty underwrote the audacious moves against Australia and Czechoslovakia in 1938, and their success redoubled his certainty. His June 1937 conversation with another man of destiny would also reassure the Fuhrer that the path he had charted pointed towards victory.

14

The Interview

The moment had arrived. Mackenzie King had only to walk two blocks up Wilhelmstrasse to get from the Aviation Ministry to the Reichspräsidentenpalais (Reich President's Palace) where he would at last have his conversation with Adolf Hitler. But the prime minister was driven one block past the palace to the Adlon Hotel, for he needed to exchange the black jacket he had worn for his meeting with Göring for the more formal attire reserved for the most important daytime occasions – the "morning dress" popular among upper-class men since the Edwardian era, consisting of a morning coat, waistcoat, striped trousers, silk top hat, and gloves. The significance of the afternoon's discussion, and the attendant necessity of making a positive impression, could not be overemphasized. There was no time for lunch; that could wait until after the meeting.

In 1937 the Fuhrer still conducted much of the business of state from the Old Reich Chancellery, so named only after the Albert Speer–designed New Reich Chancellery was begun in 1938 just to the south on the same block. The older version was a Rococo-style former palace at 77 Wilhelmstrasse purchased by the newly unified German state in 1871. Here, chancellors from Otto von Bismarck through Hitler oversaw the workings of government, and it was here that President Paul von Hindenburg had appointed Hitler chancellor in January 1933. Shortly after that appointment, Hitler commissioned Speer to construct a balcony from which to acknowledge the adoring crowds that assembled on Wilhelmstrasse hoping for a glimpse of their Fuhrer, who had taken up residence in an apartment in the chancellery.[1]

Even with this new veneration pulpit, Hitler did not consider the chancellery worthy of the very saviour of the German people, bristling that the "building looks like the headquarters of a soap company, not the center of the Reich!" Thus he frequently hosted visiting dignitaries at the more stately Reichspräsidentenpalais a few doors to the north, at 73 Wilhelmstrasse, until the new chancellery was completed. The palace, constructed in the 1730s for Prussian diplomat Count Hans Bogislav von Schwerin, was a component of a larger scheme inspired by King Friedrich Wilhelm I of Prussia to line Wilhelmstrasse with lavish aristocratic residences. The ruling Hohenzollerns purchased the estate in the mid-nineteenth century; in 1919, the recently deposed Kaiser Wilhelm II sold it to the new German republic in order to finance the purchase of the Dutch castle to which he and his fifty-nine railway carriages of personal effects had absconded. Weimar president Paul von Hindenburg resided at 73 Wilhelmstrasse from 1919 to his death in 1934, giving the palace its final name; Mackenzie King referred to it as the "Hindenburg Palace," as did many Germans.[2]

In 1939, Hitler moved from the old to the new chancellery and foreign minister Ribbentrop took over the Reichspräsidentenpalais following a garish renovation, solidifying the half-kilometre strip of Wilhelmstrasse south of the British Embassy as the nerve centre of National Socialism. Walking south from the embassy and looking west, one passed the Reichspräsidentenpalais, which abutted Wilhelmstrasse 74–76, headquarters of the German foreign service, which abutted the chancelleries. On the east side of Wilhelmstrasse stood Joseph Goebbels's Propaganda Ministry, along with the ministries of justice and education. Goring's aviation building was south of the New Chancellery, and just beyond this stood the separate headquarters of the Einsatzgruppen, SS, and Gestapo, sites where untold numbers of state enemies were tortured and killed. After reunification, the excavated foundations of this latter cluster of NSDAP surveillance and murder agencies were turned into a permanent outdoor exhibit and memorial called the Topography of Terror.[3]

Hitler's New Chancellery was a colossal, austere granite structure designed to overwhelm and unnerve his visitors. Its central hallway, as Hitler was delighted to point out, was double the length of the Hall of Mirrors at the Palace of Versailles. As bombs began to fall on Berlin, the Fuhrerbunker was constructed under the courtyard shared by the old and new chancelleries, and a shell crater in the courtyard served as the crucible for the gasoline-doused bodies of newlyweds Hitler and Eva Braun as the Soviets neared in April 1945.[4]

14.1 Adaptive (and vindictive) reuse: Hitler's New Reich Chancellery lives on in the red granite stones of the colossal Soviet war memorial in Berlin's Treptower Park. (Author photograph, 2012)

This dense collection of NSDAP administration buildings was, of course, a prime target for Allied bombers and Soviet invaders, and lay in ruins at Germany's surrender. The Soviets triumphantly carted off the red granite stones from the New Chancellery to build war memorials at Tiergarten and Treptower Park, in Berlin's east end. The latter is an immense complex of statues, gates, and interpretive tablets inscribed with Joseph Stalin's homage to Soviet genius and to the eightly thousand troops who died in the two-week assault on Berlin, seven thousand of whom were buried at the memorial grounds. The remains of the chancellery grounds were partially incorporated into the Berlin Wall fortifications, and lay vacant for four decades before the East German government built a complex of stereotypically dreary socialist apartments and small shops over much of the site. This construction project necessitated the full removal of the Fuhrerbunker, a task begun by the Soviets but abandoned because of the bunker's robust construction. Today only its concrete floor remains, buried more than twelve metres below a car park and playground. Just before Germany hosted soccer's World Cup in 2006, officials installed a marker identifying the site. Concerns over pilgrimages by neo-Nazis were trumped by worries that visiting fans would disturb the locals by combing the area looking for clues to the bunker's whereabouts.[5]

When Mackenzie King called in 1937, Hitler received him at the Reichspräsidentenpalais. An honour guard "attired in court dress," as King wrote, greeted the prime minister and secretary Pickering with formality and pomp. The building, he observed, was "like an old palace" (admittedly, this is along the lines of describing the silk top hat he was wearing as "like a silk top hat"). The Canadians were given a tour of Hindenburg's office, where the president's death mask "repose[d] on his desk" and his portrait hung on the wall. They were then presented to members of the Foreign Office and Hitler's personal staffers, and later "conducted upstairs, preceded formally by attendants," and "formally shown into [the] room" where Hitler received visitors.[6] The dignified tone King employs here says much about the gravity with which he regarded the afternoon's encounter, as well as his gratitude for being received in such a ceremonious manner. In what may be a testament to his intensive focus on the upcoming meeting, King did not comment on the pair of sandstone lions flanking the palace entrance on Wilhelmstrasse.

And then he was face-to-face with the man who had so transformed Germany and rattled the international order. Adolf Hitler, in evening dress with white tie, approached King and extended his hand. The Fuhrer welcomed the prime minister "quietly and pleasantly," and then directed him to a chair at a table. Both men, along with interpreter Schmidt, took their seats. Besides Hitler and Schmidt, there were eight other men in the room when the prime minister arrived; these, King was told, were on hand to assist the Fuhrer in his talks with various foreign representatives throughout the day. The *Manchester Guardian* reporter covering King's meeting wrote that those in attendance included Hitler's cabinet ministers Konstantin von Neurath, Otto Meissner, and Vicco von Bülow-Schwandte. Pickering and Hewel then entered, making thirteen in all, a rather large contingent for a "private interview."[7] If King regretted not permitting Ambassador Henderson to join him in order to counterbalance the negotiating teams, he did not admit it.

King opened by proffering a signed "de lux copy" of his own biography, opening it to a picture of "the cottage where I was born" and treating the Reich chancellor to the stock speech professing his intimate connections to the two Berlins and the German land and *Volk*. "Hitler looked at the book in a very friendly way," King dictated later, "and smiling at me as he turned over its pages and looked at its inscription. He thanked me for it." As historian Larry Rose observed, "It is hard to imagine what Adolf Hitler, one of the world's most powerful leaders, his mind bursting with megalomaniacal plans to rip apart the map of Europe, must have thought about spending an afternoon leafing through King's picture book."[8] Whether out of decorum or not knowing how to segue out of the prime minister's little exhibition, Hitler remained silent, waiting for King to take the conversation in a different direction.

The prime minister obliged, turning to the fundamental reason for his visit: he had come to promote "the friendliest of relations" among the countries of the world. King being King, he then proceeded to heap fulsome praise on those responsible for planning the trip and on the "constructive work" he had witnessed on his tour of the Reich. Hitler's initiatives, King assured, were "bound to be followed in other countries to the great advantage of mankind." The Fuhrer feigned modesty, and pointed out that in order to institute these great changes, Germany "had had to go through a difficult time," but that the nation was now reaping the benefits of the Nazi agenda.[9]

King pivoted to his concerns over the level of fear and suspicion gripping much of the world, and defended his reluctant decision to build up Canada's armaments by pointing to the widespread anxiety that Europeans were girding for another "Great war." He explained in no fit of modesty that he had the authority to speak for the generalized fears in his own country, for he possessed "the largest majority a Prime Minister had had in Canada." The last thing Hitler wanted, King submitted, was that the miraculous transformation of Germany he, King, had witnessed on his visit be destroyed – through warfare being the clear implication.[10]

In response, Hitler justified his own nation's "reluctant" rearmament in an extended diatribe that those subjected to his tedious evening monologues could probably recite word for word. The prejudice of the Treaty of Versailles and the calamity it brought to the

German nation could hardly be overstated. His regime was merely rectifying a wrong by building Germany's capacity to match the military strength of its rivals, reincorporating territories unjustly confiscated, and ensuring that Germans would never again be a subject people. The revanchist lecture ended, however, on a reassuring note. Since his government had undone most of the provisions of the despised Treaty of Versailles, the types of aggressive moves that had so riled his neighbours – the occupation of the Ruhr, for instance – "would not be necessary any further." Following this sentence in King's diary, typed out by Pickering, the prime minister added in pencil: "Hitler said to me, my support comes from the people – the people don't want war. – This impressed me very much & a real note of humility."[11] As one who prided himself on his ability to read and respond to popular opinion, Kind found in this an approach to governance he could readily praise.

We have already considered some of the Nazis' motivations for hosting King, and underscored in particular their desire to press the prime minister on whether Britain and its dominions would stand up to future gambles for *Lebensraum*. It is also a certainty that the Germans were employing King as a messenger to the British, knowing he would immediately share with London all he had taken away from his conversations with Reich officials. What message would Hitler most like to convey? The last thing he wanted at this point was a Britain convinced that the Nazis were determined to attack their neighbours. Such a belief would spur even greater efforts among his enemies to re-arm, cement their anti-fascist alliances, and stand firm against further territorial demands and treaty contraventions.

Little surprise, then, that Hitler treated King to a lengthy and seemingly impassioned meditation on his non-violent aims and his abhorrence for bloodshed – a common ruse of the Fuhrer's that Gerhard L. Weinberg described as "propaganda for peace and preparation for war." Hitler promised that Germany would never instigate an armed conflict, that the horrors he witnessed in the Great War he never wished to revisit. "But let me go further," the Fuhrer continued. "Let us assume a war came. What would it mean?" Nothing less, he insisted, than a vast depopulation of Europe and the annihilation of its civilization. Regardless of who prevailed, "all that would be left, would be anarchy." On this Hitler proved prescient, but did he seriously harbour such nihilistic prognostications in 1937? Elsewhere he was wont to frame the relationship between nations and races as a Darwinian struggle for mastery, a struggle that, given his certitude in Aryan supremacy, would usher in a thousand years of German domination over Europe. By the end of the war that – despite his sober vow to King – he would in fact instigate, Hitler insisted on fighting to the last man rather than surrender. The German people, he swore, would pay for their evident weakness with total annihilation, for they had failed the test that he, and nature itself, had assigned.[12] Did he genuinely entertain the possibility of Germany's obliteration even prior to the war, as his comments to King suggest? If so, the megalomania and nihilism already synonymous with the name Hitler achieves another order of magnitude.

While Hitler regaled Mackenzie King with tall tales of his passion for international concord and brotherhood, he did concede that peace was not an inevitability, that if some nations (i.e., England) prevented others (i.e., Germany) from achieving equality and realizing "legitimate aspirations ... then there might be trouble arising." King's response was identical to the one he gave Göring on the same question. Britain did not seek to control or weaken Germany, but was simply a disinterested and skilled referee seeking to prevent "some precipitate step" that could ignite a regional or even global conflict. This Hitler claimed to understand perfectly well, as "the German people felt the same way about the danger of precipitate steps."[13] (Precipitation being in the eye of the beholder, Hitler doubtless had in mind some form of "reckless" military response to fully justified Nazi initiatives).

With his repeated references to precipitate steps, King was, like an old general, fighting the last war. Europe descended into chaos in 1914 after a cascading series of moves and countermoves brought armies to the point of no return: ultimatums, communiques, mobilizations, strategies designed to ensure the fight would occur on enemy, not home, soil – all had conspired to generate a momentum seemingly beyond any single leader's control, a stumble into war for which all principals bore at least some blame. Now in 1937, King was haunted by the possibility that a false move might inadvertently start the dominoes tumbling again. The idea that, having witnessed the carnage of industrial-age conflict first hand, any state would unilaterally launch a premeditated scheme to once again wreck Europe was simply beyond belief. On this, King was not alone. Historian Laurence Rees's examination of the minutes of British cabinet meetings on the 1938 Sudetenland crisis revealed that the Chamberlain government "simply couldn't believe that a chancellor of Germany, and thus leader of a cultured European nation, could actually *want* a war."[14]

The architect of that stupefying scheme then turned to a matter on which both he and King could agree. The League of Nations, by threatening a collective military response to any nation violating its precepts, could, Hitler warned, "make a world war out of anything which should be a local affair." This had been precisely King's grievance at the Imperial Conference: the "automatic" resort to arms against aggressors recommended by some of its members rendered the League the most pressing threat to global stability – "any reference to a threat to peace," as King had warned, "would be equivalent to a declaration of war." Hitler's concerns imply that the prospect of a united and battle-ready League did indeed give him pause, that he feared the incremental treaty violations and land grabs to come might not remain "local affairs." His complaint allowed the prime minister to circle back to Anglo-German relations, as greater bilateral understanding was a far surer route to continental accord, held the prime minister, than inflexible dictates issued by an international body.[15] The King Doctrine was on full view: conflict arose from misunderstanding; frank deliberations among adversarial parties, rather than fixed, impersonal, and legally binding rules, would enhance understanding; expert go-betweens could help various interests construct a relationship based on mutual advantage.

Fortunately for Hitler and the fate of Europe, such a go-between was now before the Fuhrer. Noting that the British and Germans exhibited conspicuous difficulties comprehending one another, King submitted that "some of us in Canada understood both of them better than they did themselves." His country's (or more pointedly, his) experience as a helpful intermediary between the British and the Americans had provided just the sort of know-how that was needed here. The prime minister then provided an example of the type of bridge-building and empathy he could effect by offering a quick tutorial on the English "heart." Citing once again Foreign Minister Neurath's aborted visit to London in light of the *Leipzig* affair, King explained that British dismay over the cancellation arose because the broad global responsibilities borne by such a "great Empire" precluded getting tied up in knots over any single "small incident" like those involving the *Leipzig*. What's more, "an Englishman," King instructed, habitually suppressed his true feelings – the trait, it would appear from the prime minister's personality assessment, lay somewhere between a negotiating ploy and an intrinsic national characteristic. His point was that the British would not have cancelled a planned visit simply because one of their ships had been fired upon, as this would represent an emotional and disproportionate response to a rather insignificant matter.[16] King's exegesis of the Anglo-Saxon mind was a faithful precis of the "stiff-upper-lip" mythos, but he did not catch the internal contradiction in his case study: namely, the bitter response from London when Neurath called off his trip. British vexation about the cancellation, aired frankly in both the press and through diplomatic channels, was to German officials a patently emotional overreaction to a "small incident."

Hitler said as much. He countered that the *Leipzig* incident was in fact "a serious" rather than small event, while his foreign minister's decision to remain in Germany to help manage the crisis was an entirely logical one over which the British had made entirely too much. The Fuhrer then proceeded to tip his hand over the prospects of future negotiations with London, or with any other party for that matter, explaining why the trip's cancellation was of virtually no consequence. "There were two kinds of interviews," Hitler began, one like the one which they were enjoying now – "a free and frank exchange of views" intended to improve mutual understanding. The other was the kind that sought to "settle finally and completely some concrete problems"; in other words, an "interview" aimed at changing minds and behaviours. The latter variety – the British variety – was of no interest to him. On the most pressing issues, his mind was made up. It would, he argued, be as if he advised Canada to sever its association with "the British Isles, and that it was in your interests to do so. I could go on talking for weeks and for years," said Hitler, "but I know that it would be no use."[17] Only in retrospect would King grasp the full significance of this declaration – that no amount of talk, conciliation, goodwill, understanding, empathy or any of the other watchwords for King's mediation techniques would alter the Fuhrer's plans for annexation and conquest. The threat and use of force was the only language that Hitler, the sleepwalker pursuing the path laid out by Providence, would ever heed.

While King seemed to be making little headway in softening the Fuhrer's attitude towards the British, the two leaders once again found common ground when the talk moved to their mutual commitment to peace and the democratic process, and to their anxieties over the press and the threat posed by communism. For a second time Hitler professed that he was simply an instrument of the people, "that he was not like Stalin who could shoot his Generals and other members of his Government who disagreed with him." Again, the Fuhrer's purpose was to deflate the notion that his regime would instigate any aggression, as "the German people did not want war or commitments to possible war in advance." Such advance commitments were the very basis of King's disdain for the idea of collective security, whether exercised through the League of Nations or the British Empire. The prime minister applauded the Fuhrer's stance, noting in his diary that Hitler "was using exactly the same argument as I had use in the Canadian Parliament last Session." In his own face-to-face with Hitler, US journalist H.V. Kaltenborn determined that the Fuhrer had "no capacity for logical or consecutive thought." Mackenzie King found quite the opposite – a man whose rational reflections on domestic and foreign policy mirrored some of the prime minister's own. Then again, Kaltenborn had flustered Hitler by challenging him to justify his anti-semitism and authoritarian rule; King posed no flinty questions about ethics when he sat down with the Fuhrer.[18]

King's apparent willingness to buy the nonsense about the discrepancy between Stalinist authoritarianism and Nazi "democracy," or at least to let the comment pass even in his own diary, is hard to fathom. He knew, of course, that Hitler's regime had outlawed all opposition parties and was notorious for locking up dissidents. More than that, King himself had previously expressed disgust over the episode dubbed "The Night of the Long Knives," a 1934 liquidation of hundreds of perceived enemies within and beyond the Nazi Party. The ruthless purges were met with disbelief and rebuke among politicians and journalists the world over. King's diary from the time took note of the "accounts of Hitler's barbarism" that filled the newspapers, and prophesied that "he will meet his end by means similar to those he has employed."[19] The prime minister could not have forgotten an incident which saw Hitler's henchmen carrying out gangland-style shootings of "Generals and other members of his Government who disagreed with him," the words Hitler used to describe Stalin's purges. Did King come to consider the newspaper reports exaggerations, or misrepresentations of what the Nazis insisted was a legitimate police action against an imminent coup? Even complete fabrications?

Perhaps. The prime minister, as we know, often expressed a low view of the press, blaming journalists for manipulating public opinion and distorting the issues, thereby interfering with the task of governance. Naturally, the Fuhrer concurred. He told King that "the newspapers made no end of trouble" (the *foreign* newspapers that is, as most German dailies had been quickly transformed into Nazi mouthpieces, a fact that alarmed both Colonel Crerar and some of the Germans he had talked with two weeks earlier). The press, groused Hitler, continually raised unrealistic expectations for diplomatic solutions to complex international problems and speculated wildly on what would be achieved at upcoming meetings between various governments. The inevitable public disappointment that followed meant that it was often better, Hitler maintained, not to hold any such meetings at all.[20]

King could hardly object to this synopsis of fourth-estate meddling and distortions. The trip to Germany itself had furnished yet another example, for had he not seen with his own eyes a Nazi government and program that was far more humane, equitable, and sensible than the one depicted in the English-language newspapers? If war came, as he had noted earlier in his diary, it would be the fault of the press and their jingoistic campaign of misinformation. King had a seconder in the *Diplomatische Korrespondenz*, official organ of the German Foreign Office. "It is especially fortunate," editors wrote of King's visit, "that an important member of the British Empire, at a time when the condition and aims of the German nation are being misrepresented and falsely represented abroad, has an opportunity to observe the German people's desire and will to build up peacefully their country."[21]

King's silence on the purported divergence between the workings of the Stalin and Hitler regimes was also underwritten by his singular and lifelong aversion for communism. And once again, nothing he had witnessed on his German tour had suggested anything like a moral equivalence between fascism and the seditious, atheistic materialism peddled by the Bolsheviks. Indeed, the kind, soft-spoken chancellor before him, with his obvious dedication to the common man, seemed the farthest thing from the pitiless despots spewed up by the Soviet system. The Fuhrer, reported King, presented a "composed exterior with a deep emotional nature within." Far from the volatile, gesticulating clown depicted in the foreign press, the humble servant now conversing with the prime minister was "passive," "calm," "smiling," "thoughtful," "very nice," and "sweet." He looked King in the eye and spoke frankly. He was "distinctly a mystic," a "Joan of Arc" who sought to deliver Germany from tyranny.[22]

And he was a marvellous physical specimen to boot. Hitler "had a sort of appealing and affectionate look in his eyes," King recorded.

His face was "prepossessing," "his skin was smooth," and his eyes had a "liquid quality about them which indicates keen perception and profound sympathy." King, quick to discern nascent tyrants among his political foes back home, found nothing of the sort here. This was certainly no Stalin. (Perhaps Hitler had resolved to tone down the histrionics for foreign visitors after observing how they portrayed him in the press. After meeting Hitler in 1935, American correspondent Pierre Huss reported that "he is a fanatic, every inch of him, going into a passion or fury when the occasion demands."[23])

The Fuhrer, of course, was adamant that his government bore absolutely no relation to the one based in Moscow, and as the world's most fanatical communist-hater, was bound to assign them full blame for Europe's troubles and justify his own countermoves as essentially anti-Marxist. Accordingly, he closed the meeting with a plaintive, wrenching plea for a pan-European, anti-Bolshevik solidarity. If only the Soviets were removed from the equation! A productive relationship between Germany, Britain, and France would certainly follow. (King had stated the same in his musings on the European situation while attending the Imperial Conference.) Why, Hitler implored, had France made an alliance with Russia? (The decidedly anti-Nazi "Franco-Soviet Treaty of Mutual Assistance" had been signed in 1935.) Why could England not comprehend the dreadful menace posed by communism, or the heroic stand he and his followers had taken against it? Had the Nazis not come to power, Germany would today be another Spain, wracked by a civil war incited by Moscow that could ignite the whole continent. In a word, Hitler was to the world an inestimable, and completely unappreciated gift.[24] (That Hewel had treated King to a near-verbatim line of argument lends credence to the notion that the former had a special capacity for remaining conscious during Hitler's monotonous evening rants.)

The King-Hitler talk had been scheduled to last just thirty minutes. Such brevity for a meeting with a visiting head of state says much about the significance the Fuhrer placed on German-Canadian relations, and on meaningful dialogue with foreign governments in general by 1937. Nevertheless, it was now nearing two o'clock; the discussion had gone on for over an hour, and some in the room were beginning to give Hitler signals that other duties awaited. Sensing this, King hurriedly injected his closing arguments. First, Britain was a friend. As with Göring, he informed Hitler that the recent Imperial Conference was the most pro-German he had yet experienced, and that

Neville Chamberlain was a wise and considerate statesman possessing a "broad outlook." Nevile Henderson and the newly crowned British sovereign, he assured, were of similar mind. The Fuhrer "was very pleased" by this, King noted. Second, King offered the vague warning that if Britain or other regions of the Empire were endangered by aggression, "there is little doubt that all parts would resent it." The fact that Henderson was not present was not a sign of any imperial disunity, but of Britain's confidence that Canada shared the home country's priorities in international affairs. Finally, the prime minister assured Hitler that improved understanding was inevitable if patience and dialogue were maintained.[25]

The interview was over. As the prime minister rose to leave, Hitler thanked him for the visit and handed him a gift. It was a framed photograph of the Fuhrer gazing imperiously towards the horizon, with a personal inscription to "His Excellency the Canadian Prime Minister Dr. W.L. Mackenzie King." King shook Hitler's hand warmly, enthusing that he would always value the memento and reiterating that he was "strongly in accord" with Hitler's great work on behalf of Germany and humanity as a whole. Then another handshake, smiles, looks of affection given and received. King's ultimate conclusion? "My sizing up of the man as I sat and talked with him was that he is one who truly loves his fellow-men, and his country, and would make any sacrifices for their good."[26]

As King and Pickering exited the Reichspräsidentenpalais, they were met by an honour guard and a cluster of journalists and bystanders. One reporter snapped a photograph of a very relaxed looking King. Reporting from the scene, the *Toronto Star's* Matthew Halton wrote that the prime minister was "obviously impressed and apparently moved." King's combined sense of relief and satisfaction was, in fact, immense. A crucial meeting that he had been pondering for a year, and over which he had been fretting for weeks, had concluded. It had been a good one. As evidenced by the throng of journalists, the world was paying attention. King was now virtually certain that all would be well, a state of affairs helped along in no small measure by his own labours. For once again, his mediation efforts had proven successful: he had been both empathetic and frank with Hitler in demonstrating that patience, understanding, and peace were the only rational solutions to Germany's domestic and international challenges. The message seemed to sink in. King noted that at key junctures in his presentation,

14.2 Adolf Hitler's gift to Mackenzie King. Hamilton Fish Armstrong, editor of the US journal *Foreign Affairs*, reported that during his own interview with the chancellor Hitler kept his eyes "fixed on the upper distance, which made it seem as though he were communicating with God."[27] (Library and Archives Canada, C-011452)

14.3 Flanked by an SS honour guard, Mackenzie King poses on the steps of the Reichspräsidentenpalais following his meeting with Hitler. Walther Hewel stands three steps above at left. (Library and Archives Canada, PA-119008; also Bundesarchiv Bild 183-C09362, Müller)

the Fuhrer had nodded, smiled "in a knowing way," or "give[n] a look of recognition."[28]

Although they had not discussed any concrete measures for moderating European tensions – arms reduction, for instance, or the return of Germany to the League of Nations, or a commitment to future, high-level talks among rival powers (all of which the prime minister had called for in an uncharacteristically forceful speech before the League the previous fall) – King had not come to Berlin with any diplomatic objectives other than to establish personal contacts and bolster international goodwill. As long as world leaders developed relationships in face-to-face encounters, the details would fall into place. And his own visit was laying the groundwork. King felt certain he had made the kind of connection he had yearned for on the train from Paris to Berlin three days earlier, when he had written of "seeking the entrance to his [Hitler's] heart which I will seek to find in my conversation with him." The *Star's* Halton believed King may have indeed forged a special bond with the Fuhrer, although coming from this early and eternal adversary of Hitler and his movement, Halton's words carried a backhanded critique: "They say in Berlin," he wrote, "that Adolph Hitler never gives more than 15-minute interviews unless he meets 'a sympathetic soul.'"[29]

Befitting the magnitude of an appointment with the Fuhrer, the prime minister, Pickering, and Hewel were chauffeured the three short blocks north to the Adlon, where they enjoyed lunch al fresco. Afterward, King finally had time for a much-needed rest. He picked up his Bible and read from Psalm 91: "Thou shalt tread upon the lion and the adder, the young lion and the dragon shalt thou trample under feet."[30] He had indeed prevailed.

15

Savouring the Triumph,
with an Assist from Verdi

Like most cult leaders, Third Reich officials took considerable pains
to ensure that their potential converts were almost always accompanied, and that they ingested a constant, heavy diet of indoctrination.
Accordingly, at 5 p.m. on day three Mackenzie King was shuttled off
to yet another homage to the Nazis' glorious reinvention of Germany,
this one at the Berlin headquarters of the Hitlerjugend. More speeches
about youth training. More "strength through joy." More "beauty of
work." More circumspection and cynicism would have led the assid-
uous diarist to begin penning the literary equivalent of eye-rolls and
sighs over the monotony and blatant evangelism suffusing the repetitive exhibitions. King, however, continued to marvel, and did not
record any suspicions or fatigue over the highly scripted messaging
delivered by his Nazi docents. "As was the case wherever we went,"
he noted of the evening's excursion, "some young leader was detailed
to meet us at the Hotel, and explain what we were to see and the movement generally. I found all of these young men very frank, very alert,
clean looking, active minded, enthusiastic young people. There was a
splendid order and efficiency about everything we saw."[1] For his part,
and as was his custom, Colonel Crerar was considerably more sardonic
about the relentless and obvious propaganda he had absorbed a few
days previous, the flagrant distortions directed at visitor and citizen
alike:

> In moving around Berlin one seemed to meet a personally (Nazi) con-
> ducted party of sightseers at every turn. Groups of small boys, or girls,
> or adults of both sexes, each with obvious guides were to be met at all
> times of the day. Instruction in Germany's past greatness, in its present

emancipation and its future and inevitable expansion, seems to be organized from cradle to grave ... At the moment no pains or expense are being
spared to impress upon all who live in, or visit, Germany the national improvement which has resulted from the first four years of Hitler's leadership ... I also visited an exhibition commemorating the Nazi rise to power
and which was composed almost entirely of gruesome souvenirs of Communist "atrocities" and Nazi "martyrs." Photographs of street riots, wax
figures (not complimentary) of Red "terrorists," samples of Communist
weapons, were all displayed with explanatory placards contrasting the
terrible days of earlier years with the law, order and good government of
the present day.[2]

The Hitlerjugend headquarters was located in an 860,000-square-foot
former department store at the intersection of Torstrasse and Prezlauer
Allee in the Mitte district. Built in 1928 by Jewish retailers, this V-shaped
edifice, whose elegant curvature made it one of Berlin's finest examples
of Art Deco architecture, was soon confiscated as part of the NSDAP
aryanization program. Nazi officials chose to house the youth organization here in large part because the massive tombstone marking the
grave of twenty-two-year-old Horst Wessel, an SA street hooligan executed by members of the communist party, lay directly across the street.
Adulation for the young fascist martyr was deepened by the fact that
he had written *Kampflied* (Fight Song), a clichéd marching number renamed the *Horst-Wessel-Lied* and made one of the two official anthems
of Nazi Germany in 1933.[3]

Following the war, East German officials transformed the building into
the headquarters of their state's ruling political party, the Sozialistische
Einheitspartei Deutschlands (SED, Socialist Unity Party of Germany),
whose top brass from the general secretary on down had offices here.
It was later converted into the Institute for Marxism-Leninism, keeper
of the SED archives and research centre for DDR court historians. In
the 1990s, the descendants of the original store owners recovered the
property under a reparations program initiated in West Germany in
1952 but only extended to the East after reunification. It was eventually
purchased by a London-based chain of private clubs for arts and media
types, and subjected to a complete gutting and remodelling. Today
passers-by can spot the tips of umbrellas and the heads of sunbathers
surrounding the rooftop pool of the former Hitlerjugend headquarters
but, uncharacteristically for modern Berlin, nothing that would commemorate the building's troubled past.[4]

15.1 Meet the new boss: The former Hitlerjugend headquarters fell within
the Soviet occupation zone, and East German communists wasted no time
in repurposing the spacious building as the headquarters of East Germany's
ruling SED party. This photograph from December 1949 conveys the SED's
well-wishes on the occasion of their overlord's seventieth birthday; their
salutation reads "The leader and teacher of humanity in the fight for peace,
democracy and socialism." Although he claimed otherwise, Stalin had
actually turned seventy-one; like the SED and others of the Orwellian school
of leadership, this saviour of humanity simply revised facts – like his date
of birth – that inconvenienced him. (Bundesarchiv, Bild 183-S91405, Funck,
Heinz)

King enjoyed tea here with Hitlerjugend officials and Deputy Führer
Rudolf Hess, although it seems King did not have an opportunity for an
intimate tête-à-tête with the latter. The prime minister's 29 June diary
does not mention the long-time, fanatical Hitler stalwart to whom the
Fuhrer dictated much of *Mein Kampf*, and chances are good that any

private exchange between Hess and King would have progressed in short order to their mutual enthusiasm for "things unseen" (a conversation King's diary was most unlikely to omit). In truth, Hess appears to have anticipated the "New Age" movement by several decades: by his mid-twenties he had committed himself to a vegetarian diet of biodynamic foods and had begun dabbling in anthroposophy, herbal remedies, astrology, and the occult. Some time around the end of the First World War, Hess joined like-minded seekers in Germany's Thule Society, a cover for the secret Germanenorden Walvater von Heilige Gral (German Order of the All-Father of the Holy Grail). This loopy band of antisemitic Odin-worshippers was committed to the study and proliferation of "Ariosophy," or Aryan wisdom. In 1916 the Thule Society made the swastika its official symbol, and two years later created the political party that in 1920 Hitler would transform into the NSDAP. Like King, Hess was to embark on his own ill-starred peace initiative when in 1941 he flew solo to Scotland to negotiate with British officials, who immediately imprisoned the Deputy Führer for the duration of the war and then shipped him off to the post-war tribunal at Nuremberg. The doltish peace mission, observed historian Mattias Gardell, "has variously been interpreted as insanity, a failed attempt to impress Hitler, and a desperate attempt by the Thule Society to correct an Ariosphic revolution gone astray."[5]

Following his tea with Hess and Hitlerjungend bosses, King was driven back to the Adlon Hotel. He had an opera date at eight that evening with Göring, but the prime minister was still exhilarated over his face-to-face with Hitler and decided to go for a walk rather than rest. He headed west to Tiergarten where he chanced upon (admittedly, a phrase King would summarily reject) a "statue of the wounded lion with its mate and cubs. I noticed the date it was constructed as 1874, the year of my birth." Lions again, and numbers, and the circle of life, as King, with the assistance of some locals, located the Weber residence south of Tiergarten where he had boarded thirty-seven years earlier. He returned to the Adlon at 7:20, estimating that he had walked for five or six miles in all – no mean feat for a plump sixty-two-year-old not given to physical activity and who had already endured a demanding three days in Berlin. "During this walk," King reported, "I enjoyed exceedingly being in the woods, and listening to the birds singing, and felt a real sense of rejoicing from the way in which the interview had gone and the good, I believed, it was going to serve."[6]

15.2 Following the war, which cleared Tiergarten of most of its trees, hungry Berliners transformed the park into a vegetable garden. The Victory Column on the horizon, erected to commemorate German triumphs in the nineteenth-century wars of unification, adds cruel satire to the spectacle of deprivation. (Bundesarchiv, Bild 183-H0813-0600-009, Dryer)

Eight years later the woods and the birds were gone and the park was a smouldering moonscape, stripped of most of its trees through relentless air raids. Scavengers seeking firewood then cut down nearly all of the rest, and under British orders, hungry Berliners divided the park into vegetable garden plots. Most of the dozens of statues in the park experienced at least some bomb damage. Some monuments to military heroes were removed and buried by locals who feared the occupying Americans would demolish them; they were finally unearthed in 1993. West Berlin's first mayor, Ernst Reuter, called the destruction of the beloved park "the most painful wound that Berlin had suffered from the war."[7]

The Berlin Zoo in the southwest corner of Tiergarten was not spared. In April 1945 the grounds were littered with burned-out vehicles, charred trees, bomb craters, wreckage from its once-splendid exhibition spaces, and mounds covering the corpses of twenty-eight zoo employees and untold animals. Only ninety-one of the zoo's roughly four thousand creatures survived; from all accounts, none were bison. The reforestation of Tiergarten began in 1949, and would take a decade to complete. If King walked the same route today, he would encounter not only a restored and expanded zoo and a revivified landscape of natural beauty and refuge, but two new Tiergarten memorials. Both are dedicated to victims of National Socialism, and are situated at the park's east end: one honours gays and lesbians, the other the Sinti and Roma peoples.[8] After exiting the park and crossing Ebertstrasse (in 1937, Hermann-Göring-Strasse) to return to Pariser Platz and the Adlon, our fictional contemporary King would then pass what some consider contemporary Berlin's most evocative site, and others its most deficient: *Denkmal für die Ermordeten Juden Europas* – in English, Memorial to the Murdered Jews of Europe.

Opened in 2005, this field of 2,711 grey concrete slabs takes up nearly five acres of what was previously the heart of the Nazi bureaucracy, including a portion of the former chancellery grounds. The DDR incorporated this area into the notorious "death strip" of the Berlin Wall, and thus the space lay vacant at the time of reunification. While laid out in a grid pattern, the memorial's slabs are of different heights and tilt at random angles, and the terrain on which they lie is undulating. To wander through the site is to become disoriented in a claustrophobic, graveyard-like maze, and many visitors find the experience deeply and aptly haunting.[9]

Others condemn the memorial for being too abstract – the number of slabs, its architect Peter Eisenman maintains, was chosen randomly, and the exhibit does not include any interpretive text. Some consider it too small to represent the scale of the NDSAP's methodical murder campaign (*New Yorker* writer Richard Brody suggested six million slabs scattered throughout Berlin and environs), while others call it too large to protect from vandals, partiers, and neo-Nazis. Still others say it is superfluous given the presence of concentration camp memorials in the vicinity.[10] What the site and the discourse surrounding it reveal without question is the impossibility of adequately conveying in any

15.3 Peter Eisenman's 2005 Memorial to the Murdered Jews of Europe, facing east. (Author photograph, 2012)

commemorative site the gravity of the Holocaust, as well as a nation nonetheless willing to commit significant resources and public space to the most sordid aspects of its past. This is, after all, a massive expanse at the very heart of Germany's national capital.

Mackenzie King, of course, did not have to confront the dilemmas raised by the memorial; he was gearing up instead for an evening with one of the individuals whose actions obliged its construction. His very eventful day ended with a trip to the Staatsoper (State Opera) with Hermann Göring for a performance of Giuseppe Verdi's *Un ballo in maschera* – Italians being one of the few nationalities still in the Nazis' good books by 1937. The opera house, constructed in the early 1740s on Unter den Linden, five blocks east of the Adlon and near the Stadtschloss, was reconstructed after fire destroyed

15.4 The Nazis' notorious burning of "degenerate" books took place in the courtyard of Berlin's Staatsoper, a structure visible in faint outline in the background of this photograph. (Bundesarchiv, Bild 102-14599, Pahl, Georg)

the original in 1843. It was in the Opernplatz, the courtyard of the Staatsoper, that Joseph Goebbels had presided over the infamous book-burning of May 1933, declaring to a rabid crowd of forty thousand that "the era of extreme Jewish intellectualism is at an end." Associated Press correspondent Louis P. Lochner witnessed the event with great foreboding, declaring in a widely published despatch that "the whole civilized world was shocked" by the incineration of "books of authors displeasing to the Nazis." S. Miles Bouton of the *Baltimore Sun*, heretofore derided by Lochner as "an ardent Nazi," was utterly transformed by what he saw of NSDAP tactics and began warning "that the truth is ten times worse than the reports." In 1995,

15.5 Micha Ullman's 1995 memorial to the book-burning. (Author photograph, 2011)

a memorial designed by Israeli artist Micha Ullman was unveiled on the site. It consists of a window onto bare underground bookshelves with space for twenty thousand books – roughly the number burnt here in 1933.[11]

The opera house itself suffered extensive bomb damage as early as the spring of 1941, but in an especially macabre variation of "the show must go on," the Nazis rebuilt damaged sections and continued to sponsor performances here until late 1944, by which point much of the surrounding Mitte district had been ground into rubble. Then on 3 February of the following year, American planes, by now engaged in brazen daylight precision bombing against the increasingly defenseless enemy, unleashed the most devastating attack of the war on the German capital. Much of the government quarter, with its cluster of Nazi offices,

15.6 Cows graze outside the Staatsoper in the summer of 1945. The front
elevation of the building looks reasonably intact, save for the bullet holes
and the windows that reconstruction brigades bricked over following a 1941
bombing. However, the elevated roof to the rear, which covered the stage, is
gone. (Bundesarchiv, Bild 183-D0217-0002-007)

was razed; the Old and New Reich Chancelleries suffered multiple direct hits, with the former rendered completely unusable; after this, Hitler spent most of his remaining days underground. The same massive
raid delivered two direct hits to the Staatsoper that proved too much
for reconstruction crews, but in order to stave off the aura of impending defeat, upcoming performances were relocated to still-functioning
Berlin halls rather than cancelled. In spite of the bombing, there was
enough of the Staatsoper's skeleton – and not enough of its association
with Nazism – for DDR officials to begin reconstruction in the early

15.7 The Staatsoper undergoing renovations in summer 2017. (Author photograph)

1950s, this time with a kitschy variation on the original baroque interior described by locals as "socialist rococo."[12]

At the Staatsoper, the regal treatment of His Excellency the Prime Minister of Canada continued. Upon arriving, King wrote, he "was received by a couple of members of General Goring's staff who were more than politeness and kindness itself." He sat in the royal box next to Göring, who had taken personal control of the opera in 1933, the same year the Nazis forced all Jewish conductors to resign their positions at Berlin opera houses. Pickering and Hewel also took seats in the box. The prime minister scanned the room, savouring the hum that passed through the audience upon the entry of the aviation boss and his special guest. The performance itself King judged superb in every respect: acting, staging, singing (though he refrained, in his fashion, from including any of the details).[13]

Between acts the entourage was taken to a "special supper" also attended by British ambassador Henderson's second-in-command Sir

George Ogilvie-Forbes and his wife Clare. During the meal King was especially taken by a Göring staffer who "spoke about secret forces at work to bring about better conditions after this period of stress and strain," but the prime minister would have been better served by the counsel of Ogilvie-Forbes. Unlike Henderson and King, the junior diplomat saw through Hitler's "man-of-peace" charade and was sickened by the Nazis' Jewish policies, which as early as 1938 Ogilvie-Forbes was predicting were pointing towards mass extermination. When he temporarily spelt off an ailing Henderson as top diplomat in Berlin a year after his dinner with King, Ogilvie-Forbes would prove instrumental, wrote historian Bruce Strang, in "help[ing] to undermine Chamberlain's often inaccurate views, and to create the climate of moral revulsion and the heightened sense of danger in which the Cabinet operated."[14] Much time and room for manoeuvre, however, had been squandered.

Verdi's *Un ballo in maschera* typically runs to nearly three hours, including intermission, so King likely returned to the Adlon a little before midnight. Still too wound up to turn in, he began jotting down handwritten observations of this most extraordinary day. He recapped all of the prophetic scriptural passages, the signs, the concurrences, including yet another discovered at dinner: Sir Ogilvie-Forbes's father, it seems, was the present owner of a property in Tyrie, Scotland, once owned by King's paternal grandfather. It was "a complete circle – the completed round ... now I the grandson with the owner's son in Berlin at the time of this mission."[15]

The gravity of the day's events, the conviction that he made a breakthrough with Hitler, the pageantry and honorifics dedicated to him, the late hour, possibly drinks at dinner – all may have played a part in stimulating one of the more megalomaniacal paragraphs in King's fifty-seven years of diarizing. After bringing mostly neglected valet Nicol back into the action to laud his boss's discernment in reaching out to Hitler – "it was your vision," Nicol eulogized and King underlined – King recorded Pickering's comments putting it all into perspective. "I imagine, Mr. King," offered the secretary, "this is the greatest day of your life." Who was King to disagree? "Certainly," he wrote, "it would seem to be the day for which I was born." All the living and deceased emissaries urging a visit to Berlin and guiding his efforts had proven most wise. To top it all off, the evening's opera performance revealed itself to be nothing less than a tribute to the prime minister's victory for peace realized earlier that day. When the entire ensemble took the stage "to fill the entire Opera House with harmony and joy" during

Un ballo in maschera's closing chorus, King understood that the performers represented the earthly and spiritual "cloud of witnesses" who had assisted him – the protagonist of the drama – in fulfilling his destiny. "The last scene," he wrote, "seemed to bring invisible numbers of persons who joined in the chorus which closed the life of one who was playing the leading part. A triumphal end to it all." He finished the day's entry with a benediction: "May God's blessing rest upon this day and the nations of the world – and his peace be theirs."[16]

16

Taking Leave

What could top the realization that an opera by one of history's most renowned composers and staged by an illustrious opera company was actually about you? With such heady thoughts buzzing, King enjoyed dreams filled with similar victories and accolades. Example: He enters Ottawa's Parliament Building, which appears to be under renovation, and puts down the valise he is carrying, the one valet Nicol had purchased for him in Europe. On departing, he discovers that the valise is empty; he has mistakenly picked up a stranger's satchel, and the stranger his. The upshot? There has been an exchange of ideas, and those King furnished have led to changed minds and progress. In that moment of revelation, he sees that the renovation project to the Parliament is now complete. "The improvement in the building was clear – it was the work of reconstruction for which I was responsible."[1]

Relieved and exhausted after his big day, King had slept well, the tartan and the Lord Grey biography once again smartly fulfilling their responsibilities. After rising he jotted down a draft statement for the press, ate breakfast, and then dictated his summary of the previous day to Pickering. The diary entry, replete with especially detailed recollections of his talks with Göring and Hitler, filled thirteen and a half typed pages. King found the dictation "rather fatiguing," a sentiment his transcriber doubtless shared in spades, though of course wouldn't have dared to record.[2]

Then King was on the move again, treated to yet another testament to the splendour of the Nazi workers' paradise – this time, by visiting the main branch of the Allgemeine Elektricitäts-Gesellschaft (AEG, General Electricity Company) for morning roll call. Once again, Robert Ley

16.1 The AEG's *Beamtentor* (clerk's gate) is all that remains of the eastern portion of what was once a sprawling factory complex. (Author photograph, 2017)

accompanied King on his tour, and once again, Ley, a silent character in this ominous Strindbergian drama, didn't make the cut when it came time for King to recount the day's events to secretary Pickering.[3]

Naturally, the selection of AEG was not arbitrary. Along with other large German companies, AEG's contributions to the Nazis were instrumental in bringing Hitler to power. The quid pro quo involved lucrative contracts in support of the National Socialist rearmament program, and once war began, the vast reduction in overheads facilitated by the use of slave labourers, some twelve million of whom were compelled to work for companies throughout the Third Reich. In the 1950s, AEG joined other German companies I.G. Farben, Krupp, Siemens, and Rheinmet in a one-time payment of seventy-five million Deutschmarks to survivors.[4] The forced labour carried out by Polish prisoners at the

16.2 Berlin memorial plaque to slave labourers at AEG headquarters, surrounded by bullet holes from the Battle of Berlin. A translation of the inscription reads: "At this factory during the Second World War, AEG employed Polish forced labourers deported to Germany. They too are victims of Nazi rule." (Author photograph, 2017)

AEG plant King toured is today commemorated in a plaque on one of the remaining buildings at the Berlin complex, a once massive production facility that today occupies less than half its original footprint.

A photograph of the prime minister's visit to AEG shows him in excellent spirits, striding across the grounds with officials of similar comportment through a triumphal arch of arms raised in Nazi salutes. The next day, King finally acknowledged the seemingly omnipresent but neglected Ley, writing him a thank you note for a tour that "revealed, in striking fashion, the work which you and those associated with you are seeking to do in effecting important improvement alike

16.3 King and Pickering, in civilian clothes, tour the Allgemeine Elektricitäts-
Gesellschaft grounds with Robert Ley (holding white gloves), head of the
German Labour Front, and sports chief Hans von Tschammer und Osten, far
right. Behind them is a sizeable mural promoting the German Labour Front's
Kraft durch Freude program. (Library and Archives Canada, PA-119013)

in industrial welfare and in the well being of the workers throughout
the land." Yet again, his official commendations were virtually synonymous with his private ruminations. And yet again, Pollyanna King's
facile celebration of the new Germany and its booming economy was
gainsaid by his foil, wet blanket Harry Crerar. The colonel wrote disap-
provingly of the exorbitant corporate tax rates imposed in order to stuff
Nazi coffers, of the excessive bureaucratization of the commercial sector, of the preferentialism afforded the armaments industry, and of the
coercion from Reich officials to invest company profits in government

bonds. "It would be unwise to assume," he wrote, in a riposte to those who simplistically championed the Nazi miracle, "... that the present organization of the 'Dritte Reich' is anything to fall down before and worship."[5] Here, Crerar was likely drawing on economic information provided by Deutsch Bank managing director Oswald Rösler, a professional contact of Crerar's friend Sir Edward Peacock of the Bank of England. Rösler had been deeply troubled by the firing of the bank's Jewish directors in 1933, and his ongoing chariness about the Hitler government can be measured in part by his arrest and trial as a suspected conspirator in Operation Valkyrie – a charge dropped for lack of evidence.[6]

Following his factory tour, King headed to the British Embassy for an 11 a.m. debriefing with Henderson. The stakes were high, as the two men were huddling over precisely what King should say to the newspapers about his deliberations with National Socialist brass. The press, Henderson agreed, was a real danger to the international situation, and any disclosure about what had gone on behind closed doors demanded the most careful wording. King gave Henderson a synopsis of the previous day's discussions and his analysis of the overall situation. The ambassador "was in pretty much entire agreement" with the prime minister's sanguine views of Göring, Hitler, and the prospects for peace and cooperation.[7]

King read aloud his draft press statement. It was laudatory in its assessment of the Nazi program and its leaders, and optimistic about future dealings with Germany. Henderson liked what he heard, and suggested even more praise for "the good features" of National Socialism, particularly in labour relations. Frankly, Henderson was looking for redemption. He was still smarting from the thrashing he had received from the British press over his recent address to the Deutsch-Englische Gesellschaft applauding aspects of Nazism, and was baffled by Foreign Minister Anthony Eden's limp defence of his ambassador in the face of the Labour Party's withering attacks over the same speech. Now, in King, Henderson had a respected seconder, one who had likewise seen enough to deliver correctives to the relentlessly negative assessments of the Nazis back in the home country. The ambassador thanked King for taking the time to see Germany for himself, and urged the Canadian prime minister to offer the impressions collected on the trip to Neville Chamberlain soon as possible. By now, King had warmed considerably to Sir Nevile, judging it "particularly fortunate that Henderson is the Ambassador at the present time."[8]

In the end, King delivered to reporters a prepared statement that was both wholly positive and, in its emphasis on the need for personal relationships and its lack of specifics, wholly King:

> If I might express what I feel most deeply, it is that I wish more such visits to one another's countries could be paid by those having to do with public affairs and the circle of personal friendly contacts thereby widened. I would not confine this hope to public men, but would include those in all countries who have at heart mankind's well-being. The sole purpose of my visit has been gaining and promoting more in the way of understanding, friendship and goodwill, and in all three my expectations were more than fulfilled.[9]

King had one more call to make before his train would depart for Brussels later that day. As the prime minister served as his own secretary of state for external affairs, this was a meeting with his opposite number in that role, Baron Konstantin von Neurath, foreign minister of Germany. Born in 1873 to a Prussian aristocratic family with a history of diplomatic service, the baron completed a law degree before gaining employment with the German Foreign Office in 1901. When the First World War began, the forty-one-year-old Neurath enlisted as an officer, was badly wounded, and was awarded the Iron Cross. While no great supporter of republicanism, he agreed to serve in a variety of Weimar-era diplomatic postings – including to Britain, a land of which he grew especially fond – out of what he considered a proper Prussian lord's *noblesse oblige*. In 1932 he was recalled from London to Berlin to serve as foreign minister in Chancellor Franz von Papen's cabinet, a reactionary ensemble of blue bloods more to Neurath's taste than the officials who had led earlier, more populist Weimar regimes. Called the "cabinet of barons," it was ridiculed by those unimpressed with Papen's increasingly autocratic governance as the "cabinet of monocles."[10]

Nearing sixty by the time of this appointment, the well-mannered and dignified foreign minister expressed grave misgivings about the rising Nazi Party's thuggery and cultural philistinism. He was, on the other hand, wholly in line when it came to the party's contempt for Jews and the Treaty of Versailles, enmities all too common among veterans who swallowed the canard that their great sacrifice had been frittered away by a Weimar government beholden to international Jewry. Concord with the National Socialist agenda on these matters and his sense of duty led Neurath to consent to Hindenburg's plea that he stay on as foreign minister under new chancellor Hitler. The goal was to "box in" the volatile and untested leader by loading his cabinet with non-Nazis. Moderates within and beyond Germany rejoiced at the announcement that only three of Hitler's eleven cabinet posts had been handed to Nazis, believing the fascists had been defanged. The British began referring to the new chancellor as a "man of straw."[11]

Hitler quickly escaped the box, completing the detonation of the republic begun under Papen, liquidating the opposition, and accelerating the repression of German Jews. While Neurath was troubled by the Fuhrer's methods, he did nothing. It is a truism to say that Hitler succeeded because of collective inaction among those with the sense and the capacity to encumber his ascent, but to historian J.L. Heineman, Neurath's failure stands out. Because of the foreign minister's esteem among German elites and his close ties to President Hindenburg in particular, Heineman offered the tantalizing hypothesis that "during the first eighteen months [of Hitler's chancellorship] Neurath's resignation would have triggered a presidential crisis which Hitler might not have survived." Within a year of King's visit, Neurath would be shown the door as foreign minister – not out of ideological dissonance with the Fuhrer, but because the baron was convinced that his leader's brinksmanship over Czechoslovakia would bring war. But by then, the Fuhrer cult had rendered Hitler untouchable in the eyes of the German people, and the forced resignation did the regime no harm.[12] Counterfactual history is a notoriously inexact science, but here is a compelling illustration of the "First they came/and I did not speak out" maxim, wherein principled action by even a single individual might have infinitely altered the course of events.

Nazism's foes would eventually come for Neurath, and he would join other top Nazis in the prisoners' dock at Nuremberg. The charges laid against him involved a similar failure of backbone and conscience in a subsequent posting under Hitler. Still a loyal company man after leaving the Foreign Office, he accepted a posting as *Reichsprotektor* of Moravia and Bohemia following the successful dismemberment of Czechoslovakia. While occasionally raising objections to the brutality of the SS in the region under his "protection," he expended considerably more energy hunting big game in the Moravian forest. On account of his age, and because his role in Nazi atrocities was considered lesser than that of others tried at Nuremberg, he received a fifteen-year sentence rather than a death penalty for SS atrocities perpetrated under his watch.[13] Standing trial alongside some of history's most appalling killers, in other words, may well have saved his life.

Mackenzie King's weakness for decorum, the high born, and all things English boded well for his encounter with Neurath. So, too, did the fact that the men were contemporaries – at age sixty-four, the German minister was the only Nazi official the sixty-two-year-old King met on the trip who was his senior. They sat down in Neurath's office at Wilhelmstrasse 76, a building just north of the Old Chancellery that served as both the foreign minister's residence and the headquarters of the German foreign office he oversaw. As with the Reichspräsidentenpalais, King described the building, a two-hundred-year-old palace where iron chancellor Bismarck also once lived and worked, as "like an old palace."[14]

The prime minister was immediately taken by Neurath, judging him "an exceedingly pleasant and able man" whom King "like[d] exceedingly." Neurath's pleasant manner, facility with English, and apparent Anglophilia hit all the right notes. He was, King observed with some precision, "rather of a school different than most of the other advisors of Hitler": more mature, cosmopolitan, and soft spoken, less fervent and outwardly ideological. Still, Neurath stuck to the party script, treating King to the now-shopworn litany of German gripes, if in more genteel and polished cadences than those King had heard previously. In fact, the lament was so repetitive that one wonders why King reproduced Neurath's catalogue of miseries in such detail for his diary: the French pact with Bolshevik Russia, British and French indifference to the plight of Spain, the travesty of Versailles, the plot to deny Germany its rightful resources and sovereignty. Then the obligatory declaration of hatred for war, that Germany would never precipitate one, that it would only mean "the destruction of civilization."[15] When it came to the proclamations emanating from Nazi officialdom, *Gleichschaltung* was on full view.

By now, King's responses were also well rehearsed, although he did add one more note of reassurance. He wanted Neurath to know that US president Franklin Roosevelt and secretary of state Cordell Hull, along with others in the American administration, were "very friendly in their attitude and intention; that they really wanted to help." The US president, long an anxious observer of Hitler's machinations, would have been puzzled by the characterization. Neurath countered by pointing out that the "horrible things" said by US officials about Nazi antisemitism, rearmament, and aggression made it "impossible not to have the Germans feel a dislike for the Americans." Neurath's reading of the US administration's attitude would be confirmed little more than three months later, when FDR gave his landmark "Quarantine Speech" equating the lawlessness of Germany, Italy, and Japan with a virus that the civilized word must unite to snuff out. This was just the type of isolating, finger-pointing, and promise of collective action that exasperated King, and he made his frustrations plain in his diary following the speech. "More than ever," he wrote, "I must spike the guns of those who want boycott's [sic] & sanctions, leading to war."[16]

Having been contradicted by Neurath over the mood in Washington, King fell back on the old mantra: to move beyond such animosities "all of us should do our best to overcome prejudices, and to foster goodwill." Neurath said that he agreed. To both men, the prejudices in question were those that set German against American, Briton against Italian. Resentments towards Jews were clearly another matter. Neurath's affirmation of the need for international brotherhood came on the heels of a discussion that portrayed antisemitism as a logical response to personal encounters with Jews – as a post- rather than pre-judice. Neurath had railed against the Jewish takeover of Berlin's neighbourhoods and businesses, of the displeasure of having to sit next to them at the theatre. "Many," he explained, "were very coarse and vulgar and assertive." Their removal from the city had allowed the German people to restore normality and autonomy to their city and their lives.[17]

Neurath's accusations of coarseness, vulgarity, and assertiveness were far more apposite to the brownshirts and SS louts who had turned Berlin's public spaces into zones of intimidation, violence, and murder, and he unwittingly acknowledged as much to the prime minister. "He admitted," King recorded, "that they had taken some pretty rough steps in clearing up the situation," but the thuggery and repressive legislation that accompanied it had been a prerequisite to "inspire desire for a good life in the minds of young people." Nine years later at Nuremberg, Neurath was still defending the "necessary cleaning up of public life" that had become too influenced by Jews, but under cross-examination conceded that their removal "should have been carried out by different methods." "Why," asked the prosecution, "did you continue in a government that was using murder as an instrument of political action?" Neurath responded that "such mishaps cannot be avoided, most unfortunately."[18]

There was no cross-examination on the purging of Berlin's Jews from Mackenzie King. His interview with Neurath shifted effortlessly to their mutual affection for England and its people, and King concluded that he had "met a man whose confidence I would continue to enjoy

16.4 King developed an instant rapport with the aristocratic Neurath, with whom the prime minister shared a fondness for England (not to mention a sartorial inclination). The two were photographed immediately following their private meeting. (Library and Archives Canada, C-016776)

through the rest of my life ... He is, if there ever was one, a genuinely kind, good man. A very safe man for a Foreign Minister." The meeting was followed by lunch at Neurath's apartment in the same Foreign Office building. There King met Neurath's daughter and her husband ("exceedingly nice people"). "The luncheon party," he enthused, "was one of the pleasantest I have ever enjoyed. The whole environment was most attractive; no one could have been kinder than the hosts." Had King's visit come a few months later, he would have been dining at Neurath's new residence in the verdant Berlin suburb of Dahlem, a relocation made necessary by demolition of his office and residence in advance of the construction of Albert Speer's colossal New Reich Chancellery. Unfortunately for Neurath, the new neighbourhood was not yet completely free of Jews; fortunately for Neurath, his own move facilitated the ethnic cleansing already underway. Prosecutors at Nuremberg alleged that he purchased his new home from Jews who were intimidated into selling when Neurath showed up, accompanied by a uniformed SS officer, with an offer they dared not refuse.[19]

King returned to the Adlon in the mid-afternoon. He took a short rest, caught up on some correspondence, and began packing his bags, for he would be taking a train to Belgium later that evening. Before departing for the station, he met the press and issued the statement he had prepared with Henderson's aid; thanked the Fuhrer, Neurath, Göring, and Hess for their generous hospitality; and affirmed that his "visit had been an exceedingly enjoyable and profitable one, and above all, most reassuring." At 8 p.m. on Monday, 30 June, he left the hotel, accompanied by representatives from the Germany Foreign Office and the British Embassy. Sir George Ogilvie-Forbes was there to wish him well at Friedrichstrasse Station; Nevile Henderson was not.[20] A year later, Ogilvie-Forbes was in charge at the embassy, and even the most ardent champions of the Henderson school of Hitler diplomatics had largely recanted.

At 9:22 p.m. King was en route to Belgium and reflecting upon a visit that was "as enjoyable, informative, and inspiring" as any he had ever experienced. It had been, in fact, the most "interesting" and "significant" event of his life. Henderson, though roughed up for saying so, was right: King now saw how "far reaching ... are the reforms being worked out in Germany; and how completely they are on the right lines." While Colonel Crerar before him could not escape the overall atmosphere of "nervous tension" among Germans that "became more marked with each succeeding day" he toured Berlin, King perceived an overwhelming optimism. He had witnessed nothing less than "a new nation being created," one whose reforms "other nations would be wise" to emulate. If the gestation to nationhood had generated some "hatreds," these had arisen from reactionary opponents of progress and justice: domestically, from those who feared losing their "position and privilege" (a fear certainly well founded among German Jews), and internationally, from those who feared that Nazism's model of "liberty and equality for the classes may spread from Germany to their own lands." Most importantly of all, he had received assurances from the nation's foremost officials that they would not resort to war. As long as Hitler and Neurath were at the helm "I felt sure there would be no war, and that constructive work would continue." "I have come away from Germany tremendously relieved," he wrote. Only one thing could breach the peace, he mused yet again: the press.[21]

17

Home

On the morning of 1 July – Canada's seventieth birthday, he noted in his diary – King arrived in Brussels for a quick debriefing with Belgian officials. Here he assured King Leopold III, whose neutrality and nation had been savaged by German armies in the First World War, that Belgium need not fear a repeat performance. Hitler, King reported, "had been most emphatic in saying there would be no war." This message the prime minister broadcast far and wide, along with an appeal to continue dialogue with Germany along the lines he had established. *Toronto Star* reporter and dogged anti-Nazi Matthew Halton caught up with the prime minister in the Belgian capital and posed the question he dared not in the company of NSDAP officials. "Have they spoken frankly to you or tried to throw dust in your eyes?," asked the journalist who had dubbed his own Nazi-guided tour "a prearranged farce." King was clear. "They have really been extraordinarily frank. I don't think they have tried to hide their real motives."[1]

While in Brussels, King composed lengthy, handwritten, and effusive notes to Hitler and Neurath thanking them for their attention, lauding their impressive work, and expressing faith that the friendships inaugurated on his visit would prove lasting and constructive. The personal meetings were simply the first stage of the prime minister's program for peace; continued encouragement would ensure that the seeds he planted in Berlin would blossom. "I have tried in the letters," King confided in his diary, "to give the feeling of personal sincerity which, I believe, will go a long way toward keeping the hearts of the Germans rightly disposed." To the Fuhrer King wrote: "You have helped to remove much of the fear that in common with others I have, in some measure, shared."[2]

King had finally landed on a matter over which both he and Harry Crerar agreed. The colonel's report to Canadian officials concluded that "Hitler will not deliberately risk his actions being the cause of a major European war at the present time." But that was the extent of the concord. Crerar continued: "From what I saw and heard I should judge that it will be one, or perhaps, two years before the military organization of the country will be sufficiently ready for such a tremendous strain, a limiting factor which Hitler certainly appreciates." War could come sooner, he granted, if Hitler misjudged the will of the international community to tolerate Germany's "aggressive pursuit of external objectives." A particularly worrying sign was the "increasing liaison between important groups in Russia and Germany," a product of the Nazis' renunciation of Anglo-German rapprochement that would come to full fruition with Hitler's final pre-war diplomatic set piece, the August 1939 Ribbentrop-Molotov pact. Crerar summed up his prescient forecast of the troubles to come by warning that "the step from international blackmail to international bloodshed is all too easily accomplished." He had witnessed a nation "increasingly dangerous to the European and, indeed, the world peace. There may be nothing original in this conclusion, but it may serve to confirm similar views held by others."[3]

Needless to say, Mackenzie King was not one of them. From Brussels the jubilant prime minister took a train to Paris, where a press conference reinforced his worst fears about the inherent delinquency of journalists. King's declaration that the freedom safeguarded by the British Commonwealth must be defended was mistranslated as "*England* must be defended," turning his statement into precisely the kind of line-in-the-sand posturing he detested. He decided he would no longer bother with anything the press wrote, and at the same time determined that he should "say much more myself" about the world situation to counter the rubbish in the newspapers.[4] Again he predicted that, should war come, it would be the news media that would shoulder the tawdry fardels of guilt.

On 3 July, having been abroad for more than two months, King once again boarded the *Empress of Australia* for a six-day voyage back to Canada. He spent much of the time aboard ship dictating letters of thanks to his German hosts and of advice to officials in London. The steady exchange of cheery letters and cables to Nazi officials would continue for several months, and included personal Christmas greetings to Hitler, Göring, Neurath, and Ribbentrop. He sent memoranda to Chamberlain and Eden, reassuring them that Hitler was "a man of deep sincerity," and that his own visit had revealed the "conditions in Germany itself which accounted for much that had been done there which it was difficult to understand beyond its borders." Regarding Nazi officials as a whole he informed Eden: "I believe they are men with whom it should be possible to work with a good deal of trust and confidence."[5]

While Chamberlain and Eden wrote polite notes thanking King for his intercession efforts, internal correspondence among officials in the British Foreign Office who perused King's synopsis of his trip was far less cordial. "It is curious," noted Sir Orme Sargent, an assistant under-secretary of state, "how easily impressed & reassured Hitler's visitors are when Hitler tells them that Germany needs to expand at somebody else's expense but of course does not want war." US correspondent William Shirer was similarly brusque in his dismissal of foreign visitors who swallowed these Nazi fictions. "When the visiting firemen from London, Paris, and New York come, Hitler babbles only of peace. Wasn't he in the trenches of the last war? He knows what war is. Never will he condemn mankind to that. Peace? Read *Mein Kampf*, brothers." Shirer was relieved at the news he was being transferred (temporarily, as it turned out) to Vienna in the fall of 1937, after he and his Austrian wife Tess had spent three years in Berlin. "Personally, they have not been unhappy ones," he wrote in his diary, "though the shadow of Nazi fanaticism, sadism, persecution, regimentation, terror, brutality, suppression, militarism, and preparations for war has hung over all our lives, like a dark, brooding cloud that never clears."[6] Mackenzie King seemed to have surveyed an entirely different country.

Also aboard the *Empress of Australia* with King were some of the unseen helpers, in repose now in his cabin after their spirited choral finale at Verdi's *Un ballo in maschera*. Joining him for prayers on his first night of the voyage were his parents and grandparents, including an understandably proud grandpa Mackenzie, whose long quest for justice his grandson had now redeemed. It was, King noted, "just this little group gathered together sharing this blessed hour together" in view of the Mackenzie tartan draped across the couch. His father's presence was especially vivid, so much so that King spoke aloud to him, "prayed to him and thru' him to God the great father of us all ... Dear Father, You have been nearer to me in this last twelve hours than I have ever been conscious of your being since you passed into the Great Beyond." The prime minister now recognized that since taking his earthly leave, the elder King had been waiting to fully reveal himself until "the moment of triumph" realized in Berlin. The incredible immediacy of his father's spirit King considered a reward "for what I had done in taking him to England with me."[7]

Keeping in mind that King was "alone" and fully conscious – that this was not one of the typical visions that came to him during a seance with a practised medium or while he slept – his account of the little gathering is already a head-shaker. It was about to become odder still, veering into the territory of a full-blown hallucination. King went to bed and tossed and turned, restless and "conscious – very conscious of the nearness of father" and the wider King clan. Then, wide awake at 4 a.m., his eye was drawn to the Mackenzie tartan, which now communicated directly to the prime minister. "It seemed to say," wrote King, "this is the second watch – the King's [sic] have been with you from 12 till 4, now the Mackenzie's [sic] will be the next watch."[8]

Consoled, he lay awake, and was soon "joined" in his cabin by canine siblings Pat and Derry: "very significant was the nearness of little Derry to me. It seemed to me he & I were rejoicing together. I talked with him and little Pat but Derry for the time being seemed to claim his own right to share my love as well. It was a marvellous feeling of sharing the love which is the heart of the animal creation."[9] Again, King's mystical visitors generally popped by during dreams or mediated sessions or, as with the "cloud of witnesses" in the opera chorus, assumed the form of tangible beings in his proximity. In this instance, we have the waking prime minister rejoicing, speaking, and sharing his affection with creatures who were – it can be stated definitively – either fully decomposed or, in the case of the canine siblings, thousands of miles away in the skirts of the Gatineau Hills. And possibly, we have a talking blanket. The things the ever-vigilant but maddeningly discreet Nicol must have seen and heard during a lifetime of service to the prime minister ...

During the Atlantic crossing King also wrote a telegram to Henderson, thanking him for his hospitality and assistance. The ambassador responded the following day, writing that his was "not an easy or a peaceable job," but that King's visit and his encouraging telegram had lifted his spirits and "put the heart in me." Henderson assured the prime minister that he would continue his fight to open British minds to the positives of Nazism. King's message to Canadian governor-general Lord Tweedsmuir (John Buchan) was unequivocal: "I am perfectly certain ... that the Germans are not contemplating the possibility of war."[10]

The prime minister also wrote to French diplomat Gabriel Hanotaux, who had expressed such optimism about King's pending peace errand

17.1 In the flesh: King holds Pat and Derry in this 1938 studio photograph. As he sailed home on the *Empress of Australia*, their spirits joined him to rejoice over his virtuoso diplomatic performance in Berlin. (Library and Archives Canada, C-055544)

to Berlin when the two had met in Paris, to inform him that the mission had been accomplished. "You will be interested, I am sure," King wrote, "in hearing me say that the talk I had with Herr Hitler reassured me almost as much as my conversation with yourself at the time of my last visit." Initiatives like his own, King maintained, not threats of collective action or joint communiques of warning, were a surer route to peace. "I confess my faith in international conferences is far from being what I should like it to be. The old diplomacy, with the quiet way of negotiating between nations, may have limitations, but it had much to commend it. The fault of our day is that we have too much, not too little, in the way of publicity." Hanotaux's exuberant reply must have put the heart in King, although it included an unintended nod to the bounteous naivety King displayed in Berlin: "Never has the world been in greater need of mutual trust and that trust naturally radiates from your whole being."[11]

King's wariness towards the press and "too much publicity" was surely not moderated by a bogus story that appeared in a Paris newspaper just before the *Empress* reached its destination in Montreal. The report was summarized in an anxious telegram sent to Pickering asking that King immediately disavow claims falsely attributed to him in the Paris report: namely, "Hitler suffering insomnia unable to discuss European politics coherently and King feared Hitler might unwittingly plunge Europe into Catastrophe Stop." King's first duty when he made dry land on 9 July, then, was to once again seek to undo damage done in the foreign press.[12] As fate would have it, the phoney synopsis of King's visit proved more prescient than his own.

And then there was the damage to undo on the home front. King learnt "to [his] horror" that immediately after he had departed for the Imperial Conference, his butler McLeod and members of the RCMP tasked with safeguarding the prime minister's residence had launched into an energetic, boozy celebration. The bender went on for more than a day, "both indoors and outside"; McLeod was arrested for public drunkenness; most distressingly, "little Pat had been left alone" for the duration of the prolonged debauch. King found the betrayal especially hurtful "in the light of all I have done" for this "unfaithful & unjust steward." The prime minister simmered over how to respond for three days, consulting with friends and scripture and cogitating for page after page in his diary. Instead of sacking McLeod, King ultimately decided to subject the butler and his wife, herself no stranger to the bottle, to a sermon on finding pleasure through industriousness and piety rather than inebriants. This was followed by a reading from scripture. The whole wretched affair he considered "in some respects a greater sorrow than the one of 21 years ago" when his mother died.[13]

On home soil King allowed himself to raise matters about Germany that he had evaded – both before his hosts and in his own reflections – while touring the barbarous state. At the same time, he made it clear that, like the Canadian journalists who had followed him around Germany, he regarded the excesses of Hitler's regime as "side issues" unworthy of disrupting bilateral trade agreements and goodwill. Hitler's "dictatorship is a means to an end," he wrote " – needed perhaps to make the

Germans conscious of themselves – much I cannot abide in Nazism – the regimentation – the cruelty – oppression of Jews – attitudes toward religion etc., but Hitler ... the peasant – will rank some day with Joan of Arc among the deliverers of his people, & if he is only careful may yet be the deliverer of Europe."[14] Here again King seemed to imply that, while the Nazi Party exhibited behaviour discomfiting to a liberal democrat like himself, Hitler's wise guidance would steer the nation, and the continent, towards justice and concord.

In the months following his return, the prime minister received accolades for the visit from fellow politicians and the press. In late July he gave his fullest public account to date of his European deliberations, reassuring Canadians in a speech broadcast on CBC radio that "I believe the nations of Europe have a better understanding of each other's problems to-day than they have had for some years past. Moreover, despite all appearances, they are prepared, I believe, in an effort to work out a solution, to co-operate to a greater degree than has been the case for a long while ... Of this I am certain ... that neither the governments nor the peoples of any of the countries I have visited desire war, or view the possibility of war between each other, as other than likely to end in self-destruction, and the destruction of European civilization itself."[15] Hitler's assurances about the suicidal outcome of a continental war had clearly left their mark, and King, in hailing the new spirit of "better understanding" and cooperation, was assigning his visit at least some of the credit for the encouraging turn in international relations.

H.D.G. Crerar, meanwhile, was in the midst of compiling his much bleaker view of the prospects for European cooperation. Filed in early August, his "Report on Visit to Germany" ran to seven and a half typed, legal-sized pages and circulated widely through the upper echelons of the federal bureaucracy: to his superiors in the Canadian Army, to Defence, to Trade and Commerce, to External Affairs, and to a range of individuals within and beyond government whom Crerar thought might be interested. Did the prime minister catch wind of Crerar's contrapuntal take on the European situation? The chances are good, given the King cabinet's intensive focus on any information relating to the prospects for war. What's more, copies of the prime minister's own internal report on his German trip – culled nearly verbatim from his diary account of his interview with Hitler – were also making the rounds in those same government departments; the two reports' strikingly contradictory conclusions must have generated at least some high-level conversations. If King was privy to the contents of the competing

report, however, it seems unlikely that it would have had much impact
on his thinking. After all, the prime minister's experience in politics
and diplomacy was unmatched, while military men, he repeatedly reminded his colleagues, were typically on the hunt for pretexts to ply
their trade and ignorant of the political arts.[16]

When parliament resumed sitting in February 1938, King's visit hit the
papers again after politicians from rival parties offered congratulations
for what they considered the prime minister's fruitful, if still opaque,
deliberations with the Germans the previous summer. However, one of
King's foremost nemeses, Conservative opposition leader and former
prime minister R.B. Bennett, made a brief attempt to flummox his op-
ponent over the issue. Bennett found it jarring that the Liberal leader
would sit down with Nazi leaders despite previously warning "of the
dangers that threaten the body politic from communism, on the one
hand, and from fascism on the other. My recollection," Bennett continued, "is that he found the chief fascist in the world, Herr Hitler, a most
entertaining person and a man who is doing great work."[17]

Bennett followed this direct hit with another, calling out King's double standard of routinely denouncing domestic rivals as tyrants and
fascists while glad-handing the overseas variety: "it was not necessary
for the right honorable gentleman to travel all the way to Germany
to see what he regards as a dictator because I recall that during the
election in 1935 he pointed to me sitting opposite as a combination
of Hitler and Mussolini." In what would appear to be a coordinated
attack, Bennett's brother-in-law, Conservative Party apparatchik W.D.
Herridge, had told an audience of Toronto Conservatives three days
earlier that "Liberalism goes a long way from liberalism of freedom
when it goes to Berlin."[18]

These cogent criticisms went nowhere, and as it had during its coverage in Berlin, Canada's "newspaper of record" the *Globe and Mail* rose
to defend King's trip and his right not to disclose the contents of his
in-camera meetings. The stakes were simply too high to allow petty
domestic rivalries and political buccaneering to subvert the prime minister's efforts to still the volatile international waters.[19]

18

Failure of a Mission, or The War That Harry Crerar Foretold

Mackenzie King's confidence in the prospects for peace in Europe died hard. In March 1938, after a year of Göring's consistent prodding on the matter, Hitler was finally ready to incorporate Austria into an expanded Germany. Although his generals considered the *Anschluss* a sure incitement to war with Britain, the Fuhrer was supremely confident that the Chamberlain government would do nothing.[1]

Whether Mackenzie King's assurances of the British prime minister's "friendliness" had anything to do with the Fuhrer's conviction on the matter cannot be established. Those close to Hitler noted that by the middle 1930s he had ceased to solicit or pay heed to opinions that contradicted his own, so if the Fuhrer had already judged Chamberlain as pliable or the British indifferent to the annexation of Austria, counterclaims from King may have done little. Regardless, the Canadian prime minister had tendered no such counterclaims, and on this gamble Hitler was, of course, correct. Göring's earlier concern, raised obliquely with King, over British intervention and a subsequent cascading of imperial partners into an anti-German coalition proved unfounded. An appeal by the Austrian government for British assistance was met with an eight-word telegram: "His Majesty's Government are unable to guarantee protection."[2]

King was alarmed by the German move, but expressed confidence that the British would not resort to war, that they would find a peaceful way of dealing with the situation "a little later on."[3] His view of the Fuhrer, however, began to align itself more and more with reality. Hitler was surely a "dictator," King now reckoned in his diary entry about the *Anschluss*, no different from the men who had recently led Japan and Italy into wars of conquest. "The amazing fact of this whole situation," the prime minister continued, in a eureka moment that could have come much earlier, "is that it is all in complete accord with the book which Hitler himself has written, entitled 'Mein Kompf' [sic]."[4]

Still, King held to the conviction that Nazi bids for surrounding territory would be carried out "without bloodshed," since Third Reich officials had personally and repeatedly assured him of this the previous summer. Perhaps more remarkably, the pitifully toothless League of Nations continued to be the primary antagonist in King's assessment of the European situation. He recalled with trepidation Hitler's warning that the League's collective security mandate would turn regional scuffles into a global inferno, the same concern fundamental to the prime minister's own contempt for the world body. But to his credit, King, tireless advocate for power of communication with potential foes, had gained some appreciation for the Roosevelt school of liberal-tyrant relations. The prime minister now came to the view that the other great powers should cease business as usual with the world's dictators, believing that ostracizing these criminal regimes would eventually lead them to crumble from within.[5] While still unwilling to pledge allegiance to collective security, the prime minister had begun to sour on the notion that rational dialogue with autocrats could forestall "precipitate steps" and usher in an era of international camaraderie and understanding.

Then, in the fall of that same year, Hitler moved against Czechoslovakia. At this, King finally began to countenance the approach he had once railed against: a multinational military stand against German aggression. He insisted to his cabinet, in the face of strong pushback, that Canada must support the British if they were imperilled by German aggression regardless of the political price in Quebec.[6] For a noted ditherer whose natural reflex was political self-preservation, it was a bold and principled (if not yet public) stance.

He still held out hope, however, that the King Doctrine could avert war. When Chamberlain boarded a plane for Munich to negotiate with Hitler, the Canadian prime minister once again saw a potential vindication of his long campaign for face-to-face negotiations rather than ultimatums, adversarial alliances, and quarantines. Despite opposition from Anthony Eden, King noted, Chamberlain had from the start sought an amicable relationship with Hitler and Mussolini; now in Munich, that strategy might bear fruit. "A very few personal contacts inspiring confidence are the factors which are saving the situation today," he wrote as heads of state from Germany, Italy, France, and Britain assembled in Munich to discuss the fate of Czechoslovakia, whose representatives were conspicuously absent from the deliberations.[7]

Two days later, King's renewed confidence in the personality-driven approach continued to blossom. In his diary entry from 14 September, the eve of the Munich Conference, he cast himself, half a world away, as the true father and hub of the momentous negotiations about to begin. He reflected on the "completeness of the circle which brought me in touch with the principals in the present world situation," each encounter a fateful step towards the current conciliation efforts. King then meticulously itemized that progression, beginning with his initial correspondence with Ribbentrop in 1936, and then meeting him at the coronation, first at a reception and then one-on-one over lunch; King's deliberations at the Imperial Conference with Chamberlain and Eden over handling Germany, followed by telegrams to Nevile Henderson and Neurath from Scotland to prepare for the mission to Berlin; arrival in that city via train, welcomed by Henderson at the station; the prudence of lodging at the Adlon Hotel rather than the British Embassy; meetings with Neurath, Göring, Hess, and Hitler, "in particular, my effort to give Hitler confidence in Neville Chamberlain."[8]

King continued with a detailed inventory of the flurry of telegrams and letters he sent following the visit – to the British, assuring that Hitler did not want war, and to the Germans on the "constructive work" he had witnessed and his appreciation for their commitment to peace; the renewed British-Germany dialogue that followed, "due to the strong advice I gave Chamberlain on the importance of arranging immediate contacts"; a list of all the subsequent letters and Christmas greetings to top Nazis; Canada's bison donation, and King's standing, big-game-hunting invitation to Göring. It had all come to this, the talks in Munich on which the hopes of the entire world rested.[9] The prime minister saw his diary as the raw material for his memoirs, and the detailed taxonomy of his protracted peace initiative reads like an outline of all the components that would round out what would doubtless be the memoir's most dramatic and glorious chapter.

The final paragraph of the 14 September entry suggests King wouldn't have been surprised by an invitation to come to Munich to mediate the negotiations: "Today, I could cable Chamberlain, Henderson, von Ribbentrop and Hitler all as one, and help to afford a background of confidence and friendly purpose ... The unseen forces have unquestioningly been working together in using me in this way toward helping in the great purpose of the preservation of peace."[10]

When those same officials forged an agreement that averted imminent war – by handing the fascist bully Czechoslovakian territory negotiators had no right to offer – King was ecstatic. He cabled congratulations to Chamberlain: "The heart of Canada is rejoicing tonight at the success which has crowned your unremitting efforts for peace." In a letter to Canadian Lord Tweedsmuir, King could not help taking at least some of the credit. "How grateful I am that Chamberlain went to see Hitler!" the prime minister wrote. "You may recall how strongly I urged these personal contacts." The perceived triumph of his mission to Europe led King to consider a visit to Japanese officials, whose ruthless aggression against China had put the region, and the Western colonial powers that controlled much of it, on edge. Hitler, meanwhile, basked in another bloodless conquest, a diplomatic besting of the acquiescent British prime minister that buried any remaining hopes for meaningful internal opposition to the cult of the Fuhrer. A small group of German generals preparing to launch a coup in response to what they anticipated would be global outrage over the territorial theft now called off the operation. As Germany's dwindling opponents to Nazism concluded bitterly, "Chamberlain saved Hitler." New Zealand prime minister Michael Savage, the scourge of the 1937 Imperial Conference for castigating appeasement, castigated appeasement again in public remarks denouncing Chamberlain's capitulation.[11]

One month later, *Kristallnacht*, the anti-Jewish pogrom set in motion by Goebbels, swept Nazi-held territories. The shocking reports from European correspondents moved King deeply. "The sorrows which the Jews have to bear at this time are almost beyond comprehension," he wrote. "Something will have to be done by our country."[12]

The issue consumed him for weeks. He conferred with Franklin Roosevelt, governor general Lord Tweedsmuir, Canadian Jewish leaders, and his cabinet, but his efforts to strike the proper response pitted King's newfound empathy against political expediency and time-worn chauvinisms. He made principled declarations of Canada's duty to accept Jewish refugees, but wondered whether it would be better to ghettoize them in "an area set aside for development," or perhaps help them resettle in South America instead. He accepted Tweedsmuir's stereotypical allegation that emigrating Jews could finance their own move, as "it was amazing the amounts that they have, secreted away," in the governor general's words. King insinuated that the more magnanimous proposals coming from Washington owed to the makeup of the president's cabinet, which "is very strong as to Jewish influence." To desperate Jewish leaders from Montreal and Toronto, who had trekked to Ottawa to assure the prime minister that their communities would gladly bear the costs of bringing in ten thousand refugees, King fell back on base political calculations. He lectured them on Canada's high unemployment rate and the threat Jews posed to national unity, and coldly informed them that he "must consider the constituencies and the views of those who are supporting the Government." Yet the next day he urged his cabinet to consider accepting Jewish refugees, challenging them to reflect "the conscience of the nation, and not what might be, at the moment, politically most expedient." Cabinet demurred, and instead convinced King that Canada should help "find homes for refugees in some other land than our own." In the end, the Liberals did nothing. It was perhaps the greatest refutation in King's career of his avowal that "it is what we prevent, rather than what we do that counts most in Government."[13]

The steady flow of demoralizing news from Europe continued. Any residual illusions about talking Hitler out of further land grabs were dealt a severe blow when Nazi armies overran what remained of Czechoslovakia on 14 and 15 March 1939. Britain and France now renounced the policy of appeasement and pledged to defend Poland should Hitler continue to push eastward. The pledges distressed King, who remained, in the words of historian James Eayrs, "a true believer" in appeasement. "His confidence in Hitler," Eayrs wrote of the events of mid-March, "had been shaken less than his confidence in Chamberlain." Deputy minister of foreign affairs O.D. Skelton wrote to King that Chamberlain's hawkish turn was an emotional overreaction to the notion that "Hitler made a fool of him" over Czechoslovakia, and urged King to resist any marching orders from the wounded British leader. Others who feared being drawn into what King had earlier called "an Empire centralizing scheme" expressed similar misgivings. South African and Australian leaders lamented the new bellicosity emerging from London and urged Chamberlain not to give up on appeasing Germany. Michael Savage, conversely, felt a sense of vindication.[14]

Although King still did not grasp the degree to which Hitler would reject established international norms to fulfil his ambitions, the prime minister did understand that if European leaders could not keep the peace, Canada could hardly expect to remain neutral. On 20 March, he made what sounded like a public repudiation of isolationism and a promise to defend Britain. "If there were the prospect of an aggressor launching an attack on Britain," King declared in a prepared statement in the House of Commons, "with bombers raining death on London, I have no doubt what the decision of the Canadian people and Parliament would be. We would regard it as an act of aggression, menacing freedom in all parts of the British Commonwealth."[15]

It was not, however, an outright guarantee, as King had long maintained that it was Parliament's prerogative whether to join any foreign conflict. Nor was it an open-ended pledge to blindly follow London's lead; the prime minister's statement applied only to a potential attack on British soil. But with a commanding Liberal majority in Parliament and the backing of his cabinet, he was confident that if the British were truly endangered, Canada would come to the island's defence. He wrote in his diary that "it was necessary to make clear Canada's determination to stand with other democracies in opposing aggression and attempt at domination of the world by force." Ernest Lapointe, the most trusted and influential of King's Quebec cabinet ministers, made a similar declaration, adding that for the Liberal government, conscription was off the table should Canada go to war. While King admitted he was "a bit jealous of all the positive press attention it received," especially in English Canada, the reaction to Lapointe's address appeared to leave little doubt about Canadian opinion on the issue.[16]

Ten days later, in the face of some pointed criticism in the francophone newspapers, King appeared to hedge. His government, he clarified to Parliament, was not "prepared to support whatever may be proposed by the Government at Westminster ... Absolute statements of policy, absolute undertakings to follow other governments, whatever the situation, are out of the question." More than that, Canada was too weak and too poor "to save, periodically, a continent that cannot run itself"; such an obligation, King continued, "seems to many a nightmare and sheer madness." Had the vigorous custodian of liberty who stood before the House on 20 March been eclipsed by the latent autonomist, conciliator, and dissembler? Privately, King expressed few doubts that Canada would be at Britain's side should war come; this latest statement was meant to reassure Canadian Anglophobes that the nation's policy was not predetermined, that Canada was still a democracy whose Parliament, rather than 10 Downing, would steer policy.[17] It was also the case that the prime minister's idealism and faith in his own destiny would not let him fully forsake the King Doctrine.

In February 1939, six weeks prior to the German annexation of all Czechoslovakia, King had written directly to Adolf Hitler to remind him of their productive talk in the summer of 1937, during which the

Fuhrer had firmly renounced war. In the letter King implored Hitler yet again to take no steps that might jeopardize the great example of "human well-being" his Germany was providing for all nations. The present note should be considered, King wrote, "an expression of the faith I have in the purpose you have at heart, and of the friendship with yourself which you have been so kind as to permit me to share."[18]

Certainly there is a good deal of strategic blandishment at work here, as King's opinion of the Fuhrer had corroded steadily since the *Anschluss*. But there is also the dependable mix of artlessness and conceit inherent in the assumptions that Hitler could still be sweet-talked out of his plans for European mastery and that King was the man to do so. And in diary and private conversation, King continued to offer up groundless apologias for Hitler's increasingly belligerent conduct, apologias that seemed designed to temper some of the prime minister's own embarrassment over anointing the Fuhrer a modern Joan of Arc and Europe's saviour: Hitler was at war with the more radical members of his movement, who were goading him into progressively more dangerous moves; Hitler was at war with himself, caught up in a titanic inner struggle between his own angels and demons.[19]

The Fuhrer did not reply to the prime minister's letter until July, preoccupied not by nonexistent conflicts with his ruling coterie or his better angels, but by his imminent consumption of Bohemia and Moravia. His response simply ignored King's sundry and earnest entreaties; instead, the Fuhrer suggested that a group of Canadian students and officers come to Germany for a holiday. King, guileless optimism seemingly fully restored despite the fresh evidence of German rapaciousness, believed the response meant "that Hitler wanted to work through him to restore peace in the world," as Allan Levine observed. In his diary King wrote that this was "all part of a plan in which God was using man to effect his Will in answer to prayer ... I recognized that great care would be needed in each step and the utmost secrecy preserved ... I felt I must communicate with Chamberlain." He resolved to personally head the Canadian delegation proposed by Hitler, and began planning for a November 1939 expedition.[20]

Late August brought the Nazi-Soviet pact, and deep foreboding among those who thought Hitler would be held in check by his supposed arch-enemy to the east. King was shaken, but still believed that he had a central role in the drama, that he held some sway over the European statesmen girding for war. He cabled Chamberlain with the outlandish claim that a direct appeal for peace from the British royals could convince Hitler to stand down. He directed Chamberlain to convince George VI of the soundness of this strategy, and declared that the message would be most effective if the king flew to Berlin to deliver it in person. He cabled Mussolini, Polish president Władysław Raczkiewicz, and Hitler, urging that they find a way to live in peace. Mussolini and Raczkiewicz acknowledged the diplomatic missives; there was no response from the German chancellor.[21]

At least some part of the prime minister continued to cling to the belief that Hitler's goal was peace even after the start of the Second World War. In a seance King held with his lifelong friend Joan Patteson the day after Hitler launched his *Blitzkrieg* against Poland, grandfather William Lyon Mackenzie floated in to tell his progeny that, as with the Rebellion of 1837, "Hitler did not want to have war" but had been driven to desperation. At the same session, the earthly King was informed by his deceased parents that Hitler had been "shot [dead] by a Pole" and that "war would be averted." When these assurances proved false, King's diary entry read, "This all makes perfectly clear either that a lying spirit has come in somewhere, or that sub-conscious wishes dictate the words expressed." He swore off any further attempts to call on the dead for the duration of the war.[22]

With the Fuhrer very much alive and his armies routing hapless Poland, King the lifelong peacemaker now realized that he would need to counter some of his deepest instincts and aspirations and rally Canadians behind the Allied cause. On 8 September 1939, the day before Parliament would, as King well knew, overwhelmingly endorse Canada's declaration of war on Germany, he rose to address the House of Commons. The prime minister accepted his new role grimly but stoically, and could not help reflecting on its considerable irony:

> I never dreamed that the day would come when, after spending a lifetime in a continuous effort to promote and to preserve peace and good-will, in international as well as in industrial relations, it should fall to my lot to be the one to lead this Dominion of Canada into a great war. But that responsibility I assume with a sense of being true to the very blood that is in my veins. I assume it in the defence of freedom – the freedom of my fellow-countrymen, the freedom of those whose lives are unprotected in other countries, the freedom of mankind itself.[23]

The personal mission of peace in which King had invested so much time, energy, and hope, one constructed around his insistence upon

Chamberlain's tractability and Hitler's peaceable intent, had done nothing to stanch the plunge into war. To any objective observer it was plain that he had misfired terribly in his pre-war reading of the signs and in his advice to world leaders. Yet even after Nazi forces steam-rolled western Poland, and then in early 1940 began tactical naval and air attacks on western European targets in anticipation of their ambitious spring offensive, King mulishly defended his antebellum strategy for handling the Fuhrer. Reading the opening chapters of Nevile Henderson's just-released Berlin memoir in March of that year led King to once again defend the idea of leader-to-leader mediation – and his own genius for it – against "the technique and claptrap of diplomatic circles." "I really believe," his diary records, "though I wish I had realized it more, that my own visit to Germany and talks with these men, went further to bring the real frame of mind which might have saved disaster than what was accomplished either in London or Berlin in the strictly official relations. I may be wrong in that, but I would be surprised if Hitler, Goering and Ribbentrop themselves might not be the first to admit it."[24]

The intensity of this delusion, not so much *devoid of* as the *inverse of* all conceivable evidence, marks King's thinking here as an archetype of what eminent American historian Barbara Tuchman termed "wooden-headedness" in statecraft. In *The March of Folly: From Troy to Vietnam*, her magnificent survey of the blunders that sparked and perpetuated some of history's more infamous wars, Tuchman employs the term to describe the "self-deception" inherent to "assessing a situation in terms of preconceived fixed notions while ignoring or rejecting any contrary signs ... It is epitomized in a historian's statement about King Philip II of Spain, the surpassing wooden-head of all sovereigns: 'No experience of the failure of the policy could shake his belief in its essential excellence.'"[25]

King wasn't finished trafficking in fantasy, for the same diary entry then pivots deftly from stubborn delusion to delusion-incomprehensible-to-anyone-but-King. After submitting that Nazi leaders likely agreed that faithfulness to the King approach could have averted disaster (men whose every move in fact deliberately summoned that disaster), the prime minister continued: "At the same time, this does not mean that the Nazi regime and method were not to be trusted. It means that the machine might have been smashed in large part by the German people themselves before it became the menace it has since become."[26]

Leaving aside that the second "not" reverses the intended meaning of the first sentence (a mere grammatical slip), the notion that the prime minister's approach to interwar diplomacy could somehow have stimulated regime change in Germany is simply baffling. Just which component of King's Third Reich apologetics – the unwavering cheerleading for the regime's accomplishments, initiatives, and officials? The crowning of Hitler as humanity's saviour? The disdain for attempts by Britain and the League of Nations to undermine fascist prerogatives? – would have inspired the German people to rise up as one and smash the Nazi machine? That nothing of the substance of King's pre-war interactions with Reich officials was aired publicly to Germans or the wider world adds another layer of mystification to the notion that King's wanton National Socialist sympathizing might have sparked an anti-fascist revolution. Upon completing this diary dictation reaffirming the essential excellence of his Hitler policy, the prime minister went to bed and had a vision reiterating yet again that his fidelity to the path of truth owed to the fact that "others were working through me."[27]

Throughout the war, King continued to proclaim to anyone who would listen – in August 1942 it was a visiting Sir George Ogilvie-Forbes, now assigned to the safe hemisphere of the globe as British ambassador to Cuba – that Hitler had not wanted bloodshed. The prime minister told Ogilvie-Forbes that he truly believed the Fuhrer's July 1939 letter proposing a visit by Canadians was a good-faith, last-ditch effort to strategize with King about ways to "avoid an open rupture." On learning of Hitler's suicide in April 1945, King still portrayed the primary engineer of global cataclysm as a statesman of squandered potential, one whose stubborn refusal to heed wise counsel had brought his doom: "My thoughts were much of what I urged him to consider most, his chance to be of service to the world by championing the cause of the poor and seeking to improve the standards of many but avoiding at all costs the temptation of war."[28] For better and for worse, King's was a faith in the power of rational dialogue and human betterment that seemed to know no bounds.

The Second World War would also force Colonel Harry Crerar to confront the implications of his earlier approach to Canadian foreign policy. In the spring of 1938, he expressed satisfaction that one component of his agenda had been secured, thanks in large part to Hitler's increasing brashness: Crerar and other advocates of preparedness had "at last," he wrote, "succeeded in getting Government departments actively concerned in their national responsibilities for war." His vision of

18.1 Reluctant warrior: King inspects a guard of honour from the Régiment de la Chaudière in Redhill, England, 1 July 1941. The prime minister favoured deploying these and other Canadian soldiers only in the event of an invasion of Britain; H.D.G. Crerar thought otherwise, and would soon have his way. (Captain Laurie A. Audrain, Library and Archives Canada, PA-152440)

the scope of those responsibilities would, however, place him directly at odds with his prime minister. While both men were committed to the preservation and extension of Canadian sovereignty, for King autonomy meant a latitude to commit as much or as little to the Allied cause as the government deemed feasible (and politically prudent). To Crerar, participation as a fully sovereign and mature nation meant that Canadian troops should bear the same burdens as the British, and that his nation must cease to rely on others for its own defence. He became the leading advocate for the development of a "Big Army" that he hoped would play a leading role in the war and remain a fixture of Canadian statecraft thereafter. King didn't warm to this vision. "The true ambition of our general staff," he wrote in 1941, "was to build an army in Britain not particularly for the defence of Britain, but to be the spearhead of the attack on Germany ... all our generals were concerned about was to be in at the kill." His brusque conclusion? "Generals are almost invariably wrong."[29]

Throughout the conflict King and Crerar engaged in a continuous tug-of-war over the choice and scale of Canadian deployments. King frequently invoked the Great War's enormous price, the lives lost, and the crisis over national unity wrought by conscription, and seemed to behave as if a maximum effort from Canada was not essential to Allied victory. Crerar, too, recalled the earlier conflict, but focused on the increased national autonomy his country's contribution to victory had purchased, and maintained that a large contingent of Canadian forces was critical to the defeat of the Axis powers.[30]

It was rare for Mackenzie King to give ground on such a vital and sensitive national issue, but give ground he did. While the prime minister initially envisioned a Canadian force sent to Britain only to defend the island in the event of an invasion, Crerar – by 1940 the army's chief of the general staff – fought tirelessly and successfully for significant Canadian contributions to the defence of the British colony of Hong Kong in 1941, as well as the 1942 raid on Dieppe. As any student of Canadian history knows, both operations proved disastrous. A Japanese attack on Hong Kong in December 1941 overran the colony's defences, which included 1,975 Canadian troops, in ten days. By the time imperial forces surrendered on Christmas Day, 290 Canadians had been killed and 493 wounded, a casualty rate of nearly 40 per cent. The remainder were taken to POW camps, where an additional 260 perished from malnourishment, disease, and abuse. The suicidal Dieppe raid in August of the following year saw a casualty rate of nearly 70 per cent of the 6,100 infantrymen, nearly 5,000 of whom were Canadian. Following Dieppe, King began to fret that the supply of Canadian volunteers would not meet demand.[31]

Critics charged that the Canadians sent on both botched missions were inexperienced, inadequately trained, and their tasks poorly conceived, and these detractors assigned Crerar much of the blame. He defended his decisions to the end, pointing out that the British had been responsible for the planning and that, as the operations would have gone ahead regardless of whether he had pushed for Canadian involvement, this was simply a matter of his soldiers "doing their bit." He also offered the seemingly cold rationalization that if the Canadian army lacked experience, sending them into the heat of the battle was the surest way to remedy that deficit. At least prior to the reports from Hong Kong and Dieppe regarding capitulation and casualties, Crerar had plenty of company on this. Canadians' fascination with their soldiers' contributions to victory and nation-building in the First World War, trumpeted and often exaggerated in Canadian popular culture for two decades, led many citizens to believe that Canadian forces, the heralded "shock troops" of the First War, were invincible. With their nation's soldiers largely on the sidelines in the first years of this new war, English Canada, at least, was growing restless. As an alarmed senior Canadian officer observed, "the people in Canada are calling for blood."[32]

The sobering upshot of that call led the Liberal government to exert greater control over troop deployments, and Mackenzie King to question Crerar's qualifications for the job. The prime minister was not alone, as one British general described Crerar as "nice – and clever – but an academic soldier," while Field Marshall Bernard Montgomery, with whom Crerar worked closely, stated flatly that the Canadian was "quite unfit to command an army." Nonetheless, Crerar received several promotions as the war progressed, a trajectory aided in part by a wider lack of experience among Canadian officers and his own rather unsavoury plotting to undermine Canada's top commander, General Andrew McNaughton, whom Crerar then replaced. And despite those earlier failures and Mackenzie King's anxieties that Crerar's tolerance for casualties endangered the prime minister's 1939 pledge forswearing conscription, the commander's vigorous and successful jockeying for increased Canadian contributions continued: to the Italian theatre in 1943; to the Normandy landings a year later.[33]

Crerar habitually defended his aggressive approach to deployments on both tactical and nationalistic grounds – that the sacrifice was both vital to victory and the unavoidable price of Canadian sovereignty, and he had the weight of English Canadian opinion, at least, behind him. Naturally, his unrelenting appeals for sacrifice did not endanger his own life, and the despatch of growing numbers of Canadians to the front elevated the ever-ambitious commander's own standing and influence over strategic decision-making. Indeed, Crerar would grace the cover of *Time* magazine in 1944.[34] In modern warfare, to employ another common German expression, *so ist das nun mal*. So it goes.

In King's enduring quest to map destiny, fortune, coincidence, and the circle of life, here is an uncanny concurrence that he failed to catch: the man whose reading of the tea leaves during a pre-war visit to

Berlin directly contradicted the prime minister's own, the intelligence director who saw war coming and pressed his hesitant prime minister to make preparations for it, was also the soldier most responsible for forcing King to face the dreaded spectre of conscription. Absent Harry Crerar's indefatigable pleas for more men and more action, King may have escaped the war without having to shepherd his country through the bitter and convulsive quarrel over recruitment, the very quarrel his own 1937 mission to Berlin had sought to preclude.

Certainly, there had been wider goals in going to Germany: King had undertaken that mission in the name of humanity, hoping to ward off a conflict that could kill millions and, as he warned repeatedly, destroy civilization. But as we have seen, this broad altruism was also married to more narrow national interests. King feared a European war would throw his own country into tumult – over its obligations to Britain and the League of Nations, and over the dimensions of Canadian involvement. He had had a front-row seat in the 1917 row over conscription, a clash that split his own party and nearly broke Canada, and the resolve to never relive that crisis was always top of mind as the prime minister picked his way through the confusion of interwar foreign affairs. King was nothing if not supremely confident in his judgment and his powers of persuasion, but on balance he did not fare well against Harry Crerar: on the nature of Hitler's regime, the progression of events proved Crerar right; on the scope of Canada's commitments to the war that Crerar, not King, had foreseen, the commander's wishes ultimately prevailed, leaving King to sort out the political consequences.[35]

In confronting this new conscription fight, King's considerable tactical gifts served him well, as he partially diffused the crisis through a restrained, multistage approach. A 1942 national plebiscite proposing conscription, a measure as favoured in English Canada as it was disfavoured in Quebec, released the government from its earlier promise to field only volunteers overseas; King, however, assured Canadians that conscription would only be enacted if absolutely necessary. Only in November 1944, with Canadian forces suffering significant battle fatigue and attrition, and with a desperate Crerar writing to King that the time had come, did officials send a small contingent of conscripts to Europe. While the prime minister's incremental and ultra-cautious strategy spared the country the degree of trauma witnessed in 1917, the issue essentially paralysed his government for several weeks in the fall of 1944, and nearly dismembered the Liberal party once again along linguistic lines. Riots broke out in Montreal, many conscripts deserted, some launched a militant strike against their deployment.[36] Harry Crerar, who in 1937 had merely offered a counterpoint to King's take on interwar Germany, had become yet another of Mackenzie King's many nemeses, one who was instrumental in precipitating the prime minister's greatest domestic challenge.

King truly believed, and recent scholarship has backed him up, that he could have faced a revolt by army leadership if he did not consent to conscription in November 1944. At the very least, the mass resignation purportedly threatened by Canadian command would have led to the fall of his government; at worst, feared King, this challenge to the primacy of civilian leadership might have ignited a civil war.[37] Thus it was more than a little ironic that, by dint of their leadership of the government and military respectively, King and Crerar were seated together in a limousine during the Canadian army's victory parade through Ottawa at war's end.

It was 7 August 1945, the twenty-sixth anniversary of King's election as Liberal Party leader, as the prime minister (naturally) observed, and he was in a mood to safeguard his legacy. He utilized the opportunity provided by this compulsory companionship to extract something of a confession from Crerar: "to hear from his lips," as a gratified King dictated that evening, "that the army had been denied nothing they needed. That he could think of nothing which had not been done by the Government" throughout the war. At a luncheon following the parade, Crerar offered that "everything had worked out splendidly." King, who never forgave army leaders for forcing his hand on conscription, concurred, but pointedly informed Crerar that "it might all so easily have gone in the opposite direction and Canada would have been without any government at all."[38]

H.D.G. Crerar retired in 1946. He spent his final years continuing his crusade for readiness in the face of what he considered the next inevitable conflict – this one against the Soviet Union. He petitioned to make conscription a permanent feature of Canadian life, envisioning a large, battle-ready army able to confront communism anywhere in the world, and when the Korean War began in 1950, warned that the Third World War may have begun. Such proclamations did not capture the imagination of a war-weary public now looking for Canada to play a role more attuned to the sentiments of Mackenzie King – that of international mediator. Forever associated with the fiascos at Hong Kong and Dieppe and increasingly seen as an anachronism from a bygone era of military glorification and unquestioning loyalty and duty to country, Canada's

18.2 A fairly civil war: Major-General H.D.G. Crerar and Prime Minister W.L. Mackenzie King in Ottawa for the 7 August 1945 victory parade. The two Canadians so at odds over the German question in 1937 also disagreed on Canada's obligations to the fight against Hitler. They remained, however, on reasonably friendly terms. (Canadian War Museum 19920263-058)

leading commander in the war to defeat Hitler died a forlorn man in 1965, aged seventy-six.[39]

Given Crerar's central role in tendering Canadian soldiers to some of the war's most ill-conceived missions, the controversy surrounding him is understandable; his relative obscurity among post-war Canadians is not. During a war to determine whether the global order would be dominated by fascism or liberalism, it is arguable that the two individuals exerting the greatest influence over the nature of Canada's role and the lives of its citizens were little-remembered Harry Crerar and much-remembered Mackenzie King, two Canadian nationalists locked in a protracted battle over the shape of Canada's autonomy and place in the world.

19

Aftermath

Mackenzie King would return to Germany one last time. In the summer of 1946 he travelled to the Paris Peace Conference, where representatives from the Allied nations were negotiating with those from Nazi Germany's wartime partners. The preponderance of the world's attention, however, was on Nuremberg, where leading Nazis were facing trial, and King decided to make a side trip to observe some of the proceedings. First, however, he travelled to Berlin – this time by aircraft, and this time with Edouard Handy, his personal secretary to the very end. While both the German nation and its capital were portioned into four quadrants by the victorious Allies, Berlin now lay deep within the Soviet sector of the defeated and occupied country, and was already earning a reputation as the world capital of espionage and ground zero in the emerging Cold War standoff.

King and Handy touched down on 20 August at Templehof Airport in the US sector, the vast terminal a rare surviving vestige of the "National Socialist intimidation architecture" Hitler and Speer had planned for all of Berlin – or rather, the reimagined *Welthauptstadt Germania*. Once again, King was struck by the circle of life, "another rounding out of a great conviction." He recounted his path from Berlin, Ontario, to its German namesake – now thrice visited – although this time the circle portended not the glorious fulfilment of his own destiny, but the damnation that fate assures the wicked. His journey had brought him into the company of "Hitler and his friends," King wrote, "and now with war over, some of the latter dead and others about to be hanged. A strange story of the inevitableness of the moral law and retribution."[1]

The following day, King walked the British-occupied zone of the ruined city, a sector that included the Government District where he

19.1 Mackenzie King much preferred the "old diplomacy" of quiet, one-on-one meetings to international conferences conducted under the prying eyes of the media. If members of his cabinet felt otherwise, one wouldn't know it from this August 1946 photo from the Paris Peace Conference. *Left to right*: Under-secretary of State for External Affairs Norman Robertson, Prime Minister Mackenzie King, Minister of National Defence Brooke Claxton, and Clerk of the Privy Council and Secretary to the Cabinet Arnold Heeney. (Library and Archives Canada, C-031312)

had spent the majority of his time and conducted his most significant interviews in 1937. Did he feel any shame as he wandered through the razed remnants of his beloved Berlin? He had once been optimistic – convinced, in fact – that war would not come, and that his own diplomacy had been vital to averting the European crisis. But that wouldn't necessarily translate into a sense of personal responsibility for what had come to pass. For one thing, after 1937 he had steadily gained a more reasoned estimation of the full sum of Nazism's singular malevolence, and by now likely recognized that the momentum of its appalling vision was well beyond any single individual's capacity to reverse. For another, an ego so robustly self-affirming as King's, which permitted him to believe destiny had anointed him humanity's saviour, was unlikely to turn on its host so completely as to assign him much blame when the fates chose calamity over salvation.

All the same, there was no denying that he had gotten it all so stupendously wrong for far too long, had so publicly and eagerly played the dupe. His diary account of the tour is uncharacteristically taught and clipped, the voice of one sobered by a bitter reckoning of the full depths of humanity's capacity for wickedness – and perhaps, of the full depths of his earlier error: "It was all very familiar but an appalling sight. Tiergarten, one waste of ground. Beautiful buildings demolished beyond recognition. The whole centre of the city all but totally destroyed. I recognized building after building – complete destruction."[2]

British officials and soldiers escorted King to the Reich Chancellery grounds, where the prime minister was permitted a look into the Fuhrerbunker, Hitler's "place of final refuge," as King's diary put it. He wandered through the Fuhrer's dank and fetid underground office and bedroom and the adjoining bedroom of Eva Braun, the nature of their relationship no longer a secret. Blood on the sofa was that of Braun, King's guide presumed. "Beyond was a telephone room – complete equipment," King noted. "We also saw the room that Goebbels occupied. Bed still there." King picked up a broken chunk of wall, "an interesting souvenir," and was "given a tile from Hitler's bathroom ... I felt a sort of feeling of appalling disgust as I went through these lower rooms constructed as a sort of hide-out. Final retreat and hide out." King was struck by how the bunker's occupants "had degraded themselves," their existence "something that corresponds to vermin and rats and the like, with holes in the ground, etc. The idea of men supposed to be carrying on govt., seeking a place like that to govern."[3] For one who saw in politics a sacred duty to improve the general welfare, this was utterly alien, utterly sickening.

While touring the bunker, King appeared to tacitly acknowledge the earlier misjudgment that allowed him to believe, well into the war, that the Fuhrer's constructive agenda for Germany had been derailed by a war he did not seek. "Hitler and his gang," he now conceded, "had begun the wrong way at the start." Their logical end was "this degraded cellar" where "Hitler and his consort were burnt to death with oil." He thought of Tennyson's poem *Guinevere*, wherein the narrator's sin turns him into "the loathsome opposite" of what he had desired, and of "the Frankenstein monster. How completely the whole idea had been fulfilled there." Then it was on to the Reichspräsidentenpalais, and

19.2 King, centre, in the Reich Chancellery garden near the entrance to the Fuhrerbunker, 21 August 1946. Hitler loyalists burned the bodies of the Fuhrer and Eva Braun here as the Soviets closed in. (Library and Archives of Canada, C-029789)

immediate recollections of the honour guard and the photograph that captured King in that moment of illusory triumph, the rooms he had visited now blown wide open, the grand staircase terminating at something "completely blasted," the sky visible through to the ground floor three stories below. The British Embassy flattened, the Adlon a shell.[4]

King tried to relocate the Anton Weber residence on Konigin Augusta Strasse where he had boarded in 1900. It was all a muddle – the landmarks were gone, the street had been renamed, even the police who were guiding him initially sent him in the wrong direction. He finally located the home's remains, and had photographs taken to record the damage. The few people out in the streets looked "very weary and frightened and surly and sad." Infrastructure was still in shambles; the city, he shuddered, reeked of sewage. Waves of dysentery, typhoid, and typhus fever would continue to strike malnourished residents for another year.

19.3 King picks his way through the rubble to enter the Old Reich Chancellery, escorted by British officials and soldiers. (Library and Archives Canada, C-026748)

King came upon the so-called *Trümmerfrau* (rubble women) who, under the watch of occupying troops, methodically sorted through "piles of bricks" to salvage what might be of use in the reconstruction. Crews hauled the remainder of the debris to the city's western outskirts and dumped them overtop a never-completed, Albert Speer-designed military college, a structure too solid to demolish via explosives. The project to clear the western sector of Berlin and entomb the college would go on for nearly three decades and create Berlin's highest peak, the 120-metre-high and aptly named Teufelsberg (Devil's Mountain).[5]

In the late afternoon King and Handy took off from Templehof for the city of Nuremberg, in the American-occupied zone of the conquered nation. As they gained altitude, they were given an aerial view of the. row upon row of crumbling husks of brick and masonry that had once formed one of the world's most dazzling cities.[6]

19.4 While wandering through what was left of Berlin in 1946, King observed the work of the *Trümmerfrau*, women aged fifteen to fifty whom Allied occupiers charged with cleaning up Germany's levelled cities. This photograph is of "Frau Beier," who is clearing the Reich Chancellery grounds that King had twice walked. It was taken after Beier was named "Berlin's best rubble woman," an honour presented on International Women's Day in 1950. Five years after Germany's surrender, there is obviously much work yet to be done. (Bundesarchiv, Bild 183-S94177, Rudolph)

19.5 King inspects an honour guard of US soldiers after touching down in Nuremberg to observe the international tribunal of leading Nazis. (Courtesy of the Robert H. Jackson Center, roberthjackson.org)

They touched down at 6 p.m., met by an honour guard and a dinner invitation from Justice Francis Biddle, lead American judge at the Nuremberg trials. King and Handy dined that evening with Biddle and his fellow magistrates, who advised the prime minister to "maintain an attitude of complete passivity" when observing the accused on trial the next day so as not to give any indication that he had met any of them. In view of his ill-starred pre-war discussions with key defendants, King was happy to comply. "I was fortunate in not having to meet the eyes of any of those whom I knew," he recalled afterward.[7]

The following morning King was in the gallery at Nuremberg's Palace of Justice to take in modern history's most infamous and influential tribunal. It was the last day to present evidence in the trial of the twenty-three Nazis considered the most prominent living architects of the war and Holocaust. Looking down on the men he had once predicted would be lifelong friends – Göring, Ribbentrop, Neurath – King found it all "a horrible and pathetic, tragic sight." They had given themselves over to "one leader – a maniac – a devil incarnate," bringing destruction to themselves, Germany, the world, and the moral order. Neurath, now seventy-three, was as hollowed a husk as Berlin itself, "an appalling fate" for a once-honourable gentleman who "had got in with the wrong gang." Neurath's earlier professions of rabid antisemitism, frank admission that his government had employed "pretty rough steps in clearing up the [Jewish] situation," and supervision of the deportation of Czechoslovakian Jews weren't enough for King to equate Hitler's first foreign minister with the other emblems of depravity in the dock. "Goering," King observed, "had shrunk to almost half the size as I remember him," the consequence of a prison diet designed to keep him alive long enough to properly execute. Erstwhile King confidant Ribbentrop was a "shadow of himself."[8]

After the morning's proceedings, King was shown the prison at the Palace of Justice. He was taken to the cell where Deutsche Arbeitsfront chief Robert Ley, the prime minister's frequent but unacknowledged companion in the summer of 1937, had hanged himself from the toilet pipe the previous autumn. "Anything more ignominious could not be imagined," declared the shaken prime minister, at last invoking Ley by name in his diary.[9]

King then approached the cell holding Rudolph Hess. Hess had been absent from the dock that morning at Nuremberg, as he was on numerous occasions during the trial. King noted only that Hess was allegedly feigning illness; more specifically, the former Deputy Fuhrer had for some time claimed recurrent bouts of amnesia, part of an ongoing campaign to prove he was mentally unfit and should thus be spared the death penalty. As he passed the cell, King could not avoid making eye contact, and Hess, who had previously denied recognizing even Göring, Ribbentrop, or any others on trial with him, appeared to temporarily give the game away. "When I looked in," King shuddered, "his eyes suddenly blazed up as though he recognized me in a moment. They were like coals of fire ... I shall never forget the look on his face. I took care not to wait a second but to move right on." Hess's other persistent claim – that he was in such physical decay that he should receive leniency – proved equally dubious. Sentenced to life in prison, he would live forty-one more years behind bars before taking his own life at age ninety-three.[10]

Reflecting on the austere cells, the "nauseating odour" that permeated the building and the executions that surely awaited those most responsible for Nazism's scarcely believable abasement of humanity, King "could think of no torture comparable," adding, "How right it is to what they have given others to endure." He and Handy were whisked to Nuremberg's airfield and boarded a Paris-bound flight, their three-day inspection of Adolf Hitler's bequest to Germany complete.[11]

Epilogue:
Perspectives

Mackenzie King was right to go to Berlin in 1937. The dangers of affording the Nazis increased international legitimacy were far outweighed by the dangers of a continental war, and any effort to stave off such a conflict through dialogue should be applauded. To both Göring and Hitler, King offered warnings that Canadians would likely rise to any threats to British territory or interests; that these warnings were somewhat ambiguous and probably not very consequential says more about the prerogatives of Canada's parliamentary democracy and the nation's relative powerlessness than the prime minister's woolliness or diplomatic ineffectiveness. King sought to moderate Nazi officials' evident hostility towards London's continued efforts at dialogue, and cannot be faulted for failing to appreciate that by the time of his visit Reich leaders had closed the door on any further attempts to work constructively with Britain.

But King got far more wrong than right. He was artless about assurances offered by Nazi officials who were already notorious as serial deceivers of the world community, and about the obvious preparations for battle discerned by other observers of the National Socialist youth and work camps. He was troublingly indifferent to the state persecution of Jews and other 'undesirables,' to the worldwide uproar over a Nazi Olympics, and to the blatant violations of international treaties and laws meant to check aggression. He wandered German soil in seemingly full-blown amnesia to outrages between 1933 and 1937 that had shocked the world and that he himself had previously castigated in his diary: abuse of minorities, Hitler- and race-worship, murderous purges of party and government, brazen remilitarization of the Rhineland. Instead, he departed Germany in July 1937 believing he had glimpsed the future in the Nazis' paternalistic, transparently doctrinaire, Aryans-only labour-betterment schemes, and praising Hitler as a beacon for humanity. No one fought harder at the Imperial Conference against the idea of collective and punitive responses to Germany's international criminality; King was convinced that a dictatorship that had demonstrated continuous and abundant disdain for world opinion and the anxieties of its neighbours could simply be talked out of further transgressions. Afforded the rare chance to sit down with Adolf Hitler, he offered little of diplomatic substance, no strategies for de-escalating the mounting hostility or working through the myriad points of friction other than an appeal to international bonhomie. King told Hitler that Chamberlain was pliable, and Chamberlain that Hitler could be trusted. He cleaved to a preposterously inflated belief in his destiny and his ability to shepherd global relations towards harmony.

To blame King for failing to usher in that harmony would be just as preposterous, a similar exaggeration of the prime minister's capacity to alter the march of events. Moreover, King was not the only one to counsel the governments of Britain and Germany along these lines. The failure to "box in" Hitler was a collective one, born of a terror of war, understandable confusion over ultimate Nazi aims, wishful thinking, and at least some capacity to abide the inhumanity intrinsic to National Socialism.

Yet a scholar and public servant who had dedicated his career to ideas completely at odds with the cult of militarism, death, and tyranny he witnessed in 1937 should have done better. Others in his position certainly had. After touring Germany in 1936, American reporter Howard K. Smith claimed that the typical visitor progressed through four stages in their opinion of Nazism: first, admiration for the order, cleanliness, and prosperity; second, recognition of the alarming quantity of "uniforms and guns" that signalled preparation for war; third, realization that "young humans, millions of them, were being trained ... to kill as a reflex ... to smash, crush, destroy, wreck"; and finally, "a strange, stark terror" that the world did not grasp the exigent threat from a regime that "screamed defiance at my [democratic] world from the housetops. One had to be deaf not to hear it." Some visitors, Smith allowed, never progressed beyond stage one; these, he declared rather uncharitably, possessed "the profundity of a tea-saucer."[1] On balance, it is grossly unfair to equate Mackenzie King's faculties with those of a tea saucer. In the context of his prewar relationship with Hitler's Germany, however, it must be admitted that it took the prime minister an awfully long time to graduate from stage one.

Colonel H.G.D. Crerar heard Nazism's defiant screams loud and clear. The colonel, whose education and experience in diplomacy were clearly eclipsed by the prime minister's own, saw plainly on a visit to Germany just before King's what National Socialism meant and where it was headed, and predicted with precision when the world could expect the war of words to escalate into war proper. Admittedly, Crerar, perennial advocate for increased military spending and preparedness, had a tendency to see the threat of war wherever he looked. Like a broken clock accurate twice a day, continual warnings of the battle to come will sometimes be proven right. But in this instance, Crerar furnished the hard and plain evidence that King could not or would not perceive, and that any objective observer should have found troubling: prodigious regimentation, propaganda, and thought control; seething hatred for internal and external enemies; vast resources allocated to armaments and military infrastructure; coercion to compel private corporations to fund that armaments program; a shackled press; foreign policy by blackmail; imminent absorption of Austria; Nazi-Soviet rapprochement; a blind readiness to follow the Fuhrer wherever he leads; a palpable tension about where the Fuhrer might lead. Crerar ended his report by doubting whether his trip had been of much use, so obvious and unoriginal were his observations to those paying attention.

Mackenzie King's sunny appraisal of National Socialism was not the consequence of any intrinsic penchant for offering the benefit of a doubt. He had no problem rendering harsh judgments against those with whom he disagreed; his diary teems with savage verdicts about a host of real and perceived foes. And his fascist cheerleading was not simply the product of Hitler's noted capacity to mesmerize. Canadian historian J.L. Granatstein offered the following apologia for the prime minister's dismal performance in Berlin: "King, I think, was taken in by Hitler, but then he's one of a very long series of politicians ranging from Chamberlain to Churchill to most of the politicians in the world in the 1930s. Hitler could be extraordinarily persuasive, could fool all sorts of people, and he fooled Mackenzie King."[2] This rationalization overlooks the fact that the prime minister had had more than four years to observe Hitler's movements from afar, and two full days to see it in the flesh, before sitting down with the Fuhrer. As his diary makes clear, it didn't take Hitler's mystical powers of seduction to make King an enthusiastic champion of the National Socialism experiment. He offered nothing but praise in his detailed and private record of his Berlin initiative, from the first day to the last. The Fuhrer's demeanour, "smooth skin," and "liquid eyes" simply reinforced King's fascination with the policies and the movement he described repeatedly as a model for all other countries.

Granatstein's other excuse for King's shoddy diplomatics – that "a very long series of politicians" also got Hitler wrong – finds echoes elsewhere. The *Canadian Encyclopedia*, for instance, takes this "King-had-company" line: *"Like many other leaders of the time*, King was impressed by Hitler when the two met in Berlin, Germany on 29 June 1937." Yet these justifications elide not only the many others who were emphatically unimpressed by the Fuhrer, but also the extraordinary degree to which King was "taken in by Hitler," to reiterate Grantatstein. Historian Abraham Ascher, who as a teen fled Hitler's Germany with his family, included King, along with several "prominent Britons," on his list of "leading appeasers." Ascher observed, however, that many of those most conciliatory towards Hitler expressed "comments about him [that] were often distinctly unflattering, sometimes not very different from those of diplomats who despised the dictator and urged condemnation of his repressive policies."[3]

The same could not be said of Mackenzie King. His affirmative public comments about his encounter with German fascism and its commandant were not sugar-coated diplomatic niceties meant to gloss over more unsympathetic private impressions, and he continued to cling to vestiges of his catastrophic delusions even after the Luftwaffe began dropping bombs on Warsaw. While Chamberlain viewed appeasement as the best hand he could play in difficult circumstances, King saw it as the best option, period. No other head of state from the democratic west endorsed the policy more unreservedly, or spoke more highly of Adolf Hitler. As historian Claude Bissell observed, "Of all the innocents abroad, King was the most innocent. Whereas his British predecessors had refrained from praising the Nazi regime, King sounded, in his summing up, like a disciple of Oswald Mosely."[4] King's visit in and of itself, undertaken in an age wracked by fear and uncertainty and lacking many of the modern mechanisms and institutions aimed at preventing war and mass violations of human rights, could have been defended by a leader who made it plain that talk did not amount to legitimization or endorsement, and that talk would include a forthright disavowal of the policies liberal democracies claimed to abhor. The Canadian prime minister failed to voice any such qualifications.

King's ability to champion Nazism arose from a complex constellation of factors, ranging from his overwhelming fears of leftist revolution and another world war to his support for improved labour conditions, from his love of elites and weakness for flattery to his own antisemitism. He was intoxicated by the undeniable gravity of his mission, a gravity amplified *ad absurdum* by the fantasy that he held the fate of the world in his hands. In crafting his approach to the troubles in Europe, King seemed to put less stock in the material evidence before him than on the false assurances of chronic fraudsters, along with cues from blankets, clouds, imaginary friends, and a host of other hallucinatory signs and wonders. These attitudes and approaches produced a mission by a Canadian prime minister that could hardly have been less illuminating or fruitful.

Following the war King had hoped to personally avert, his 1937 mission to Berlin was largely forgotten. Given the global attention paid to King's trip at the time, the virtual absence of the visit in the historical record is puzzling. Sir Nevile Henderson's memoir of his days in Berlin, candidly titled *Failure of a Mission 1937–1939* and running to 334 pages, finds no room for King's trip. Ian Kershaw's magisterial two-volume biography of Hitler, an account roughly two thousand pages long that, once Hitler is made chancellor, is a virtual day-by-day record of his activities, is likewise silent on King. So, too, is American war correspondent William Shirer's similarly encyclopaedic *The Rise and Fall of the Third Reich*. A random sampling of forty-three of the more prominent post-war non-Canadian histories of international relations in the 1930s, appeasement, and the road to the Second World War found just one reference to King's personal encounter with the Fuhrer.[5]

Why the silence? Canadians have a habit of claiming that those outside the country – particularly from Britain and the United States, the nationals whose esteem they secretly crave most – habitually underplay Canada's influence on world affairs. In this instance, they are partially correct. A Churchill or Roosevelt in Berlin would clearly gain notice in the record. But those leaders would doubtless have exerted more influence than King over the subsequent course of events – if not with German leaders, then at the very least with members of the international coalition that would come to coalesce in opposition to Nazi expansion. King's trip did nothing to alter the plot, save perhaps boosting Hitler's confidence that Chamberlain would respond as he did to pending German provocations, and providing succour to those in Britain who considered the threat from Nazism overblown.

More surprising than the lacunae in foreign accounts is the handling of the affair by historians from King's own country. For decades the visit was habitually ignored in even the most comprehensive post-war Canadian works on the King era, while the few writers who attempted to come to terms with what would appear to be a tacit legitimation of the repugnant regime did so briskly, before moving on to recount the grit and determination of Canada's war effort. And the story they told of the prime minister in Germany was generally the same: King's mission was a well-intentioned and bluntly delivered, though ultimately futile, warning to Hitler of the steely resolve of the English-speaking world in the face of Nazi aggression.[6] That certainly sounds commendable, but this reassuring tale hardly captures the authentic gist of King's initiative. In this instance, national insecurity rears its head again. As King botched the most important issues and came off looking like a dupe, few analysts were inclined to turn their gaze towards the fiasco or to afford it the cold scrutiny it deserved. In truth, Canada's first significant foray into international peacemaking was at best an embarrassing waste of time, and at worst, additional fuel for the conflagration ahead.

More recent historians' assessments of King's encounter with the monstrous engineers of Nazism, those that had access to and took seriously the fascist-friendly musings in King's diary, are entirely justified in their damnations of the prime minister and his credulity. In these works the affair, although still handled briskly, has been labelled "one of King's most contested foreign policy decisions," "a central blemish on his record," "one of the strangest diplomatic missions in Canadian history," and "probably the most controversial of all his actions in external relations."[7]

Terry Reardon gave King too much slack in writing that "King's thoughts were written soon after the meeting, and he can be forgiven for his enthusiastic assessment," but the writer was on surer ground in noting that "it is baffling that he could have written in that vein when he knew that the Nazis were operating concentration camps for political prisoners, and that laws had been placed on the books since 1933 to deny Jews the freedoms which the rest of the citizens enjoyed." Larry Rose conceded that the "comments King confided to his diary are cringe-inducing," and Tim Cook concurred, noting that "King's schoolgirlish description [of Hitler] still has the power to make one squirm." J. Wagner reported that even German diplomats stationed in Ottawa found the depth of the prime minister's fervour for their Fuhrer "amusing."[8] The Mackenzie King crowned Canada's greatest prime minister by historians in the *Maclean's* magazine surveys, the judicious statesman and political sage, never made it to Berlin, and his grave misreading of the most critical issue of his era should prompt at least some attenuation of the praise for his legendary perspicacity. Here, the type of forthright soul-searching conducted by Germans following their own deadly embrace of fascism provides a marked counterpoint to the uncomplicated tributes to King's political IQ that populate Canadian history books.

What, then, of the Liberal leader's other celebrated administrative gift – his capacity to divine the public mood? Both the reporters of King's era and the historians writing prior to the publication of his diaries lacked a full appreciation for the prime minister's endorsement of fascism, and their coverage and opinions of his trip to Germany thus lack the expressions of disbelief and mortification present in the most recent accounts. Even so, the response from Canadian journalists, politicians, and the general public in 1937 – and many later historians – was conspicuously bereft of any criticisms of the prime minister's decision to be feted by Nazi leaders, or of his refusal to raise even the slightest public (and as it turns out, private) objections to the intensively documented ruthlessness that had marked more than four years of Hitler's reign.

This absence of controversy, placed in the context of the broader forbearance among Canadians for the types of racial chauvinism that found their fullest expression in Nazism, suggests that King's amalgam of myopia, timidity, and callousness was not merely a personal failing, that the responsibility for and consequences of this diplomatic miscarriage are not King's alone to bear. When modern writers contend that King's illusions about the Nazis marked him as "naive," "absurd," "imperceptive," blissfully unaware," and "the most innocent" of Nazi Germany's visitors,[9] they reinforce the "Weird Willie" caricature that Canadians love to satirize, but these writers, whether by intention or not, are also saying a good deal about the prevailing cultural assumptions among interwar Canadians. In this instance at least, comforting rationalizations about the blunder in Berlin that focused primarily on the prime minister's peculiarities and psychoses will only take us so far. King may have served as Canada's longest-serving leader – literally and figuratively its first citizen – but this did not grant him any special capacity to manufacture personal sensibilities and traits independent of his social and cultural context; in fact, that very political durability suggests a striking congruence with his time and place (as his more recent champions correctly point out in the *Maclean's* surveys).

The debates over Mackenzie King's legacy and how his dalliance with Hitler fits into it will doubtless continue. Some will argue that four days in Berlin and their damaging impact on King's stance towards

Germany in the two years that followed should not define a political career marked by many successes and many years in power. Others will point to the continuities in King's thinking that prepared him for his fascist flirtation and that never fully vanished. Here, his antisemitism, which regrettably survived the Holocaust more or less intact, provides the clearest example. King's unwillingness to amend his opinions and learn from mistakes was evident in other areas as well. While the Second World War made abundantly clear to citizens and state officials the world over the need for a truly engaged international forum, and all independent states joined the newly minted United Nations, King's wooden-headedness on the matter, to repeat Barbara Tuchman's label, rendered him an outlier. "I really feel," he carped in August 1946, "the U.N. threatens to become as great a menace as the League of Nations."[10]

Menace? In truth, it was because of heads of state like King that the League proved far too weak to constitute the kind of menace that would have been indispensable: the menace to expansionist tyrants its designers had envisioned. King's continued obduracy on the matter following the second global conflict in his lifetime recalls another truth from Tuchman's *March of Folly*, although one with which the prime minister, instrument of destiny, might not fully agree. "There is," she wrote, "always freedom of choice to change or desist from a counterproductive course if the policy-maker has the moral courage to exercise it. He is not a fated creature blown by the whims of Homeric gods."[11]

Perhaps more arresting than King's undiminished scorn for collective security are his musings, voiced in the same diary entry condemning the UN, about relations between the Soviets and the West. As the former allies in the war against Hitler slid towards full-blown cold war, the prime minister mulled over the prospect of travelling to Moscow to sound out Stalin.[12] We should probably be grateful that this was a mission never undertaken.

Notes

Prologue

1 Olivia Blair, "Justin Trudeau's Statement to Donald Trump Could Make Americans Think Twice about Emigrating to Canada," *Independent*, 10 November 2016.
2 Carol Giacomo, "Angela Merkel's Message to Trump," *New York Times*, 9 November 2016, emphasis added.
3 Mount, *Canada's Enemies*, 53; Abella and Troper, *None Is Too Many*.
4 Brett, *Photography and Place*, 27; Bruce, *Through the Lion Gate*, 202.

1 Of Lions and Lyons

1 William Lyon Mackenzie King papers, Library and Archives Canada, https://www.bac-lac.gc.ca/eng/discover/politics-government/prime-ministers/william-lyon-mackenzie-king/Pages/diaries-william-lyon-mackenzie-king.aspx, 27 June 1937. Henceforth cited as King diary.
2 King diary, 18, 22, 27 June 1937.
3 Nietzsche, *Thus Spoke Zarathustra*, 31.
4 Nagorski, *Hitlerland*, 324, 327.

2 Arrival

1 King diary, 27 June 1937; Frisse, "The Missing Link."
2 "Kitchener Mayor Notes 100th Year of Name Change – Kitchener-Waterloo." *CBC News*. http://www.cbc.ca/news/canada/kitchener-waterloo/kitchener-ontario-berlin-name-change-100-years-tom-reitz-berry-vrbanovic-1.3744212, accessed 29 January 2017.

3 Levine, *King*, 29–31; Goodall, *William Lyon Mackenzie King*, 13.
4 Stacey, *A Very Double Life*, 18–19; Levine, *King*, 77.
5 Levine, *King*, 53–4.
6 Ibid., 88–91.
7 MacMillan, *History's People*, 42.
8 Levine, *King*, 143. One of the more consistent leitmotifs in King's diary is self-censure over his appearance, public speaking performances, and food and beverage consumption.
9 MacMillan, *History's People*, 34. The "King-Byng Affair," during which King worked feverishly to retain his prime ministership despite finishing second in the 1925 election to Arthur Meighan's Conservatives, and despite the pleas of Governor General Lord Julian Byng, is perhaps the most noted case of King's sometimes slippery politicking. See Levine, *King*, 146–51.
10 Stephen Azzi and Norman Hillmer, "Ranking Canada's Best and Worst Prime Ministers," *Maclean's*, 7 October 2016, https://www.macleans.ca/politics/ottawa/ranking-canadas-best-and-worst-prime-ministers/, accessed 5 February 2017; Norman Hillmer and Stephen Azzi, "Canada's Best Prime Ministers," *Maclean's*, 10 June 2011, https://www.macleans.ca/news/canada/canadas-best-prime-ministers/, accessed 5 February 2017.
11 Stewart, "Names Written in Water," 34, 36. On the trajectory of King's reputation since his death, see Dummitt, "The Importance of Not Being Earnest," and Dummitt, *Unbuttoned*.
12 Reardon, *Winston Churchill and Mackenzie King*, 17.
13 Reynolds, *Mackenzie King*, xv; Stacey, *A Very Double Life*; Stacey, review of *The Mackenzie King Record*, 309 (quote). King's diary could also be called Canada's answer to the Nixon White House tapes. Both artefacts expose in granular detail the thoughts and activities of a head of state that are extraordinarily frank and sometimes shockingly petty, bigoted, and narcissistic (though King's diary lacks the profanity and admissions of criminal behaviour that lard up the Nixon recordings). Moreover, neither tapes nor diary have anything in the way of an equivalent in the national public record. President Roosevelt secretly recorded White House press conferences, and Eisenhower did the same for a handful of meetings. Kennedy taped important meetings and telephone calls, and Johnson, too, recorded a good deal of his telephone conversations – roughly eight hundred hours in total. No president, however, bequeathed to posterity anything like the indiscriminate record of phone calls, daily meetings, and private conversations amassed by Nixon's voice-activated taping archive, which ran to over three thousand hours and captured the kind of

in-camera exchanges only conducted by those who are certain their words would forever remain off the record. Likewise, Canadian prime ministers have penned memoirs, and researchers have mined their personal correspondence and internal memoranda, but no other prominent Canadian politicians bestowed a daily log of their most confidential thoughts and experiences. As such, the reigns of both Nixon and King cannot truly be placed in context. In the absence of similar records – ones disclosing their innermost sentiments, along with clandestine activities never intended for public consumption – do we really know that other prime ministers and presidents steered clear of the type of strange conduct often revealed here? Given the scope and scale of the peculiarities in question the odds are long, but we should be fair. Others holding these offices enjoyed the luxury of discretion that fate, and their own guileless record-keeping, did not allow Nixon or King. On US presidents' weakness for the tape recorder, see Domenico Montanaro, "The Shadowy History of Secret White House Tapes," National Public Radio, https://www.npr.org/2017/05/13/528222995/the-shadowy-history-of-secret-white-house-tapes, accessed 22 January 2018.

14 First two quotes cited in Evan Thomas, "The First Modern President," *New York Times Book Review*, 19 November 2017, 20; third quote ibid.
15 King diary, 24 April 1937.
16 Conferences held before 1907 were called Colonial Conferences. See Ollivier, *The Colonial and Imperial Conferences*.
17 Shirer, *Rise and Fall of the Third Reich,*1056; Bloch, *Ribbentrop*, 17; Weizsäcker cited in Sonnenfeldt, *Witness to Nuremberg*, 25; Kershaw, *Making Friends with Hitler*, 331.
18 King diary, 10 May 1937.
19 Cited in Levine, *King*, 281. On Ribbentrop, see Kershaw, *Making Friends with Hitler*, 160.
20 King diary, 26 May 1937.
21 King diary, 14 September 1938; Ribbentrop cited in Beloff, *Imperial Sunset*, 273.
22 King diary, 10 May 1937.
23 Eayrs, *In Defence of Canada*, 44.
24 Dickson, *A Thoroughly Canadian General*, xv–xvii.
25 Ibid., xvi (quote), 14, 17, 48.
26 Ibid., 110–12.
27 Crerar, Report on Visit to Germany, 126; On his pre-trip correspondence with Peacock, see Library and Archives Canada, Crerar fonds, MG30 E157, vol. 10, file "Notes on Visit to Germany" (2F-L, 2K: Visit to Germany).

28 King diary, 12 July 1929, 8 January 1936, 5 July 1937 (King quote); Levine, *King*, 264 (quote on treatment of staff); Mutimer, *Canadian Annual Review of Politics*, 44; Lumley, *Canadian Who's Who*, 987.
29 Robertson, *Memoirs of a Very Civil Servant*, 53.
30 King diary, 25 June 1937.
31 Jack Pickersgill, cited in Levine, *King*, 265.
32 King diary, 25 June 1937.
33 Bilski, *Berlin Metropolis*, 119; Korboński, *The Polish Underground State*, 88.
34 Clementi, *Holocaust Mothers and Daughters*, 325n21.
35 Ladd, *The Companion Guide to Berlin*, 95; Schulte, "Soldiers and War Criminals," 222 (quote).
36 King diary, 27 June 1937.
37 King diary, 14 June 1937; waiter cited in O'Donnell, *The Bunker*, 111; Floud cited in Levine, *King*, 8.
38 Geerken, *Hitler's Asian Adventure*, 34–8.
39 Ibid., 34–49, 52.

3 Beholding the Nazi Miracle

1 King diary, 27, 28 June 1937.
2 Ibid., 27 June 1937; Kater, *Hitler Youth*, 2, 5 (quote).
3 King diary, 27 June 1937; Eayrs cited in Vacante, *National Manhood*, 110; King cited in Vacante, *National Manhood*, 111; Fromm, *Blood and Bouquets*, 246; Halton cited in Halton, *Dispatches from the Front*, 83.
4 King diary, 30 June 1937; Hillson cited in Stone, *Responses to Nazism in Britain*, 116.
5 Lorimer and Roberts cited in Stone, *Responses to Nazism in Britain*, 116; Crerar, Report on Visit to Germany, 122. Grüger's business card can be found in Library and Archives Canada, Crerar fonds, MG30 E157, vol. 10, file "Notes on Visit to Germany" (2F-L, 2K: Visit to Germany).
6 Cruttwell, *A History of the Great War*, 64; Crerar, Report on Visit to Germany, 124, 122.
7 King diary, 27 June 1937.
8 Menkis and Troper, *More than Just Games*, 4–9, 16–18; Large, *Nazi Games*, 49–59 (IOC cited 51); Menkis and Troper, "Racial Laws vs. Olympic Aspirations," 56–7 (Hitler cited p. 56).
9 "The Movement to Boycott the Berlin Olympics of 1936," *Holocaust Encyclopedia*, https://www.ushmm.org/wlc/en/article.php?ModuleId=10007087, accessed 24 January 2018; Kurtz cited in Menkis and Troper, "Racial Laws vs. Olympic Aspirations," 71.

10 Menkis and Troper, "Racial Laws vs. Olympic Aspirations," 72–4; Large, *Nazi Games*, 290–1; Vansittart cited in Ladd, *Ghosts of Berlin*, 143.

11 Amanda Grzyb, "From Kristallnacht to the *MS St Louis*," 82; King diary, 22 April 1933, 17 December 1933.

12 Menkis and Troper, "Racial Laws vs. Olympic Aspirations," 58–63, 67; Kershaw, *Making Friends with Hitler*, 32; Halton cited in Halton, *Dispatches from the Front*, 78, 79.

13 Halton, *Dispatches from the Front*, 77–87.

14 Levine, *Scrum Wars*, 128 (first quote); Menkis and Troper, *More than Just Games*, 122, 151; Menkis and Troper, "Racial Laws vs. Olympic Aspirations," 74 (second quote).

15 Lapointe cited in MacFarlane, *Ernest Lapointe*, 99; first King quote cited in MacFarlane, *Ernest Lapointe* , 52; second cited in Cook, *Warlords*, 195.

16 Canada, House of Commons Debates, 1937, III, 2737–9.

17 "The Front Page," *Saturday Night*, 3 July 1937, 1.

18 Ladd, *Ghosts of Berlin*, 142–4 (quote p. 142).

19 Ibid.

20 Hesse-Lichtenberger, *Tor!*, 67.

21 Menkis and Troper, *More than Just Games*, 141; King diary, 27 June 1937. Tschammer's funeral is shown in a photograph held at the Bundesarchiv, Bild 183-J06059, "Berlin, Beisetzung der Urne Hans von Tschammer und Osten."

22 Friedrich, *Hitler's Berlin*, 415n110. The Weber house address, Konigin Augusta Strasse 70, is listed in the King diary, 22 March 1900, and is plotted on Alexius Kiessling, "1897 Map of Berlin in Germany" (Verlag v. Alexius Kießling). It was located at the intersection of Friedrich Wilhelm Strasse (now Klingelhöfer Strasse) and Konigen Augusta Strasse, sometimes shown as Kaiseren Augusta Strasse before being renamed Admiral von Schröder Strasse in 1933. Following the Second World War, it became Köbistrasse. As with many other Berlin streets, addresses along this route were reconfigured after the Second World War.

23 Schäche and Selene, *An Italian Palazzo in Germany*, 27; Ladd, *Ghosts of Berlin*, 141–2. The address for Konrad Adenauer Stiftung is Klingelhöfer Strasse 23, under a completely renumbered street grid.

4 Shrugging Off the British Yoke

1 Fromm, *Blood and Bouquets*, 244.

2 Henderson cited in Ascher, *Was Hitler a Riddle?*, 68; King diary, 27 June 1937.

3 King diary, 27 June 1937.

4 Historic marker, Wilhelmstrasse, British Embassy, Berlin (including Henderson quote).
5 King diary, 4 June 1937.
6 Ibid., 7 June 1937.
7 Ibid., 8 June 1937.
8 Ibid., 10 June 1937.
9 Ibid., 4, 7, 8, 10 June 1937; Eayrs, *In Defence of Canada*, 58.
10 Eayrs, *In Defence of Canada*, 37–9, 60 (first quote), 91 (second).
11 Ferguson, *Bastards and Boneheads*, 168.
12 Wood, *Militia Myths*, 242, 252; Renan cited in Vernes, *Ernest Renan*, 101; King diary 7 June 1937; Canada, *House of Commons Debates*, 1936, II, 1333.
13 Eayrs, *In Defence of Canada*, 38; King diary, 7 June 1937.
14 King diary, 8 June 1937; van Ginneken, *Historical Dictionary of the League of Nations*, 119. Franz Cede sums up the reasons for the League's failure: "Its structural weakness (e.g., the unanimity rule for decision taking both in the Council and the Assembly), the deficient regulation of the prohibition to use military force and the lack of universal membership." Each reason has roots in the unwillingness of nation-states to cede some of their traditional powers and prerogatives to a supranational referee (Cede, "Historical Introduction," 4).
15 Eayrs, *In Defence of Canada*, 58–9; King diary, 8 June 1937.
16 King diary, 10–11 June 1937; Berendsen, *Mr. Ambassador*, 128–9.
17 *London Spectator*, 18 June 1937.
18 Beloff, *Imperial Sunset*, 239–45.
19 Amstutz, *International Ethics*, 65–6.
20 King diary, 27 June 1937; Levine, *King*, 259.
21 King diary, 11 June 1937.
22 Ibid., 27 June 1937.
23 Ibid.
24 Ibid.

5 The Holy Errand

1 Levine, *King*, 4, 40 (King cited).
2 King diary, 11 June 1937. For a helpful recent study of William Lyon Mackenzie's ideology, see Wallace, *Scottish Presbyterianism and Settler Colonial Politics*, chap. 5.
3 Levine, *King*, 68, 96 (Jones cited).
4 Cook, *Warlords*, 188; King diary, 14 June 1928.

5 King, *Industry and Humanity*, 22, 69.

6 Ibid., 70, 26.

7 Natale, *Supernatural Entertainments*.

8 Stacey cited in Dummit, *Unbuttoned*, 217; French cited ibid., 218.

9 Cited in Levine, *King*, 144, 386.

10 Raber, *Shakespeare and Posthumanist Theory*, 83–4 (quote); Jones and Flaxman, *11:11*, 153.

11 Jones and Flaxman, *11:11*, 153.

12 King diary, 11 June 1937.

13 Ibid.

14 Ibid., 11, 14, 22, 27 June 1937.

15 Ibid., 26 June 1937; Trevelyan, *A Very British Family*, 69, 92.

16 King diary, 26 June 1937. As the well-known US statesman and Nobel laureate Elihu Root had died in February 1937, the speech King heard in March was probably delivered by Elihu Root Jr., like his father a prominent New York lawyer and public figure (Hill, *A Very Private Public Citizen*, 191).

17 King diary, 26 June 1937.

18 Ibid.

19 Ibid., 27 June 1937, emphasis in original.

20 Reardon, *Winston Churchill and Mackenzie King*, 83; Kershaw, *Making Friends with Hitler*, 142.

21 King diary, 11, 15 June 1937.

22 King diary, 23 (first quote), 25 (second), 24 (third) June 1937; Parker, *Albert Camus*, 225–6n12; Wesseling, "Gabriel Hanotaux."

23 Library and Archives Canada, O.D. Skelton fonds, MG 30 D33 13, vol. 4, file "Foreign Policy Discussions in London, 1935" (Folder 3: External Affairs Correspondence and Position Papers).

24 King cited in Esberey, *Knight of the Holy Spirit*, 210 (first quote), 211 (third); King diary, 11 March 1936.

6 Sympathy for the Devil

1 Henderson, *Failure of a Mission*, 14 (first quote); King diary, 27 June 1937.

2 King diary, 27 June 1937.

3 Cited in Eayrs, *In Defence of Canada*, 61.

4 Kershaw, *Hitler*, 199; Kershaw, *Making Friends with Hitler*, 253.

5 King diary, 5, 10, 29 June 1937, 2 July 1937.

6 Whitaker, *A Sovereign Idea*, 48; King diary, 20 October 1937.

7 I am grateful to one of the blind reviewers of the manuscript of this book who pointed out the paradox of King's disdain for the press despite his

family's connections to the profession; John Farrell makes a similar point about the incongruity between the sensibilities of journalists and those of his subject in *Richard Nixon*, 203. For an overview of King's tortured relationship with the Canadian media, see Levine, *Scrum Wars*, 124–50.

8 Esberey cited in Levine, *Scrum Wars*, 129.

9 King diary, 11 June 1937; Hal Frank, "The Passing Show," *Saturday Night*, 17 July 1937, 1.

10 Cited in Levine, *King*, 278, 217, 218, 228.

11 Cited in Granatstein and Morton, *Canada and the Two World Wars*, 178; Whitaker and Marcuse, *Cold War Canada*, 58, 7. As these latter authors write, Canada's War Measures Act (1939–46) gave the government far greater leeway in suppressing opposition – fittingly, given King's ideological bent, mostly the leftist variety – than was permitted in the United States or Britain. King deployed these considerable powers to the hilt in his government's thoroughly illiberal prosecution of Canadians accused of spying for the Soviets in the so-called Gouzenko Affair. For a recent and provocative look at the incident, see Molinaro, "How the Cold War Began."

12 King diary, 4, 5 June 1937.

13 Ibid.; Graham, *The Spanish Civil War*, 30; Whitaker, Kealey, and Parnaby, *Secret Service*, 139–40.

14 Kramer, "From Guernica to Hiroshima to Bagdad," 119; King diary, 5 May 1937; Southworth, *Guernica! Guernica!*, xiv.

15 King diary, 5 June 1937.

16 Gindin, *The Canadian Auto Workers*, 61; King diary, 5, 24 June 1937; King, *Industry and Humanity*, 20.

17 Timpe, *Nazi-Organized Recreation*, 186.

18 King diary, 27 June 1937.

19 Cited in Levine, *King*, 180–1.

20 Levine, *King*, 77; King diary, 15, 16 June 1937.

21 Waddington "An Idyllic and Unruffled Atmosphere," 44; King diary, 10 May 1937; Library and Archives Canada, William Lyon Mackenzie King Correspondence, MG 26-J1, vol. 236 (4–11 May 1937), "Lord Lothian to Mackenzie King," 11 May 1937, microfilm reel C-3728, pp. 203063–203101.

22 Library and Archives Canada, William Lyon Mackenzie King Correspondence, "Lord Lothian to Mackenzie King," 11 May 1937.

23 King diary, 15 June 1937; Dummit, *Unbuttoned*, 206, 295 (King cited).

24 King diary, 27, 29 June 1937.

25 King diary, 27 June 1937.

26 Ibid.

7 Haunted Berlin

1 Ladd, *Ghosts of Berlin*, 72–81; Jones et al., *An Introduction to Political Geography*, 103; Charney, "Napoleon: Emperor of Art Theft," 69.
2 Charney, "Napoleon: Emperor of Art Theft," 74–6; Jones et al., *An Introduction to Political Geography*, 103.
3 Ladd, *Ghosts of Berlin*, 75.
4 Ibid.
5 Ibid., 85.
6 Matthias, *The Hotel as Setting*, 7, 22, 30
7 Miller, *Agent 110*, 229; Harsch, *At the Hinge of History*, 44.
8 Robinson, *Reluctant Nazi*, chap. 17, n.p.; Demps and Paeschke, *The Hotel Adlon*, 96; Mourby, *Rooms with a View*, "The Adlon Hotel, Berlin," n.p.
9 Large, *Berlin*, chap. 5, n.p.; Denslagen, *Romantic Modernism*, 215.
10 Large, *Berlin*, chap. 5, n.p.

8 *Arbeit Macht Frei*

1 King diary, 28 June 1937.
2 Ibid.
3 Levine, *King*, 260; King diary, 29, 30 June 1937.
4 Taylor, *Hitler's Engineers*, 23; Lepage, *Hitler's Armed Forces Auxiliaries*, 74–7.
5 Patel, *Soldiers of Labor*, 112.
6 Lepage, *Hitler's Armed Forces Auxiliaries*, 76; Patterson, *Slavery and Social Death*; Bergen, "Social Death and International Isolation," 4.
7 Patel, *Soldiers of Labor*, 88; Lepage, *Hitler's Armed Forces Auxiliaries*, 77.
8 Dudeck, "National Socialist Youth Policy," 40; Wolfgang Sheibe, cited in Dudeck, "National Socialist Youth Policy," 41.
9 Dudeck, "National Socialist Youth Policy," 40–4 (quote p. 41).
10 Patel, *Soldiers of Labor*, 70; G.S Cox, "Are the German Labour Camps Militaristic?," *London Spectator*, 2 November 1934, 10.
11 Giles, *Students and National Socialism*, 142; Guillebaud, *Social Policy of Nazi Germany*, 68.
12 King diary, 28 June 1937.
13 Library and Archives Canada, William Lyon Mackenzie King Correspondence, MG 26-J1, vol. 239 (3 July–24 December 1937), "Correspondence with Herr Muller-Brandenburg," 2 July 1937, microfilm reel C-3728, pp. 205662–70; Coetzee, *The German Army League*, 59.

14 Author translation. Original German version: *Wir lieben die Freiheit, wir lieben den Frieden, / wir wollen die zukunft des Vaterlandes schmieden. / Deutschland voran! ... Morgen schon stehen wir dann Mann an Mann in den Reihen der jüngsten Soldaten; / Wir ziehen das feldgraue Ehrenkleid an, und wir schultern Gewehre statt Spaten ... / Wird zum Appell einst die Trommel gerührt, Kamerad, zäum' dein Pferd, aufgesessen! / Da gibt es kein Zaudern, der Zage verliert, Mannesmut wird im Felde gemessen* (lyrics from "Third Reich Song Cards," www.akpool.co.uk, http://www.akpool.co.uk/postcards/26455586-lied-postcard-spaten-und-wehr-deutschland-voran-kaethe-sommer-herms-niel, accessed 5 May 2018).

15 Library and Archives Canada, William Lyon Mackenzie King Correspondence, MG 26-J1, vol. 239 (3 July–24 December 1937), "Correspondence with Herr Muller-Brandenburg," 17 September 1937, microfilm reel C-3728, pp. 205662–70.

16 Ibid., 18 November 1937.

17 "Summer Camp in the GDR," DDR Museum, https://www.ddr-museum.de/en/blog/archive/summer-camp-gdr-pioneer-republic-wilhelm-pieck-werbellinsee, accessed 12 January 2018; Alpadia Language Schools, "Alpadia Berlin-Werbellinsee," https://www.alpadia.com/en/summer-camps/learn-german/germany/berlin-werbellinsee.htm, accessed 18 February 2018.

18 King diary, 28 June 1937; Richter, Carstensen, and Hitzer, *Germany*; Rogers, *Mackenzie King*; Levine, *King*, 224.

19 Timpe, *Nazi-Organized Recreation*, 2.

20 Ibid., 8–9; Crerar, Report on Visit to Germany, 122.

21 Patel, *Soldiers of Labor*, 241–3.

22 Large, *Nazi Games*, 49–59.

23 King diary, 28 June 1937.

24 Whitaker, "The Liberal Corporatist Ideas of Mackenzie King," 154.

25 Whitaker, *A Sovereign Idea*, 50–51.

26 Ibid, 51; Levine, *King*, 50–1.

27 King, *Industry and Humanity*, xv.

28 Ibid., xvii, 58.

29 King diary, 18, 6 June 1937; last quote cited in Whitaker, *A Sovereign Idea*, 64.

30 Whitaker, *A Sovereign Idea*, 55, 60.

31 Cited in ibid., 56.

32 Ibid., 61. For a careful delineation of the many regional expressions of this new labour militancy, see Heron, *The Workers' Revolt in Canada*.

33 Bannister, "Canada as Counter-Revolution," 64–97.

34 Dummitt, "The Importance of Not Being Earnest," 62. On the durability and elasticity of Canada's liberal project, see McKay, "The Liberal Order Framework."
35 King, *Industry and Humanity*, 3, xvii, 14, 11.
36 Ibid., 12, emphasis in original.
37 King diary, 28 June 1937.

9 Whither the Jews

1   The term gained prominence after the 1944 publication of Gunnar Myrdal's *An American Dilemma*.
2   For a summary of these practices and incidents, see Teigrob, *Living with War*, chap. 7.
3   Ibid.
4   Kohn, *This Kindred People*, 24; cited in Levine, *King*, 56.
5   Canadian Museum of Immigration at Pier 21, "Chinese Immigration Act, 1923," http://www.pier21.ca/research/immigration-history/chinese-immigration-act-1923.
6   Teigrob, *Living with War*, 35–6.
7   Whitman, *Hitler's American Model*, 9–10. I am indebted to one of the blind reviewers of this book for making this connection clear.
8   Price, *Orienting Canada*, 25; Ward, *White Canada Forever*, 149; cited in Levine, *King*, 183.
9   Cited in Levine, *King*, 287 (first quote), 169 (third); King diary, 2 December 1935.
10 Levine, *King*, 275; Bergen, "Social Death and International Isolation," 13–14, 20–1, 23, 25–6; Robinson, *A History of Antisemitism in Canada*, 59–84; Anastakis, *Death in the Peaceable Kingdom*, 138.
11 Levine, *King*, 286 (first King quote), 292; Hamerow, *Why We Watched*, 152; Neatby, *William Lyon Mackenzie King*, 304 (second King quote); Abella and Troper, *None Is Too Many*, vi.
12 Renan, "What Is a Nation?," 11.
13 Breitman and Lichtman, *FDR and the Jews*, 315.
14 King diary, 17 November 1938. For a similar view of Lord Londonderry's opinion of Nazi antisemitism, see Kershaw, *Making Friends with Hitler*, 147.
15 Cited in Knight, *How the Cold War Began*, 113, and in Levine, *King*, 375.
16 Teigrob, *Warming Up to the Cold War*, 190.
17 King diary, 16 June, 1937.
18 Ibid.

19 Ibid., 29 June 1937, emphasis added.
20 Ibid., 30 June 1937.

10 The Uses and Abuses of Mackenzie King

1 King diary, 29 June 1937.
2 Urbach, *Go-Betweens for Hitler*, 204, 201–2.
3 Kershaw, *Hitler*, 313–16.
4 Rose, *The Literary Churchill*, 177; Zuccotti, *Under His Very Windows*, 103.
5 Waddington, "An Idyllic and Unruffled Atmosphere," 59–60; King diary, 29 June 1937.
6 Kershaw, *Hitler*, 833–41.
7 Ladd, *The Ghosts of Berlin*, 150; Niven, *Facing the Nazi Past*, 71–81.
8 Ladd, *Ghosts of Berlin*, 150–1 (quote p. 150).
9 King diary, 29 June 1937; Mao cited in Angang, *Mao and the Cultural Revolution*, 32n31.
10 King diary, 29 June 1937; Fromm, *Blood and Bouquets*, 246.
11 Kershaw, *Hitler*, 338; Bloch, *Ribbentrop*, 111–20.
12 Kershaw, *Hitler*, 369.
13 Ibid., 369, 385 (Hitler quote); Italian official cited in Bloch, *Ribbentrop*, 134.
14 Henderson, *Failure of a Mission*, 68–9.
15 King diary, 29 June 1937.

11 Canada Makes Headlines

1 See, for example, "Canadian Premier in Berlin," *The Times* (London), 1 July 1937; "Mr. King Meets Hitler," *Manchester Guardian Weekly*, 2 July 1937; "Canadian Leaves Berlin," *New York Times*, 1 July 1937.
2 King diary, 30 June 1937.
3 Levine, *King*, 85.
4 Cited in Esberey, *Knight of the Holy Spirit*, 211; "Nazi Swastikas and Union Jacks Greet Premier's Arrival in Berlin," *Globe and Mail*, 28 June 1937; "Nazi Pastors to Face Trial for Defiance," *Globe and Mail*, 28 June 1937.
5 Kershaw, *Hitler*, 381–2.
6 Cited in Shirer, *The Rise and Fall of the Third Reich*, 239; Stoltzfus, *Hitler's Compromises*, 77.
7 King diary, 25 August 1936, 29 June 1937.
8 Shirer, *The Rise and Fall of the Third Reich*, 239–40; Barnett, *For the Soul of the People*, 34–5; Halton cited in Halton, *Dispatches from the Front*, 84.

9 "Premier Gets Hitler's Views," *Globe and Mail*, 30 June 1937; "L'hon.
   M. King et la question de nos tarifs, " *La Presse*, 28 June 1937; "102 pasteurs
   allemands écroués en huit jours," *La Presse*, 29 June 1937.
10 "King attend Berlin l'arrivée de Hitler," *Le Droit*, 28 June 1937; "King en
   France et Allemagne," *Le Droit*, 29 June 1937; George Hambleton, "Premier in
   Berlin, to Meet Hitler Tomorrow," *Ottawa Citizen*, 28 June 1937; "Nazi Camp
   Visited by King," *Winnipeg Free Press*, 28 June 1937; "King Greeted in Berlin,"
   Winnipeg Free Press, 29 June 1937; Halton, *Dispatches from the Front*, 123.
11 "For Peace with Germany," *Ottawa Citizen*, 29 June 1937.
12 "Mr. King's Conversations," *Globe and Mail*, 3 July 1937.
13 Kershaw, *Making Friends with Hitler*, 142.
14 "Leaders and Crisis," *Saturday Night*, 17 July 1937, 1; Rideau Banks, "Not
   Settling the World," *Saturday Night*, 3 July 1937, 5. Richard Kottman
   reveals the holder of the *Saturday Night* reporter's waggish pseudonym in
   Reciprocity and the North Atlantic Triangle, 163n21.
15 Kershaw, *Making Friends with Hitler*, 25–7; King diary, 14 June 1936.

12 Atavistic Beasts: *Der Dicke* and His Bison

1 Lorraine Boissoneault, "When the Nazis Tried to Bring Animals Back from
   Extinction," *Smithsonian*, 31 March 2017, https://www.smithsonianmag.
   com/history/when-nazis-tried-bring-animals-back-extinction-180962739/,
   accessed 5 February 2018.
2 Bruce, *Through the Lion Gate*, 129, 159, 154; Tristin Hopper, "How Canada
   Unwittingly Helped to Build a Nazi Jurassic Park," *National Post*, 5 June
   2017 (quote); King diary, 29 June 1937.
3 King diary, 29 June 1937.
4 Ibid.
5 Ibid.; Rürup, *Berlin 1945*, 91; Ladd, *Ghosts of Berlin*, 146.
6 Crerar, Report on Visit to Germany, 124.
7 Donath, *Architecture in Berlin 1933–1945*, 15; Philpott, *Relics of the Reich*, 67;
   Ladd, *Ghosts of Berlin*, 146.
8 Donath, *Architecture in Berlin 1933–1945*, 15 (quote); Philpott, *Relics of the
   Reich*, 66.
9 Ladd, *The Ghosts of Berlin*, 146.
10 King diary, 29 July 1937.
11 Evans, *Telling Lies about Hitler*, 99; Geck, *Dulag Luft, Auswertestelle West*,
   119; Maulucci, "German Diplomats," 150 (quote); Jesus Baigorri-Jalon,
   "Velleman," in Franz Pochhaker, ed., *Routledge Encyclopedia of Interpreting*

Studies (New York: Routledge, 2015), 432. To apply to the SDIM, go to http://www.sdi-muenchen.de/home/.

12 Kershaw, *Hitler*, 112; Turley, *From Nuremberg to Nineveh*, 45–6.

13 Kershaw, *Hitler*, 224–5, 964; Overy, *Goering*, 231–40; Manvell and Fraenkel, *Goering*, 61, 392 (quote).

14 Library and Archives Canada, William Lyon Mackenzie King Correspondence, MG 26-J1, vol. 235 (3 July–24 December 1937), "Correspondence with Hermann Goring," 3 July 1937, microfilm reel C-3725, pp. 201661–6; Henderson, *Failure of a Mission*, 80; Fromm, *Blood and Bouquets*, 245.

15 King diary, 29 July 1937.

16 Kershaw, *Hitler*, 359, 366 (quote); Borgwardt, *A New Deal for the World*, 200.

17 Kershaw, *Hitler*, 364–7.

18 Rosenbaum, *Waking to Danger*, 117; Hart, *A Trading Nation*, 108–11, 122.

19 King diary, 29 June 1937.

20 Ibid., emphasis added.

21 Ibid.

22 Crerar, Report on Visit to Germany, 126; Hitler, *Mein Kampf*, 3.

23 Kershaw, *Hitler*, 403.

24 King diary, 29 June 1937.

25 Ibid.

26 King diary, 29 June 1937; Göring to Londonderry cited in Kershaw, *Making Friends with Hitler*, 195.

13 Baiting Godwin's Law

1 Mike Godwin, "I Seem to Be a Verb: 18 Years of Godwin's Law," *Jewcy. com*, 30 April 2008. http://jewcy.com/jewish-arts-and-culture/i_seem_be_verb_18_years_godwins_law, accessed 16 February 2018.

2 Altman, *The German Stranger*, 7; Geoffrey Wheatcroft, "On the Use and Abuse of Munich," *New Republic*, 3 December 2013; Renshon, "The Psychological Origins of Preventative War," 201–30; Rosenfeld, *Hi Hitler!*, 340.

3 Record, "The Use and Abuse of History."

4 Gordon, *The Second Coming of the KKK*, chapter 2, n.p.; Erin Gloria Ryan, "How Many Nazis Are There in America, Really?," *Daily Beast*, 15 August 2017, https://www.thedailybeast.com/how-many-nazis-are-there-in-america-really, accessed 14 February 2018; Sonam Sheth and Jeremy Berke,

"'A Right to Speech Is Not a Right to Violence': Politicians Condemn Violence at White Nationalist Protest in Charlottesville," *Business Insider*, 12 August 2017, http://nordic.businessinsider.com/politicians-condemn-charlottesville-white-nationalist-protest-2017-8/, accessed 14 February 2018.

5 Record, "The Use and Abuse of History," 170.

6 On the efficacy of sanctions, see Hufbauer et al., *Economic Sanctions Reconsidered*. Unsurprisingly, the authors find that the United States, the lynchpin of the post-war global economy, has been the most successful single implementer of economic sanctions. They find that American sanctions have achieved their primary objectives against the Netherlands (1948–49), Ceylon (1961–65), India (1965–67), South Korea (1975–76), Taiwan (1976–77), El Salvador (1987–88), Malawi (1992–93), and Guatemala (1993). Also unsurprising is that these victories came at the expense of countries with considerably weaker economies and militaries; some of the more prominent arms treaties from the Cold War include the Partial Test Ban Treaty (1963), the Anti-Ballistic Missile Treaty (1972), Strategic Arms Limitation Talks Agreement (1972), the Intermediate-Range Nuclear Forces Treaty (1987), and the Ottawa Treaty (1997) banning land mines. As of writing, the 2015 Iran Nuclear Deal prohibiting that country's development of nuclear weapons is still on the books, although the United States has withdrawn from the agreement.

7 Kershaw, *Hitler*, xli; King diary, 29 June 1937.

8 King diary, 29 June 1937; Levine, *King*, 268, 72; Kershaw, *Hitler*, 80.

9 Levine, *King*, 86, 231, 188; Kershaw, *Hitler*, 218, 222.

10 Levine, *King*, 34–5 (quote), 33.

11 Physician cited in Kershaw, *Hitler*, 5, 15; King cited in Esberey, *Knight of the Holy Spirit*, 212.

12 King diary, 7 July 1939; Levine, *King*, 384.

13 Cited in "Mackenzie King on His Dog, 'My Little Friend Pat,'" CBC Digital Archives, http://www.cbc.ca/archives/entry/mackenzie-king-on-his-dog-my-little-friend-pat, accessed 9 March 2018.

14 Kershaw, *Hitler*, 56 (Hitler cited), 747.

15 O'Donnell, *The Bunker*, 166; King diary, 29 July 1937; Kaplan, *Landscapes of Holocaust Postmemory*, 15.

16 Cited in Speer, *Inside the Third Reich*, 94; Weikart, *Hitler's Religion*.

17 Cited in de Vos, *Cobblestones*, 120.

18 Kershaw, *Hitler*, 146, 158.

14 The Interview

1 Taylor, *The Word in Stone*, 130–1; Childers, *The Third Reich*, 224.
2 Cited in Speer, *Inside the Third Reich*, 34; Macdonogh, *The Last Kaiser*, 425–6; King diary, 29 June 1937; Ladd, *The Ghosts of Berlin*, 135, 174.
3 Ladd, *The Ghosts of Berlin*, 161–3.
4 Ibid., 130.
5 Crimmins, "Reinterpreting the Soviet War Memorial," 54–6; Ladd, *The Ghosts of Berlin*, 131; Andrew Anthony, "From the Buried Bunker, Hitler's Ghost Still Haunts Berlin's Psyche, 70 Years On," *The Guardian*, 25 April 2015.
6 King diary, 29 June 1937.
7 "Mr. King Meets Hitler: A 'Valuable' Talk," *Manchester Guardian Weekly*, 2 July 1937; King diary, 29 June 1937.
8 King diary, 29 June 1937; Rose, *Mobilize!*, 136.
9 King diary, 29 June 1937.
10 Ibid.
11 Ibid.
12 Weinberg, *Germany, Hitler, and World War II*, 68; King diary, 29 June 1937; Kershaw, *Hitler*, 910.
13 King diary, 29 June 1937.
14 Rees, *Hitler's Charisma*, 154, emphasis in original; Clark's *The Sleepwalkers* offers one of the better depictions of the 1914 stumble into war.
15 King diary, 29 June 1937.
16 Ibid.
17 Ibid.
18 Ibid.; Kaltenborn cited in Nagorski, *Hitlerland*, 87.
19 Ascher, *Was Hitler a Riddle?*, 115–16; Kershaw, *Hitler*, 313. Kershaw, *Making Friends with Hitler*, 32–3; King diary, 5 July 1934.
20 King diary, 29 June 1937; Crerar, Report on Visit to Germany, 122.
21 Cited in "Canadian Premier Talks with Hitler," *New York Times*, 30 June 1937.
22 King diary, 29 June 1937.
23 King diary, 29 June 1937; Huss cited in Nagorski, *Hitlerland*, 171.
24 King diary, 29 June 1937.
25 Ibid.
26 Ibid.
27 Cited in Nagorski, *Hitlerland*, 116.
28 Halton cited in Halton, *Dispatches from the Front*, 123; King diary, 29 June 1937.

29 Eayrs, *In Defence of Canada*, 38–9; King diary, 26 June 1937; Halton cited in Halton, *Dispatches from the Front*, 123.

30 King diary, 29 June 1937.

15 Savouring the Triumph

1 King diary, 29 June 1937.

2 Crerar, Report on Visit to Germany, 122.

3 Alyson Krueger, "A Soho House's Hitler Youth," *Tablet: Visual Art and Design*, 10 May 2012, http://www.tabletmag./jewish-arts-and-culture/99108/a-soho-houses-hitler-youth, accessed 11 February 2018.

4 Ibid.; "Holocaust Restitution: German Reparations," *Jewish Virtual Library*, http://www.jewishvirtuallibrary.org/german-holocaust-reparations, accessed 11 February 2018.

5 Gardell, *Gods of the Blood*, 26.

6 King diary, 29 June 1937.

7 Cited in Brett, *Photography and Place*, 27.

8 Bruce, *Through the Lion Gate*, 202; Brett, *Photography and Place*, 44; Niven, *Facing the Nazi Past*, 218; Haakenson, "(In)Visible Trauma," 151.

9 Carolin Emcke and Stefan Berg, "Extracting Meaning from Concrete Blocks," *Der Spiegel*, 2 May 2005, http://www.spiegel.de/international/spiegel/remembering-the-holocaust-extracting-meaning-from-concrete-blocks-a-354837.html, accessed 17 February 2018.

10 Neumärker, "Germany's Memorial"; Richard Brody, "The Inadequacy of Berlin's 'Memorial to the Murdered Jews of Europe,'" *The New Yorker*, 12 July 2012, https://www.newyorker.com/culture/richard-brody/the-inadequacy-of-berlins-memorial-to-the-murdered-jews-of-europe, accessed 5 June 2018.

11 Fraser, *The Buildings of Europe*, 37; Goebbels cited in Battles, *Library*, 164; Bouton cited in Nagorski, *Hitlerland*, 107; Neill, *Urban Planning and Cultural Identity*, 51.

12 Kershaw, *Hitler*, 900–1; Beck, *Under the Bombs*, 124; Rebecca Schmidt, "Staatsoper Berlin Finally Reopens. Sort Of," *New York Times*, 3 September 2017.

13 King diary, 29 June 1937; Janik, "The Symphony of a Capital City," 156.

14 King diary, 29 June 1937; Strang, "Two Unequal Tempers," 132.

15 "Un ballo in maschera," *Royal Opera House*, http://www.roh.org.uk/productions/un-ballo-in-maschera-by-katharina-thoma, accessed 14 February 2018; King diary, 29 June 1937.

16 King diary, 29 June 1937.

16 Taking Leave

1 King diary, 30 June 1937.
2 Ibid.
3 In equating King's journey to Germany with the works of Swedish play-wright August Strindberg, I am thinking in particular of the author's later works, which are suffused with themes of evil, suffering, the unconscious, symbolism, mysticism, and the occult. See Lewis, *Cambridge Introduction to Modernism*, 187–189.
4 Kershaw, *Hitler*, 222, 651; Imre Karacs, "German Firms Count Cost of Slave Labour," *The Independent* (UK), 9 November 1997.
5 Library and Archives Canada, William Lyon Mackenzie King Correspondence, MG 26-J1, vol. 236, "Correspondence with Robert Ley," 2 July 1937, microfilm reel C-3726, p. 203021; Crerar, Report on Visit to Germany, 125.
6 James, *The Nazi Dictatorship*, 154, 217. Rösler's business card can be found in Library and Archives Canada, Crerar fonds, MG30 E157, vol. 10, file "Notes on Visit to Germany" (2F-L, 2K: Visit to Germany).
7 King diary, 30 June 1937.
8 Ibid.
9 Cited in "Canadian Leaves Berlin," *New York Times*, 1 July 1937.
10 Davidson, *The Trial of the Germans*, 168; Zalampas, *Adolf Hitler and the Third Reich*, 20.
11 Kershaw, *Hitler*, 254; Davidson, *The Trial of the Germans*, 168; Goda, *Tales from Spandau*, 94; Steve Crawshaw, "Nazis Provide a Lesson for More than Just the Germans: Steve Crawshaw in Bonn Reflects on the 60th Anniversary of Hitler Becoming Chancellor," *Independent*, 25 January 1993.
12 Kershaw, *Hitler*, 398; Goda, *Tales from Spandau*, 96.
13 Goda, *Tales from Spandau*, 97.
14 Pflanze, *Bismarck and the Development of Germany*, 36; King diary, 30 June 1937.
15 King diary, 30 June 1937.
16 Ibid., 30 June 1937, 19 October 1937.
17 King diary, 30 June 1937.
18 Ibid; Nuremberg proceedings cited in Goda, *Tales from Spandau*, 95.
19 King diary, 30 June 1937; Goda, *Tales from Spandau*, 96.
20 "Mr. Mackenzie King on His Berlin Talks," *The Times* (London), 1 July 1937; King diary, 30 June 1937.
21 King diary, 30 June 1937.

17 Home

1 King diary, 2 July 1937; Halton and King cited in Halton, *Dispatches from the Front*, 124.
2 King diary, 1 July 1937; King to Hitler cited in Eayrs, *In Defence of Canada*, 46.
3 Crerar, Report on Visit to Germany, 126.
4 King diary, 2 July 1937.
5 Cited in Eayrs, *In Defence of Canada*, 46.
6 Sargent cited in Stacey, *Canada and the Age of Conflict*, 213; Shirer cited in Nagorski, *Hitlerland*, 226.
7 King diary, 4 July 1937.
8 Ibid.
9 Ibid.
10 Library and Archives Canada, William Lyon Mackenzie King Correspondence, MG 26-J1, vol. 235 (22 June–4 July 1937), "Correspondence with Nevile Henderson," 3 & 4 July 1937, microfilm reel C-3725, pp. 202024–27; King cited in Eayrs, *In Defence of Canada*, 46.
11 Library and Archives Canada, William Lyon Mackenzie King Correspondence, MG 26-J1, vol. 235 (16 November–7 December 1937), "Correspondence with Gabriel Hanotaux," 16 November 1937, microfilm reel C-3725, pp. 201877–83; Hanotaux response ibid., n.d., translated by King staffer.
12 Library and Archives Canada, William Lyon Mackenzie King Correspondence, MG 26-J1, vol. 237 (9 July–9 September 1937), "Telegram, Morris McDougall to Edward Pickering," 9 July 1937, microfilm reel C-3726, pp. 203356–61.
13 King diary, 30 August–1 September 1937.
14 King diary, 14 July 1937.
15 Cited in Eayrs, *In Defence of Canada*, 46–7.
16 Crerar's report, along with the signatures of officials who read it, is found in Library and Archives Canada, Crerar fonds, MG30 E157, vol. 10, file "Notes on Visit to Germany" (2F-L, 2K: Visit to Germany). King's report, "Memorandum by Mackenzie King on His Interview with Adolf Hitler, Berlin, 29 June 1937," is reprinted in Eayrs, *In Defence of Canada*, 226–31. On King's attitudes towards military officials, see Walker, "Revolt of the Canadian Generals, 1944," 59, 70.
17 Canada, *House of Commons Debates*, 1938, I, 471.
18 Ibid.; "A Jolt for Mr. Herridge," *Globe and Mail*, 12 February 1938.
19 "King Won't Tell What He Talked About with Hitler," *Globe and Mail*, 15 February 1938.

18 Failure of a Mission

1 Kershaw, *Hitler*, 408.
2 Ibid., 322, 410 (quote).
3 King diary, 11 March 1938.
4 Ibid.
5 Ibid.
6 Ibid., 28 September 1938
7 Ibid, 12 September 1938.
8 Ibid., 14 September 1938.
9 Ibid., 14 September 1938.
10 Ibid.
11 King cited in Cook, *Warlords*, 201; King cited in Esberey, *Knight of the Holy Spirit*, 214; Kershaw, *Hitler*, 446; Barry Gustafson, "Savage, Michael Joseph," in *Dictionary of New Zealand Biography*, first published 1998, in *Te Ara: The Encyclopedia of New Zealand*, https://teara.govt.nz/en/biographies/4s9/savage-michael-joseph, accessed 27 June 2018.
12 King diary, 12 November 1938.
13 King diary, 14, 17, 20, 23, 24 November 1938.
14 Hucker, *Public Opinion*, 134; Eayrs, *In Defence of Canada*, 73; Skelton cited in Eayrs, *In Defence of Canada*, 73; Waters, *Australia and Appeasement*, 4, 167.
15 Cited in Rose, *Mobilize!*, 262.
16 King diary, 20 March 1939; second quote cited in Levine, *King*, 285.
17 Canada, *House of Commons Debates*, 1939, IV, 2613; Eayrs, *In Defence of Canada*, 75–6.
18 Cited in Eayrs, *In Defence of Canada*, 76–7.
19 King diary, 19 August 1937, 19 May 1939; Keyserling, "Mackenzie King's Spiritualism," 26–7.
20 Levine, *King*, 297; King cited ibid.
21 Ibid., 298.
22 King diary, 4 September 1939; Stacey, *A Very Double Life*, 209.
23 Cited in Reardon, *Winston Churchill and Mackenzie King*, 92.
24 King diary, 29 March 1940.
25 Tuchman, *The March of Folly*, 7.
26 King diary, 29 March 1940.
27 Ibid.
28 Ibid., 19 August 1942; cited in Levine, *King*, 364.
29 Crerar cited in Dickson, *A Thoroughly Canadian General*, 112; Dickson, "Harry Crerar and an Army for Strategic Effect," 41; Walker, "Revolt of the Canadian Generals, 1944," 59, 70 (King cited).

30 Dickson, "Harry Crerar and an Army for Strategic Effect," 40.

31 Zuehlke, *Tragedy at Dieppe*, 14, 3; King diary, 17 September 1942.

32 Dickson, "Harry Crerar and an Army for Strategic Effect," 44–5; Keshen, *Propaganda and Censorship*, 125, 215; cited in Zuehlke, *Tragedy at Dieppe*, 58.

33 Cited in Dickson, *A Thoroughly Canadian General*, 231; Dickson, "Harry Crerar and an Army for Strategic Effect," 46.

34 Dickson, "Harry Crerar and an Army for Strategic Effect," 46; "Canada's Crerar," *Time* Magazine, 18 September 1944.

35 Eayrs, *In Defence of Canada*, 60.

36 Byers, *Zombie Army*, 228; Russel, "BC's 1944 'Zombie' Protests."

37 Walker, "Revolt of the Canadian Generals, 1944."

38 King diary, 7 August 1945.

39 Dickson, *A Thoroughly Canadian General*, 454–66.

19 Aftermath

1 King diary, 20 August 1946.

2 Ibid., 21 August 1946.

3 Ibid.

4 Ibid.

5 Ibid.; Reinisch, *The Perils of Peace*, 198, 247; Ladd, *Ghosts of Berlin*, 172.

6 King diary, 21 August 1946.

7 King diary, 21, 22 August 1946.

8 Ibid., 21 August 1946.

9 Ibid.

10 Pick, *Pursuit of the Nazi Mind*, 153–65; King diary, 22 August 1946; Goda, *Tales from Spandau*, 111.

11 King diary, 22 August 1946.

Epilogue

1 Cited in Nagorski, *Hitlerland*, 221–2.

2 J.L. Granatstein, "The Prime Ministers of Canada: Important Portraits of the Nation's Leaders, 6. King or Chaos," 7th Floor Media, http://www.prime-ministers.ca/king/bio_6.php?context=c, accessed 21 February 2018.

3 "Mackenzie King," *The Canadian Encyclopedia*, http://www.prime-ministers.ca/king/bio_6.php?context=c, accessed 21 February 2018; Ascher, *Was Hitler a Riddle?*, 8.

4 Bissell, *The Imperial Canadian*, 93.

5 Ovendale, *Appeasement and the English-Speaking World*, 54–6.
6 Prior to the 1980s, the vast majority of accounts fell into these two camps, although similar assessments continue to the present. A sampling of monographs and general surveys that conspicuously ignore the trip include McInnis, *Canada*; Neatby, *The Politics of Chaos*; Granatstein et al., *Twentieth Century Canada*; Finlay Sprague, *The Structure of Canadian History*; Thompson and Randall, *Canada and the United States*; and Morton, *A Short History of Canada*. Accounts that include very brief, similarly worded, and generally laudatory descriptions of King's "blunt" warning to Hitler include Brebner, *Canada*, 469; Hardy, *Mackenzie King of Canada*, 165–6; Neatby, *William Lyon Mackenzie King*, 223; Granatstein, *Mackenzie King*, 128; and Bothwell et al., *Canada 1900–1945*, 313.
7 Frisse, "The Missing Link," 19; Roazen, *Canada's King*, 15; Cook, *Warlords*, 200; Esberey, *Knight of the Holy Spirit*, 209.
8 Reardon, *Winston Churchill and Mackenzie King*, 83; Cook, *Warlords*, 200; Wagner, *Brothers Beyond the Sea*, 122.
9 Levine, *King*, 297; Hutchinson, *The Incredible Canadian*, 227; Wagner, *Brothers Beyond the Sea*, 122; Douglas and Greenhous. *Out of the Shadows*, 11; Bissell, *The Imperial Canadian*, 93.
10 King diary, 23 August 1946.
11 Tuchman, *The March of Folly*, 407.
12 King diary, 23 August 1946.

Bibliography

Primary Sources

Library and Archives Canada
    William Lyon Mackenzie King papers
    O.D. Skelton papers
    Department of External Affairs records
    Photography collection
    Newspaper collection
Toronto Reference Library
    Newspaper collection
Bundesarchiv, Germany (Koblenz and Berlin)
    Ribbentrop files
    Newspaper collection
    Photography collection

Secondary Sources

Abella, Irving, and Harold Troper. *None Is Too Many: Canada and the Jews of Europe, 1933–1948,* Toronto: Lester and Orpen Dennys, 1982.

Altman, William H.F. *The German Stranger: Leo Strauss and National Socialism.* Lanham: Lexington, 2011.

Amstutz, Mark R. *International Ethics: Concepts, Theories, and Cases in Global Politics.* 5th ed. New York: Rowman & Littlefield, 2018.

Anastakis, Dimitry. *Death in the Peaceable Kingdom: Canadian History since 1867 through Murder, Execution, Assassination, and Suicide.* Toronto: University of Toronto Press, 2015.

Angang, Hu. *Mao and the Cultural Revolution.* Vol. 1, *Mao's Motivation and Strategy.* Honolulu: Silkroad, 2017.

Ascher, Abraham. *Was Hitler a Riddle?: Western Democracies and National Socialism.* Stanford: Stanford University Press, 2012.

Bannister, Jerry. "Canada as Counter-Revolution: The Loyalist Order Framework in Canadian History, 1750–1840." In *Liberalism and Hegemony: Debating the Canadian Liberal Revolution,* edited by Jean-François Constant and Michel Ducharme, 64–97. Toronto: University of Toronto Press, 2009.

Barnett, Victoria. *For the Soul of the People: Protestant Protest against Hitler.* New York: Oxford University Press, 1992.

Battles, Matthew. *Library: An Unquiet History.* New York: W.W. Norton, 2004.

Beck, Earl Ray. *Under the Bombs: The German Home Front, 1942–1945.* Lexington: University Press of Kentucky, 1986.

Beloff, Max. *Imperial Sunset: Dream of Commonwealth, 1921–42.* London: Macmillan, 1989.

Berendsen, Carl. *Mr. Ambassador: Memoirs of Sir Carl Berendsen.* Wellington, New Zealand: Victoria University Press.

Bergen, Doris. "Social Death and International Isolation: Jews in Nazi Germany, 1933–1939." In Klein, *Nazi Germany, Canadian Responses,* 3–45.

Bilski, Emily D. *Berlin Metropolis: Jews and the New Culture, 1890–1918.* Berkelely: University of California Press, 1999.

Bissell, Claude. *The Imperial Canadian: Vincent Massey in Office.* Toronto: University of Toronto Press, 2016.

Bloch, Michael. *Ribbentrop.* London: Bantam, 1994.

Borgwardt, Elizabeth. *A New Deal for the World: America's Vision for Human Rights.* Cambridge, MA: Harvard University Press, 2007.

Bothwell, Robert, Ian Drummond, and John English. *Canada 1900–1945.* Toronto: University of Toronto Press, 1987.

Brebner, J.B. *Canada.* Rev. ed. Ann Arbor: University of Michigan Press, 1970.

Breitman, Richard, and Allan J. Lichtman. *FDR and the Jews.* Cambridge, MA: Belknap, 2013.

Brett, Donna West. *Photography and Place: Seeing and Not Seeing Germany after 1945.* New York: Routledge, 2016.

Bruce, Gary. *Through the Lion Gate: A History of the Berlin Zoo.* Oxford: Oxford University Press, 2017.

Byers, Daniel. *Zombie Army: The Canadian Army and Conscription in the Second World War.* Vancouver: UBC Press, 2016.

Cede, Franz, "Historical Introduction." In *The United Nations: Law and Practice,* edited by Franz Cede and Lilly Sucharipa-Behrmann, 3–10. The Hague: Kluwer Law International, 2001.

Charney, Noah. "Napoleon: Emperor of Art Theft." *Journal of Art Crime* 13 (Spring 2005): 69–72.

Childers, Thomas. *The Third Reich: A History of Nazi Germany*. New York: Simon and Schuster, 2017.

Clark, Christopher. *The Sleepwalkers: How Europe Went to War in 1914*. New York: Harper, 2012.

Clementi, Federica K. *Holocaust Mothers and Daughters: Family, History, and Trauma*. Waltham: Brandeis University Press, 2013.

Coetzee, Marilyn Shevin. *The German Army League: Popular Nationalism in Wilhelmine Germany*. Oxford: Oxford University Press, 1990.

Cook, Tim. *Warlords: Borden, Mackenzie King, and Canada's World Wars*. Toronto: Allen Lane, 2012.

Crerar, H.D.G. Report on Visit to Germany 16–21st June, 1937, published as "Colonel H.D.G. Crerar's Visit to Nazi Germany, 1937," *Canadian Military History* 5.2 (Autumn 1996): 121–6.

Crimmins, Courtney Glore. "Reinterpreting the Soviet War Memorial in Berlin's Treptower Park after 1990." In *Remembering the German Democratic Republic: Divided Memory in a United Germany*, edited by David Clarke and Ute Wölfel, 54–65. New York: Palgrave Macmillan, 2011.

Cruttwell, C.R.M.F. *A History of the Great War: 1914–1918*. Chicago: Chicago Review, 2007.

Davidson, Eugene. *The Trial of the Germans: An Account of the Twenty-two Defendants before the International Military Tribunal at Nuremberg*. Columbia: University of Missouri Press, 1997.

Demps, Laurenz, and Carl-Ludwig Paeschke, *The Hotel Adlon*. Berlin: Nicolai, 2004.

Denslagen, Wim. *Romantic Modernism: Nostalgia in the World of Conservation*. Translated by Donald Gardner. Amsterdam: Amsterdam University Press, 2009.

de Vos, Dirk. *Cobblestones: A Personal and Political Journey*. Victoria: FriesenPress, 2015.

Dickson, Paul Douglas. "Harry Crerar and an Army for Strategic Effect." *Canadian Military History* 17.1 (2008): 37–48.

– *A Thoroughly Canadian General: A Biography of General H.D.G. Crerar*. Toronto: University of Toronto Press, 2007.

Donath, Matthias. *Architecture in Berlin 1933–1945: A Guide through Nazi Berlin*. Translated by Miriamne Fields. Berlin: Lukas, 2006.

Douglas, W.A.B., and Brereton Greenhous. *Out of the Shadows: Canada in the Second World War*. 2nd ed. Toronto: Dundurn, 1996.

Dudeck, Peter. "National Socialist Youth Policy and the Labour Service: The Work Camp as an Instrument of Social Discipline." In *Education and Fascism: Political Identity and Social Education in Nazi Germany*, edited by Heinz Sünker and Hans-Uwe Otto, 36–53. New York: Routledge, 1997.

Dummitt, Christopher. "The Importance of Not Being Earnest: Postwar Canadians Rethink Mackenzie King's Christian Manhood." In *Canadian Men and Masculinities: Historical and Contemporary Perspectives*, edited by Christopher J. Greig and Wayne Martino, 61–75. Toronto: Canadian Scholars' Press, 2012.

– *Unbuttoned: A History of Mackenzie King's Secret Life*. Montreal/Kingston: McGill-Queen's University Press, 2017.

Eayrs, James. *In Defence of Canada*. Vol. 2, *Appeasement and Rearmament*. Toronto: University of Toronto Press, 1965.

Esberey, Joy E. *Knight of the Holy Spirit: A Study of William Lyon Mackenzie King*. Toronto: University of Toronto Press, 1980.

Evans, Richard. *Telling Lies about Hitler: The Holocaust, History and the David Irving Trial*. London: Verso, 2002.

– *The Third Reich in Power*. London: Penguin, 2006.

Farrell, John A. *Richard Nixon: The Life*. New York: Doubleday, 2017.

Ferguson, Will. *Bastards and Boneheads: Canada's Glorious Leaders Past and Present*. Vancouver: Douglas and McIntyre, 1999.

Finlay, J.F., and D.N. Sprague. *The Structure of Canadian History*. 6th ed. Scarborough: Prentice Hall Canada, 2000.

Fraser, Derek. *The Buildings of Europe: Berlin*. Manchester: Manchester University Press, 1996

Friedrich, Thomas. *Hitler's Berlin: Abused City*. New Haven: Yale University Press, 2012.

Frisse, Ulrich. "The Missing Link: Mackenzie King and Canada's 'German Capital.'" In *Mackenzie King: Citizenship and Community*, edited by John English, Kenneth McLaughlin, and P. Whitney Lackenbauer, 18–34. Toronto: Robin Brass Studio, 2002.

Fromm, Bella. *Blood and Bouquets: A Berlin Social Diary*. New York: Citadel, 2002.

Gardell, Mattias. *Gods of the Blood: The Pagan Revival and White Separatism*. Raleigh: Duke University Press, 2003.

Geck, Stefan. *Dulag Luft, Auswertestelle West: Vernehmungslager der Luftwaffe für westalliierte Kriegsgefangene im Zweiten Weltkrieg*. Frankfurt am Main: Peter Lang, 2007.

Geerken, Horst. *Hitler's Asian Adventure*. Translated by Bill McCann. Norderstedt: Books On Demand, 2017.

Giles, Geoffrey J. *Students and National Socialism in Germany*. Princeton: Princeton University Press, 1985.

Gindin, Sam. *The Canadian Auto Workers: The Birth and Transformation of a Union*. Toronto: Lorimer, 1995.

Gismondi, Mark D. *Ethics, Liberalism and Realism in International Relations*. New York: Routledge, 2011.

Goda, Norman J.W. *Tales from Spandau: Nazi Criminals and the Cold War*. Cambridge: Cambridge University Press, 2007.

Goodall, Lian. *William Lyon Mackenzie King: Dreams and Shadows*. Toronto: Dundurn, 2003.

Gordon, Linda. *The Second Coming of the KKK: The Ku Klux Klan of the 1920s and the American Political Tradition*. New York: Liveright, 2017.

Graham, Helen. *The Spanish Civil War: A Very Short Introduction*. Oxford: Oxford University Press, 2005.

Granatstein, J.L. *Mackenzie King: His Life and World*. Toronto: McGraw-Hill Ryerson, 1977.

Granatstein, J.L., Irving M. Abella, David J. Bercuson, R. Craig Brown, and H. Blair Neatby. *Twentieth Century Canada*. Toronto: McGraw-Hill Ryerson, 1983.

Granatstein, J.L., and Desmond Morton. *Canada and the Two World Wars*. Toronto: Key Porter, 2003.

Grzyb, Amanda. "From Kristallnacht to the MS St Louis Tragedy: Canadian Press Coverage of Nazi Persecution of Jews and the Jewish Refugee Crisis, September 1938 to August 1939." In Klein, Nazi Germany, *Canadian Responses*, 78–113.

Guillebaud, C.W. *The Social Policy of Nazi Germany*. Cambridge: Cambridge University Press, 1941.

Haakenson, Thomas. "(In)Visible Trauma: Michael Elmgreen and Ingar Dragset's Memorial to the Homosexuals Persecuted under the National Socialist Regime." In *Memorialization in Germany since 1945*, edited by Bill Niven and Chloe Paver, 146–56. New York: Palgrave Macmillan, 2010.

Halton, David. *Dispatches from the Front: Matthew Halton, Canada's Voice at War*. Toronto: McClelland and Stewart, 2014.

Hamerow, Theodore S. *Why We Watched: Europe, America, and the Holocaust*. New York: W.W. Norton, 2008.

Hardy, Henry Reginald. *Mackenzie King of Canada: A Biography*. Toronto: Greenwood, 1970.

Harsch, Joseph C. *At the Hinge of History: A Reporter's Story*. Athens: University of Georgia Press, 1993.

Hart, Michael. *A Trading Nation: Canadian Trade Policy from Colonialism to Globalization*. Vancouver: UBC Press, 2002.

Henderson, Nevile. *Failure of a Mission: Berlin 1937–1939*. London: G.P. Putnam's Sons, 1940.

Heron, Craig, ed. *The Workers' Revolt in Canada, 1917–1925*. Toronto: University of Toronto Press, 1998.

Hesse-Lichtenberger, Ulrich. *Tor!: The Story of German Football*. London: WSC Books, 2003.

Hitler, Adolf. *Mein Kampf*. Edited by William Langer. New York: Reynal and Hitchcock, 1941.

Hucker, Daniel. *Public Opinion and the End of Appeasement in Britain and France*. New York: Routledge, 2016.

Hufbauer, Gary Clyde, Jeffrey Schott, Kimberly Ann Elliott, and Barbara Oegg. *Economic Sanctions Reconsidered*. 3rd ed. Washington, DC: Peterson Institute for International Economics, 2009.

Hutchinson, Bruce. *The Incredible Canadian: A Candid Portrait of Mackenzie King*. Toronto: Longmans, Green, 1952.

James, Harold. *The Nazi Dictatorship and the Deutsche Bank*. Cambridge: Cambridge University Press, 2004.

Janik, Elizabeth. "The Symphony of a Capital City." In *Berlin: The Symphony Continues: Orchestrating Architectural, Social, and Artistic Change in Germany's New Capital*, edited by Carol Anne Costabile-Heming, Rachel J. Halverson, and Kristie A. Foell, 143–64. Berlin: Walter de Gruyter, 2004.

Jones, Marie, and Larry Flaxman. *11:11, The Time Prompt Phenomenon: The Meaning behind Mysterious Signs, Sequences, and Synchronicities*. Pompton Plains: New Page, 2009.

Jones, Martin, Rhys Jones, Michael Woods, Mark Whitehead, Deborah Dixon, and Matthew Hannah. *An Introduction to Political Geography: Space, Place and Politics*. 2nd ed. London: Routledge, 2015.

Kaplan, Brett Ashley. *Landscapes of Holocaust Postmemory*. New York: Routledge, 2010.

Kater, Michael. *Hitler Youth*. Cambridge, MA: Harvard University Press, 2006.

Kershaw, Ian. *Hitler*. London: Penguin, 2009.

Kershaw, Ian. *Making Friends with Hitler: Lord Londonderry, the Nazis and the Road to World War II*. New York: Penguin, 2004.

Keshen, Jeffrey A. *Propaganda and Censorship during Canada's Great War*. Edmonton: University of Alberta Press, 1996.

Keyserlingk, Robert H. "Mackenzie King's Spiritualism and His View of Hitler in 1939." *Journal of Canadian Studies* 20.4 (Winter 1985–86): 26–44. https://doi.org/10.3138/jcs.20.4.26.

King, Mackenzie. *Industry and Humanity: A Study in the Principles Underlying Industrial Reconstruction*. Boston: Houghton Mifflin, 1918.

Klein, L. Ruth, ed. *Nazi Germany, Canadian Responses: Confronting Antisemitism in the Shadow of War*. Montreal/Kingston: McGill-Queen's University Press, 2012.

Knight, Amy. *How the Cold War Began: The Gouzenko Affair and the Hunt for Soviet Spies*. Toronto: McClelland and Stewart, 2005.

Kohn, Edward. *This Kindred People: Canadian-American Relations and the Anglo-Saxon Ideal, 1895–1903*. Montreal/ Kingston: McGill-Queen's University Press, 2004.

Korboński, Stefan. *The Polish Underground State: A Guide to the Underground, 1939–1945*. Translated by Marta Erdman. Boulder: East European Quarterly, 1978.

Kottman, Richard. *Reciprocity and the North Atlantic Triangle, 1932–1938*. Ithaca: Cornell University Press, 1968.

Kramer, Ronald. "From Guernica to Hiroshima to Bagdad: The Normalization of the State Crime of Terror Bombing Civilians." In *State Crime in the Global Age*, edited by William J. Chambliss, Raymond Michalowski, and Ronald Kramer, 118–33. New York: Routledge, 2013.

Ladd, Brian. *The Companion Guide to Berlin*. Rochester: Boydell & Brewer, 2004.

– *Ghosts of Berlin: Confronting German History in the Urban Landscape*. Chicago: University of Chicago Press, 1997.

Large, David Clay. *Berlin*. New York: Basic, 2000.

– *Nazi Games: The Olympics of 1936*. New York: Norton, 2007.

Lepage, Jean-Denis G.G. *Hitler's Armed Forces Auxiliaries: An Illustrated History of the Wehrmachtsgefolge, 1933–1945*. Jefferson: McFarland, 2015.

Levine, Allan. *King: William Lyon Mackenzie King, A Life Guided by the Hand of Destiny*. Vancouver/Toronto: Douglas & McIntyre, 2011.

– *Scrum Wars: The Prime Ministers and the Media*. Toronto: Dundurn, 1996.

Lewis, Pericles. *Cambridge Introduction to Modernism*. Cambridge: Cambridge University Press, 2007.

Lumley, Elizabeth. *The Canadian Who's Who*. Toronto: University of Toronto Press, 1997.

Macdonogh, Giles. *The Last Kaiser: William the Impetuous*. London: Weidenfeld and Nicolson, 2001.

MacFarlane, John. *Earnest Lapointe and Quebec's Influence on Canadian Foreign Policy*. Toronto: University of Toronto Press, 1999.

MacMillan, Margaret. *History's People: Personalities and the Past*. Toronto: Anansi, 2015.

Manvell, Roger, and Heinrich Fraenkel. *Goering: The Rise and Fall of the Notorious Nazi Leader*. London: Skyhorse, 2012.

Matthias, Bettina. *The Hotel as Setting in Early Twentieth-Century German and Austrian Literature*. Rochester: Camden House, 2006.

Maulucci, Thomas. "German Diplomats and the Myth of the Two Foreign Offices." In *A Nazi Past: Recasting German Identity in Postwar Europe*, edited by David A. Messenger and Katrin Paehler, 139–68. Louisville: University Press of Kentucky, 2015.

McInnis, Edgar. *Canada: A Political and Social History*. Toronto: Clarke, Irwin, 1959.

McKay, Ian. "The Liberal Order Framework: A Prospectus for a Reconnaissance of Canadian History." *Canadian Historical Review* 81.4 (December 2000): 616–45. https://doi.org/10.3138/chr.81.4.616.

Menkis, Richard, and Harold Troper. *More than Just Games: Canada and the 1936 Olympics*. Toronto: University of Toronto Press, 2015.

Menkis, Richard, and Harold Troper. "Racial Laws vs. Olympic Aspirations in the Anglo-Canadian Press of Fall 1935." In Klein, *Nazi Germany, Canadian Responses*, 46–77.

Miller, Scott. *Agent 110: An American Spymaster and the German Resistance in WWII*. New York: Simon and Schuster, 2017.

Molinaro, Dennis. "How the Cold War Began ... with British Help: The Gouzenko Affair Revisited." *Labour/Le Travail* 79 (Spring 2017): 143–55. https://doi.org/10.1353/llt.2017.0005.

Morton, Desmond. *A Short History of Canada*. 6th ed. Toronto: McClelland and Stewart, 2006.

Mount, Graeme. *Canada's Enemies: Spies and Spying in the Peaceable Kingdom*. Toronto: Dundurn, 1993.

Mourby, Adrian. *Rooms with a View: The Secret Life of Grand Hotels*. London: Icon, 2017.

Mutimer, David. *Canadian Annual Review of Politics and Public Affairs 2002*. Toronto: University of Toronto Press, 2003.

Myrdal, Gunnar. *An American Dilemma: The Negro Problem and Modern Democracy*. New York: Harper, 1944.

Nagorski, Andrew. *Hitlerland: American Eyewitnesses to the Nazi Rise to Power*. New York: Simon & Schuster, 2012.

Natale, Simone. *Supernatural Entertainments: Victorian Spiritualism and the Rise of Modern Media Culture*. Philadelphia: Penn State University Press, 2016.

Neatby, H. Blair. *The Politics of Chaos: Canada in the Thirties*. Toronto: Macmillan, 1972.

– *William Lyon Mackenzie King.* Vol. 3, *1932–1939: Prism of Unity.* Toronto: University of Toronto Press, 1976.

Neill, William J.V. *Urban Planning and Cultural Identity.* New York: Routledge, 2004.

Nietzsche, Friedrich. *Thus Spoke Zarathustra (Selections)/Also sprach Zarathustra (Auswahl): A Dual-Language Book.* Edited and translated by Stanley Appelbaum. Mineola: Dover, 2006.

Niven, Bill. *Facing the Nazi Past: United Germany and the Legacy of the Third Reich.* New York: Routledge, 2003.

Neumärker, Uwe. "Germany's Memorial to the Murdered Jews of Europe: Debates and Reactions." *Filozofija I Drustvo* 23.4 (2012): 139–47. https://doi.org/10.2298/fid1204139n.

O'Donnell, James. *The Bunker: The History of the Reich Chancellery Group.* Boston: Houghton Mifflin, 1978.

Ollivier, Maurice. *The Colonial and Imperial Conferences from 1887–1937.* Ottawa: Queen's Printer, 1954.

Ovendale, Ritchie. *Appeasement and the English-Speaking World: Britain, the United States, the Dominions, and the Policy of Appeasement 1937–1939.* Cardiff: University of Wales Press, 1975.

Overy, Richard. *Goering: Hitler's Iron Knight.* London: I.B. Taurus, 2012.

Parker, Emmett. *Albert Camus: The Artist in the Arena.* Madison: University of Wisconsin Press, 1966.

Patel, Kiran Klaus. *Soldiers of Labor: Labor Service in Nazi Germany and New Deal America, 1933–1945.* Translated by Thomas Dunlap. Cambridge: Cambridge University Press, 2005.

Patterson, Orlando. *Slavery and Social Death: A Comparative Study.* Cambridge, MA: Harvard University Press, 1982.

Peterson Hill, Nancy. *A Very Private Public Citizen: The Life of Grenville Clark.* Columbia: University of Missouri Press, 2012.

Pflanze, Otto. *Bismarck and the Development of Germany.* Vol. 3, *The Period of Consolidation, 1871–1880.* Princeton: Princeton University Press, 1990.

Philpott, Colin. *Relics of the Reich: The Buildings the Nazis Left Behind.* Barnsley: Pen and Sword, 2017.

Pick, Daniel. *The Pursuit of the Nazi Mind: Hitler, Hess, and the Analysts.* Oxford: Oxford University Press, 2012.

Price, John. *Orienting Canada: Race, Empire, and the Transpacific.* Vancouver: UBC Press, 2011.

Raber, Karen. *Shakespeare and Posthumanist Theory.* London: Bloomsbury, 2018.

Reardon, Terry. *Winston Churchill and Mackenzie King: So Similar, So Different.* Toronto: Dundurn, 2012.

Record, Jeffrey "The Use and Abuse of History: Munich, Vietnam and Iraq." *Survival* 49.1 (2007): 163–80. https://doi.org/10.1080/00396330701254628.

Rees, Laurence. *Hitler's Charisma: Into the Abyss.* New York: Vintage, 2014.

Reinisch, J. *The Perils of Peace: The Public Health Crisis in Occupied Germany.* Oxford: Oxford University Press, 2013.

Renan, Ernst. "What Is a Nation?" Translated by Martin Thom. In *Nation and Narration*, edited by H.K. Bhabba, 8–22. London: Routledge, 1990.

Renshon, Jonathan. "The Psychological Origins of Preventative War." In *Understanding the Bush Doctrine: Psychology and Strategy in an Age of Terrorism*, edited by Stanley A. Renshon and Peter Suedfeld, 201–30. New York: Routledge, 2007.

Reynolds, Louise. *Mackenzie King: Friends and Lovers.* Victoria: Trafford, 2005.

Richter, Friedrich, Pay Christian Carstensen, and Hans Hitzer. *Germany.* Translated by W.D. Bayles. Berlin: Volk und Reich, n.d. [1936].

Roazen, Paul. *Canada's King: An Essay in Political Psychology.* Oakville: Mosaic, 1998.

Robertson, Gordon. *Memoirs of a Very Civil Servant: Mackenzie King to Pierre Trudeau.* Toronto: University of Toronto Press, 2000.

Robinson, Gabrielle. *The Reluctant Nazi: Searching for My Grandfather.* Brimscombe Port, Stroud: History Press, 2011.

Robinson, Ira. *A History of Antisemitism in Canada.* Waterloo: Wilfrid Laurier University Press, 2015.

Rogers, Norman M. *Mackenzie King.* Toronto: George N. Morang and T. Nelson & Sons, Ltd., 1935.

Rose, Jonathan. *The Literary Churchill: Author, Reader, Actor.* New Haven: Yale University Press, 2014.

Rose, Larry D. *Mobilize!: Why Canada Was Unprepared for the Second World War.* Toronto: Dundurn, 2013.

Rosenbaum, Robert. *Waking to Danger: Americans and Nazi Germany, 1933–1941.* Santa Barbara: ABC-CLIO, 2010.

Rosenfeld, Gavriel D. *Hi Hitler!: How the Nazi Past is Being Normalized in Contemporary Culture.* Cambridge: Cambridge University Press, 2015.

Rürup, Reinhard, ed. *Berlin 1945: Eine Dokumentation.* Berlin: Willmuth Arenhövel, 1995.

Russel, Peter A. "BC's 1944 'Zombie' Protests against Overseas Conscription." *BC Studies* 122 (Summer 1999): 49–76.

Schäche, Wolfgang, and Maria Selene. *An Italian Palazzo in Germany: The Embassy in Berlin.* Turin: Umberto Allemandi, 2006.

Schulte, Theo J. "Soldiers and War Criminals: The Ongoing Debate about the *Wehrmacht* in the Second World War." In *The German Lands and Eastern*

Europe: Essays on the History of Their Social, Cultural and Political Relations, edited by Karen Schönwälder and Roger Bartlett, 217–37. New York: St. Martin's Press, 1999.

Shirer, William. *The Rise and Fall of the Third Reich: A History of Nazi Germany.* New York: Simon and Schuster, 1960.

Sonnenfeldt, Richard W. *Witness to Nuremberg.* New York: Arcade, 2006.

Southworth, Herbert Rutledge. *Guernica! Guernica!* Berkeley: University of California Press, 1977.

Speer, Albert. *Inside the Third Reich.* Translated by Richard Winston and Clara Winston. Toronto: Macmillan, 1970.

Stacey, C.P. *Canada and the Age of Conflict: A History of Canadian External Policies.* Vol. 2. Toronto: University of Toronto Press, 1981.

– "The Divine Mission: Mackenzie King and Hitler." *Canadian Historical Review* 61.4 (December 1980): 502–12. https://doi.org/10.3138/chr-061-04-03.

– Review of J.W. Pickersgill, D.F. Forster, *The Mackenzie King Record. II. 1944– 1945. Canadian Historical Review* 50.3 (September 1969): 307–9.

– *A Very Double Life: The Private World of Mackenzie King.* Toronto: University of Toronto Press, 1976.

Stewart, Ian. "Names Written in Water: Canadian National Leaders and Their Reputations among Party Members." *Journal of Canadian Studies/Revue d'études canadiennes* 41.1 (Winter 2007): 31–50. https://doi.org/10.3138/jcs.41.1.31.

Stoltzfus, Nathan. *Hitler's Compromises: Coercion and Consensus in Nazi Germany.* New Haven: Yale University Press, 2016.

Stone, D. *Responses to Nazism in Britain, 1933–1939: Before War and Holocaust.* New York: Palgrave, 2012.

Strang, Bruce. "Two Unequal Tempers: Sir George Ogilvie-Forbes, Sir Nevile Henderson and British Foreign Policy, 1938–39." *Diplomacy & Statecraft* 5.1 (March 1994): 107–37. https://doi.org/10.1080/09592299408405911.

Taylor, Blaine. *Hitler's Engineers: Fritz Todt and Albert Speer, Master Builders of the Third Reich.* Philadelphia: Casemate, 2010.

Taylor, Clarence. *Reds at the Blackboard: Communism, Civil Rights, and the New York City Teachers Union.* New York: Columbia University Press, 2011.

Taylor, Robert R. *The Word in Stone: The Role of Architecture in the National Socialist Ideology.* Berkeley: University of California Press, 1974.

Teigrob, Robert. *Living with War: Twentieth-Century Conflict in Canadian and American History and Memory.* Toronto: University of Toronto Press, 2016.

– *Warming Up to the Cold War: The Canadian and American Coalition of the Willing, from Hiroshima to Korea.* Toronto: University of Toronto Press, 2009.

Thompson, John Herd, and Stephen J. Randall. *Canada and the United States: Ambivalent Allies.* 3rd ed. Athens: University of Georgia Press, 2002.

Timpe, Julia. *Nazi-Organized Recreation and Entertainment in the Third Reich.* London: Palgrave Macmillan, 2017.

Trevelyan, Laura. *A Very British Family: The Trevelyans and Their World.* London: I.B. Taurus, 2006.

Tuchman, Barbara W. *The March of Folly: From Troy to Vietnam.* New York: Random House, 1984.

Turley, Mark. *From Nuremberg to Nineveh: War, Peace and the Making of Modernity.* London: Vandal, 2008.

Urbach, Karina. *Go-Betweens for Hitler.* Oxford: Oxford University Press, 2015.

Vacante, Jeffery. *National Manhood and the Creation of Modern Quebec.* Vancouver: UBC Press, 2017.

van Ginneken, Anique H.M. *Historical Dictionary of the League of Nations.* Toronto: Scarecrow, 2006.

Vernes, Maurice. *Ernest Renan.* New York: Twayne, 1968.

Waddington, G.T. "'An Idyllic and Unruffled Atmosphere of Complete Anglo-German Misunderstanding': Aspects of the Operations of the Dienststelle Ribbentrop in Great Britain, 1934–1938." *History* 82.265 (1997): 44–72. https://doi.org/10.1111/1468-229X.00027.

Wagner, J. *Brothers Beyond the Sea: National Socialism in Canada.* Waterloo: Wilfrid Laurier University Press, 1981.

Walker, Richard J. "The Revolt of the Canadian Generals, 1944: The Case for the Prosecution." In *The Insubordinate and the Noncompliant: Case Studies of Canadian Mutiny and Disobedience, 1920–Present*, edited by Howard Coombs, 55–100. Toronto: Dundurn, 2007.

Wallace, Valerie. *Scottish Presbyterianism and Settler Colonial Politics: Empire of Dissent.* London: Palgrave Macmillan, 2018.

Ward, Peter W. *White Canada Forever.* 3rd ed. Montreal/Kingston: McGill-Queen's University Press, 2002.

Waters, Christopher. *Australia and Appeasement: Imperial Foreign Policy and the Origins of World War II.* London: I.B. Taurus, 2012.

Weikart, Richard. *Hitler's Religion: The Twisted Beliefs That Drove the Third Reich.* Washington, DC: Regency, 2016.

Weinberg, Gerhard. *Germany, Hitler, and World War II: Essays in Modern German and World History.* Cambridge: Cambridge University Press, 1995.

Wesseling, H.L. "Gabriel Hanotaux: A Historian in Politics." *Itinerario* 25.1 (March 2001): 65–84. https://doi.org/10.1017/s016511530000557x.

Whitaker, Reginald. "The Liberal Corporatist Ideas of Mackenzie King." *Labour/Le Travail* 4.4 (1979): 165–85. https://doi.org/10.2307/25139900.

– *A Sovereign Idea: Essays on Canada as a Democratic Community*. Montreal/ Kingston: McGill-Queen's University Press, 1992.

Whitaker, Reginald, Gregory S. Kealey, and Andrew Parnaby. *Secret Service: Political Policing in Canada from the Fenians to Fortress America*. Toronto: University of Toronto Press, 2012.

Whitaker, Reginald, and Gary Marcuse. *Cold War Canada: The Making of a National Insecurity State, 1945–1957*. Toronto: University of Toronto Press, 1994.

Whitman, James Q. *Hitler's American Model: The United States and the Making of Nazi Race Law*. Princeton: Princeton University Press, 2017.

Wood, James. *Militia Myths: Ideas of the Citizen Soldier*. Vancouver: UBC Press, 2010.

Zalampas, Michael. *Adolf Hitler and the Third Reich in American Magazines, 1923–1939*. Madison: Popular Press, 1989.

Zuccotti, Susan. *Under His Very Windows: The Vatican and the Holocaust in Italy*. New Haven: Yale University Press, 2002.

Zuehlke, Mark. *Tragedy at Dieppe: Operation Jubilee, August 19, 1942*. Toronto: Douglas & McIntyre, 2012.

Index